Lecture Notes in Business Information Processing 84

Series Editors

Malu Castellanos
Umeshwar Dayal
Volker Markl (Eds.)

Enabling Real-Time Business Intelligence

4th International Workshop, BIRTE 2010
Held at the 36th International Conference
on Very Large Databases, VLDB 2010
Singapore, September 13, 2010
Revised Selected Papers

Springer

Volume Editors

Malu Castellanos
Hewlett-Packard
1501 Page Mill Rd, MS-1142
Palo Alto, CA 94304, USA
E-mail: malu.castellanos@hp.com

Umeshwar Dayal
Hewlett-Packard
1501 Page Mill Rd, MS-1142
Palo Alto, CA 94304, USA
E-mail: umeshwar.dayal@hp.com

Volker Markl
Technische Universität Berlin
Einsteinufer 17
10587 Berlin, Germany
E-mail: volker.markl@tu-berlin.de

ISSN 1865-1348 e-ISSN 1865-1356
ISBN 978-3-642-22969-5 e-ISBN 978-3-642-22970-1
DOI 10.1007/978-3-642-22970-1
Springer Heidelberg Dordrecht London New York

Library of Congress Control Number: 2011933364

ACM Computing Classification (1998): H.3, J.1, H.2

Typesetting: Camera-ready by author, data conversion by Scientific Publishing Services, Chennai, India

Printed on acid-free paper

Springer is part of Springer Science+Business Media (www.springer.com)

Preface

Business intelligence (BI) has evolved into a multi-billion dollar market over the last decade. Since the early beginnings of data warehousing, business needs have constantly posed new requirements on state-of-the-art business intelligence systems. In today's competitive and highly dynamic environment, providing insight does not merely require analysis of the existing data. Deriving actionable intelligence demands the efficient processing of a vast amount of information in order to arrive at a timely representation of the state of an enterprise as well as of emerging trends. Prediction models must be used in order to assist with the derivation of actions from the current state of the enterprise and the market, taking into account the uncertainty of the prediction. Moreover, the increasing use of Twitter, blogs, and other media means that BI cannot restrict itself to only dealing with structured information. More and more information sources of varying kind have to be integrated, starting with the vast amount of textual information in corporate intranets and the Web. However, due to media convergence, future BI will also have to consider audio and video streams as further information sources. The end goal is to support better and timelier decision making, enabled by the availability of up-to-date, high-quality information.

Although there has been progress in this direction and many companies are introducing products toward meeting this goal, there is still a long way to go. In particular, the whole lifecycle of BI requires new techniques and methodologies capable of dealing with the new requirements imposed by the new generation of BI applications. From the capturing of real-time business data to the transformation and delivery of actionable information, all the stages of the BI cycle call for new algorithms and paradigms as the basis of new functionalities including BI over text data, ensuring information quality, dealing with the uncertainty of prediction models, nested complex events, and optimizing complex ETL workflows, just to name a few.

The series of BIRTE workshops aims to provide a forum for researchers to discuss and advance the foundational science and engineering required to enable real-time BI and the novel applications and solutions that build on these foundational techniques. Following the success of our previous workshops co-located with the VLDB conferences in Seoul, Auckland, and Lyon, our fourth workshop was held in Singapore on September 13, 2010.

The program included three keynotes, two from academia and one from industry. The first one opened the morning session and was presented by Ralf Schenkel and Srikanta Bedathur (representing Gerhard Weikum) on temporal knowledge for timely intelligence. The second one opened the afternoon session and was given by Alfons Kemper and Thomas Neumann on a high-performance main memory database system based on virtual memory snapshots. And closing the workshop was the keynote of Julio Navas on a federated event and data management system for the extended enterprise. The program included six research papers.

We wish to express special thanks to the Program Committee members for helping us prepare an interesting program. To our keynote speakers, presenters and attendees, we express our appreciation for sharing their work and the lively discussions that made this workshop a great forum for exchanging new ideas. We thank the VLDB 2010 organizers for their help and organizational support. Finally, we would like to extend many thanks to Mark Jesionowski for maintaining the workshop's website and to Alexander Löser, our Publication Chair.

June 2011

Malu Castellanos
Umeshwar Dayal
Volker Markl

Organization

Organizing Committee

General Chair

Umeshwar Dayal	Hewlett-Packard, USA

Program Committee Chairs

Malu Castellanos	Hewlett-Packard, USA
Volker Markl	TU Berlin, Germany

Program Committee

Christof Bornhövd	SAP Labs, USA
Ben Chin Ooi	National University of Singapore, Singapore
Mike Franklin	UC Berkeley, USA
Dimitrios Georgakopoulos	CSIRO, Australia
Chetan Gupta	HP Labs, USA
Howard Ho	IBM, USA
Alfons Kemper	TU München, Germany
Christian König	Microsoft, USA
Wolfgang Lehner	TU Dresden, Germany
Alexander Löser	University of Technology Berlin, Germany
Renee Miller	University of Toronto, Canada
Torben B. Pedersen	Aalborg University, Denmark
Elke Rundensteiner	WPI, USA
Donovan Schneider	SalesForce, USA
Eric Simon	SAP, France
Nesime Tatbul	ETH Zürich, Switzerland
Florian Waas	Greenplum, USA

Publication Chair

Alexander Löser	Technische Universität Berlin, Germany

Table of Contents

Temporal Knowledge for Timely Intelligence

Gerhard Weikum[1], Srikanta Bedathur[1], and Ralf Schenkel[2]

[1] Max Planck Institute for Informatics
[2] Saarland University
Saarbruecken, Germany
{weikum,bedathur}@mpi-inf.mpg.de,
schenkel@mmci.uni-saarland.de

Abstract. Knowledge bases about entities and their relationships are a great asset for business intelligence. Major advances in information extraction and the proliferation of knowledge-sharing communities like Wikipedia have enabled ways for the largely automated construction of rich knowledge bases. Such knowledge about entity-oriented facts can greatly improve the output quality and possibly also efficiency of processing business-relevant documents and event logs. This holds for information within the enterprise as well as in Web communities such as blogs.

However, no knowledge base will ever be fully complete and real-world knowledge is continuously changing: new facts supersede old facts, knowledge grows in various dimensions, and completely new classes, relation types, or knowledge structures will arise. This leads to a number of difficult research questions regarding temporal knowledge and the life-cycle of knowledge bases. This short paper outlines challenging issues and research opportunities, and provides references to technical literature.

1 Knowledge Bases and Linked Data

The proliferation of knowledge-sharing communities like Wikipedia and the advances in automated information extraction from Web pages open up an unprecedented opportunity: we can systematically harvest facts from the Web and compile them into a comprehensive, formally represented knowledge base about the world's entities, their semantic properties, and their relationships with each other. Imagine a *Structured Wikipedia* that has the same scale and richness as Wikipedia itself but offers a precise and concise representation of knowledge, e.g., in the RDF format. This would enable expressive and highly precise querying, e.g., in the SPARQL language (or appropriate extensions), with additional capabilities for informative ranking of query results. Large common-sense knowledge bases have been an elusive goal in AI for many years [16,21], and have now become practically feasible (see the recent overviews [2,13,32]).

A comprehensive knowledge base should know all individual entities of this world (e.g., Carly Fiorina), their semantic classes (e.g., CarlyFiorina isa BusinessWoman, CarlyFiorina isa PoliticalCandidate), relationships between entities (e.g., CarlyFiorina workedFor HewlettPackard, CarlyFiorina graduatedAt MIT, CarlyFiorina runsFor SenateOfCalifornia), as well as validity times and confidence values for the correctness of such facts (e.g., CarlyFiorina wasCEOof HewlettPackard [July-1999,January-2005]).

M. Castellanos, U. Dayal, and V. Markl (Eds.): BIRTE 2010, LNBIP 84, pp. 1–6, 2011.

Moreover, the knowledge base should come with logical reasoning capabilities and rich support for querying and knowledge discovery. Specific instantiations of this roadmap could focus on scholarly knowledge about researchers, organizations, projects, publications, software, etc., or on business knowledge about companies, their staff, customers, products, market properties, and other business relationships. Such a knowledge base would be a great asset and enabling infrastructure for all kinds of business-intelligence and other forms of semantic applications.

A number of recent projects have embarked on this endeavor and already made significant impact. These include commercial knowledge services such as *cyc.org*, *wolframalpha.com*, *freebase.com*, and *trueknowledge.com*. Notable research projects include *dbpedia.org* [3], *www.mpi-inf.mpg.de/yago-naga* [22], *wikitaxonomy* [19], work at UW Seattle [4,8,34], MSR Beijing [35], Google [7,25], and others (see [13,32] for further references). Our own *YAGO-NAGA* project [31] has developed methodologies for extracting facts from Wikipedia categories and infoboxes and integrating them with concepts and classes from the WordNet thesaurus. The YAGO base contains more than 2 million entities, properly assigned to semantic classes of a taxonomic backbone, and more than 20 million relationships between entities [23]. Extensive sampling for manual assessment showed that the precision of the facts is well above 95 percent; so the knowledge base is of near-human-quality. A recently completed new edition, coined YAGO2, has integrated *geo-spatial* and *temporal* information and contains more than 200 million facts. DBpedia has even more facts (more than a billion triples), by its extensive harvesting of Wikipedia infoboxes, but it contains noisier parts and is less elaborated than YAGO on the semantic typing side. YAGO types have been imported into DBpedia as specific RDF triples.

DBpedia is a major hub in the *Linked-Data* cloud [6] which comprises a wide variety of semantic databases in RDF format, along with extensive cross-linkage (see *linked-data.org*). The references that span data sources are at the entity-level, thus providing much deeper semantics than mere URL-based hyperlinks (notwithstanding the fact that the syntactic representation uses URIs). This way, complementary knowledge about the same real-world entity can be brought together by following the *sameAs* properties across different sources. This is a powerful paradigm for pay-as-you-go knowledge integration, and it is gaining great attention in computational biology, across social network providers, and in the publication and media industry.

2 Challenge: Dynamic Knowledge Gathering

Knowledge bases can be leveraged to *semantically annotate* entities and facts in natural-language texts such as news or blogs, and can enhance the automatic extraction of new relationships on the fly. This entails matching entity mentions in the text against the names of potential meanings in the knowledge base, to obtain a set of candidate entities. Then, a *disambiguation* method needs to be applied to select the most likely entity for each mention. The disambiguation itself can harness the knowledge base by comparing the textual context of a mention with the ontological context of a candidate entity (e.g., the classes to which the entity belongs, related entities, etc.) in order to compute similarities and rankings.

This theme of "exploit existing knowledge for gathering new knowledge" has also been pursued for further growing knowledge bases from arbitrary Web sources and natural-language texts. To this end, pattern-based extraction has been combined with logic-based consistency constraints in various models, including probabilistic graphical models [14,33], constrained learning [9,10], and Max-Sat-based reasoners [24]. Our own work on the SOFIE tool [24,18] has developed a novel way of mapping the joint reasoning on fact candidates, goodness of extraction patterns, and entity disambiguation onto a carefully designed weighted Max-Sat problem, along with an efficient customized approximation algorithm. This method is capable of gathering ten thousands of new facts from the Web, within a few hours. It can also be used to annotate texts with relational patterns, as a way of explaining evidence for extracted facts to users [15].

Despite these exciting steps towards more dynamic knowledge gathering, the area still poses very challenging open issues. First of all, scalability and robustness remain difficult if not elusive. It is not obvious how to scale out, on a cloud-like distributed platform, the more sophisticated steps like probabilistic inference over graphical models or reasoning over logical consistency constraints. The robustness goal involves achieving both high precision and high recall, and minimizing the dependency on human supervision (e.g., training data). For today's techniques, outlined above, precision is high for specific target relations, but recall is limited. For example, we can automatically and dynamically harvest high-quality facts for specific relations such as *isCEOof: person* $\times$ *company* or *hasAcquired: company* $\times$ *company*. Perhaps the biggest limitation at this point, is that all high-precision methods depend on seed facts for given relations. They cannot discover new relation types, and they cannot easily find new entities either. For the latter, the difficulty is to distinguish whether a given name on a Web page is an approximate match for an already known entity, a new name for a known entity, or a totally new entity. There have been attempts at pursuing "open information extraction" without any prior specification of extraction targets [4,5], but these methods have not reached convincing precision.

For tapping on information that cannot be crawled and is accessible only via functions (e.g., latest songs of pop musicians, their ratings, etc.), an intriguing idea is to dynamically couple the knowledge base with external Web Services [20]. To connect entities, facts, and their terminologies in different languages, methods for multilingual knowledge harvesting have been studied [1,11]. For learning common properties of concepts (e.g., sugar is sweet, bananas are yellow or green), statistical methods can analyze large n-gram corpora [26]. Finally, for multimodal knowledge, such as photos of general concepts (e.g., reptiles, churches, stars) or named entities (i.e., individual people, mountains, cultural landmarks, etc.), consistency-learning methods have been used for populating given knowledge bases [12,27]. All of these are early approaches on a long-term agenda.

3 Challenge: Temporal Knowledge

No knowledge base will ever be fully complete and real-world knowledge is continuously changing: new facts supersede old facts, knowledge grows in various dimensions, and completely new classes, relation types, or knowledge structures will arise. This leads to a number of difficult research questions. How do we automatically maintain a knowledge base as we discover evidence for new facts in enterprise or Web sources? How can we leverage the existing knowledge in assessing new hypotheses? How do we decide when we should overwrite facts in the knowledge base and when we should add new facts? How do we capture the temporal validity of facts? For example, when exactly did an enterprise acquire a company? During which time period did someone serve as CEO of a given company? How do we aggregate and reason about a set of possibly inconsistent observations for such temporal information? How do we explore and search knowledge with a temporal perspective?

The knowledge-gathering methods outlined in the previous sections make the simplifying assumption that facts are time-invariant. This is appropriate for some relation types, for example, for finding birthdates of famous people, but inappropriate for evolving facts such as presidents of countries or CEOs of companies. In fact, time-dependent relations seem to be far more common than time-invariant ones. For example, finding all spouses of famous people, current and former ones, involves understanding temporal relations. Likewise, business-intelligence queries often need temporal facts, for example, to answer analytical needs of the following kind: Which companies entered the tablet-PC market at which points in time? Who were the CEOs and technical key people of these companies at these points (and in the preceding year)? When did these companies acquire other companies with tablet-PC-related technologies or form business alliances with them?

Wikipedia infoboxes, lists, and category names provide a fair amount of time-annotated facts that can serve as seeds for tapping on the temporal information in the full text of Wikipedia articles, online news, and other natural-language sources (e.g., biographies or CVs on Web homepages). This process entails extraction steps, aggregation of multiple pieces of evidence, and also consistency-aware reasoning. Extracting the validity time of facts requires detecting explicit temporal expressions such as dates as well as implicit expressions in the form of adverbial phrases such as "last Monday", "next week", or "years ago". Moreover, one often has to deal with incomplete time information (e.g., the begin of someone holding a political office but no end-of-term date given, although the person may meanwhile be dead), and with different time resolutions (e.g., only the year and month for the begin of the term, but the exact date for related events). As Web and news sources typically offer ample redundancy, it seems natural to aggregate many observed cues for a temporal fact in a statistical manner. However, the appropriate way of doing this is a widely open issue. Finally, a potentially rewarding but very difficult issue is how to reason about interrelated time points or intervals. For example, the constraint that each person has at most one legal spouse now becomes a more complex condition that the validity intervals of the isMarriedTo instances for the same person must be non-overlapping. This kind of time-aware consistency checking would have great benefits for assessing hypotheses about fact candidates and eliminating false positives.

This entire complex of gathering and distilling temporal knowledge from Web sources is a major research challenge. So far, only partial aspects have been tackled [17,28,29,30]. In the long run, temporal knowledge is crucial for timely intelligence in business and other fields (e.g., Web sociology, media analytics, etc.); so the outlined direction should be a high-priority item on our research agenda.

References

1. Adar, E., Skinner, M., Weld, D.S.: Information Arbitrage across Multi-Lingual Wikipedia. In: WSDM 2009 (2009)
2. First Workshop on Automated Knowledge Base Construction, Grenoble (2010), `http://akbc.xrce.xerox.com`
3. Auer, S., Bizer, C., Kobilarov, G., Lehmann, J., Cyganiak, R., Ives, Z.G.: DBpedia: A nucleus for a web of open data. In: Aberer, K., Choi, K.-S., Noy, N., Allemang, D., Lee, K.-I., Nixon, L.J.B., Golbeck, J., Mika, P., Maynard, D., Mizoguchi, R., Schreiber, G., Cudré-Mauroux, P. (eds.) ASWC 2007 and ISWC 2007. LNCS, vol. 4825, pp. 722–735. Springer, Heidelberg (2007)
4. Banko, M., Cafarella, M.J., Soderland, S., Broadhead, M., Etzioni, O.: Open Information Extraction from the Web. In: IJCAI 2007 (2007)
5. Banko, M., Etzioni, O.: Strategies for Lifelong Knowledge Extraction from the Web. In: Int. Conf. on Knowledge Capture (2007)
6. Bizer, C., Heath, T., Berners-Lee, T.: Linked Data - The Story So Far. Int. J. Semantic Web Inf. Syst. 5(3) (2009)
7. Cafarella, M.J., Halevy, A.Y., Wang, D.Z., Wu, E., Zhang, Y.: WebTables: Exploring the Power of Tables on the Web. PVLDB 1(1) (2008)
8. Cafarella, M.J.: Extracting and Querying a Comprehensive Web Database. In: CIDR 2009 (2009)
9. Carlson, A., Betteridge, J., Wang, R.C., Hruschka Jr., E.R., Mitchell, T.M.: Coupled Semi-supervised Learning for Information Extraction. In: WSDM 2010 (2010)
10. Chang, M.-W., Ratinov, L.-A., Rizzolo, N., Roth, D.: Learning and Inference with Constraints. AAAI, Menlo Park (2008)
11. de Melo, G., Weikum, G.: MENTA: Inducing Multilingual Taxonomies from Wikipedia. In: CIKM 2010 (2010)
12. Deng, J., Dong, W., Socher, R., Li, L.-J., Li, K., Li, F.-F.: ImageNet: A Large-scale Hierarchical Image Database. In: CVPR 2009 (2009)
13. Doan, A., Gravano, L., Ramakrishnan, R., Vaithyanathan, S. (eds.): Special Issue on Information Extraction, SIGMOD Record, vol. 37(4) (2008)
14. Domingos, P., Lowd, D.: Markov Logic: An Interface Layer for Artificial Intelligence. Morgan & Claypool (2009)
15. Elbassuoni, S., Hose, K., Metzger, S., Schenkel, R.: ROXXI: Reviving Witness Documents to Explore Extracted Information. PVLDB 3(2) (2010)
16. Lenat, D.B.: CYC: A Large-Scale Investment in Knowledge Infrastructure. Commun. ACM 38(11) (1995)
17. Ling, X., Weld, D.S.: Temporal Information Extraction. AAAI, Menlo Park (2010)
18. Nakashole, N., Theobald, M., Weikum, G.: Find your Advisor: Robust Knowledge Gathering from the Web. In: WebDB 2010 (2010)
19. Ponzetto, S.P., Strube, M.: Deriving a Large-Scale Taxonomy from Wikipedia. AAAI, Menlo Park (2007)
20. Preda, N., Kasneci, G., Suchanek, F.M., Neumann, T., Yuan, W., Weikum, G.: Active Knowledge: Dynamically Enriching RDF Knowledge Bases by Web Services. In: SIGMOD 2010 (2010)
21. Russell, S., Norvig, P.: Artificial Intelligence: A Modern Approach. Prentice Hall, Englewood Cliffs (2010)
22. Suchanek, F.M., Kasneci, G., Weikum, G.: YAGO: a Core of Semantic Knowledge. In: WWW 2007 (2007)

23. Suchanek, F., Kasneci, G., Weikum, G.: YAGO: A Large Ontology from Wikipedia and WordNet. Journal of Web Semantics 6(39) (2008)
24. Suchanek, F., Sozio, M., Weikum, G.: SOFIE: a Self-Organizing Framework for Information Extraction. In: WWW 2009 (2009)
25. Talukdar, P.P., Pereira, F.: Experiments in Graph-based Semi-Supervised Learning Methods for Class-Instance Acquisition. In: ACL 2010 (2010)
26. Tandon, N., de Melo, G.: Information Extraction from Web-Scale N-Gram Data. In: SIGIR Workshop on Web N-Grams (2010)
27. Taneva, B., Kacimi, M., Weikum, G.: Gathering and Ranking Photos of Named Entities with High Precision, High Recall, and Diversity. In: WSDM 2010 (2010)
28. Verhagen, M., et al.: Automating Temporal Annotation with TARSQI. In: ACL 2005 (2005)
29. Wang, Y., Zhu, M., Qu, L., Spaniol, M., Weikum, G.: Timely YAGO: Harvesting, Querying, and Visualizing Temporal Knowledge from Wikipedia. In: EDBT 2010 (2010)
30. Wang, Y., Yahya, M., Theobald, M.: Time-aware Reasoning in Uncertain Knowledge Bases. In: VLDB Workshop on Management of Uncertain Data (2010)
31. Weikum, G., Kasneci, G., Ramanath, M., Suchanek, F.: Database and Information-Retrieval Methods for Knowledge Discovery. CACM 52(4) (2009)
32. Weikum, G., Theobald, M.: From information to Knowledge: Harvesting Entities and Relationships from Web Sources. In: PODS 2010 (2010)
33. Wick, M.L., McCallum, A., Miklau, G.: Scalable Probabilistic Databases with Factor Graphs and MCMC. PVLDB 3(1) (2010)
34. Wu, F., Weld, D.S.: Automatically Refining the Wikipedia Infobox Ontology. In: WWW 2008 (2008)
35. Zhu, J., Nie, Z., Liu, X., Zhang, B., Wen, J.-R.: StatSnowball: a Statistical Approach to Extracting Entity Relationships. In: WWW 2009 (2009)

One Size Fits all, Again!
The Architecture of the Hybrid OLTP&OLAP Database Management System HyPer

Alfons Kemper and Thomas Neumann

Fakultät für Informatik
Technische Universität München
Boltzmannstraße 3, D-85748 Garching, Germany
{kemper,neumann}@in.tum.de

Abstract. Real time business intelligence demands to execute OLAP queries on a current, up-to-date state of the transactional OLTP data. The currently exercised separation of transaction processing on the OLTP database and BI query processing on the *data warehouse* that is only periodically refreshed violates this goal. We propose to enhance the transactional database with highly effective query processing capabilities. We contrast different architectures proposed for achieving the real-time BI goal: versioning of the data and thereby separating the query from the transactions workload, continuous DW refreshing, heterogeneous workload management, update staging by periodically merging the update delta into the queryable main database, update and query batching, and our newly developed virtual memory snapshot mechanism based on hardware-supported shadowed pages. In our HyPer main memory database management system, the OLAP queries are executed on an arbitrarily current database snapshot that is created by forking the OLTP process. This snapshot is efficiently maintained by the operating system's copy on write mechanism that is supported by the MMU hardware. To assess the performance of such hybrid DBMSs we propose a new OLTP&OLAP benchmark that combines the transaction processing functionality of the TPC-C benchmark with the query workload of the TPC-H benchmark in one mixed workload. Based on this benchmark we substantiate the claim that it is indeed possible to architect a hybrid system that can achieve the transaction throughput of dedicated in-memory OLTP systems and, in parallel, execute a BI workload on the same data at the same performance as dedicated OLAP systems, such as in-memory column stores.

1 Motivation

There have been strong arguments by industry leaders, e.g., Hasso Plattner of SAP [Pla09], that our current support for Business intelligence is inappropriate. The currently exercised separation of transaction processing on the OLTP database and BI query processing on the *data warehouse* that is only periodically refreshed violates this goal. We propose to enhance the transactional database with highly effective query processing capabilities. Real-time/operational business intelligence demands to execute OLAP queries on the current, up-to-date state of the transactional OLTP data. Therefore, mixed workloads of OLTP transaction processing and OLAP query processing on

M. Castellanos, U. Dayal, and V. Markl (Eds.): BIRTE 2010, LNBIP 84, pp. 7–23, 2011.

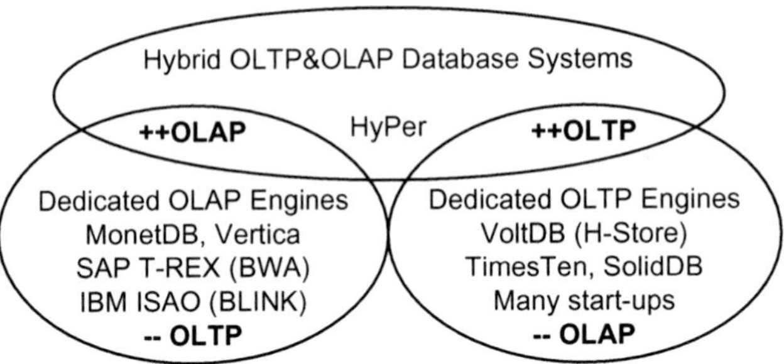

Fig. 1. Best of Both Worlds: OLAP and OLTP

the same data (or the same replicated data state) have to be supported. This is somewhat counter to the recent trend of building dedicated systems for different application scenarios.

The quest for a hybrid mixed workload system that reconciles the best of both worlds, high-thoughput OLTP engines and high-performance OLAP query processors, is depicted in Figure 1. In the OLAP "world" there are highly efficient OLAP query processors based on column store technologies, as pioneered by MonetDB [BMK09]. In the OLTP "world" recent (and established) main-memory database systems such as VoltDB [KKN+08] (or the time-proven TimesTen) excel in OLTP transaction throughput. The goal that we set out to pursue was the design of a database system that achieves the same excellent OLTP **and** OLAP performance in one system in parallel on the same data to enable the "*information at your fingertips*" performance requirements of an operational store.

We contrast different architectures proposed for achieving the real-time BI goal: versioning of the data and thereby separating the query from the transactions workload, continuous DW refreshing, heterogeneous workload management, update staging by periodically merging the update delta into the queryable main database, batch processing of updates and queries, and our newly developed virtual memory snapshot mechanism based on hardware-supported shadowed pages. The latter approach constitutes a main-memory database system which receive renewed interest due to recent hardware developments. Currently, hardware vendors offer cost-effective servers with a TB of RAM for only ca. $50,000. This makes it possible to maintain the transactional data of even the largest applications in main memory of one (or a few) server(s). The RAMcloud [OAE+09] development at Stanford is based on a similar observation by estimating, for example, Amazon's transactional data as follows: At 15 billion revenue per year and an average item price of $15 the yearly data volume of 1 billion order-lines can be stored in about 64 GB (assuming that an order-line is as compact as it is in the TPC-C benchmark).[1] We do not propose to abandon data warehouses as there is a need to collect, clean, and transform vast amounts of non-transactional data for in depth data

[1] This estimate neither includes the additional storage space for less dynamic data as Customer and Product information nor the ability to compress the data, as is typically done in main-memory systems.

analysis, such as data mining. Our goal is to enhance in-memory transactional database systems with highly effective BI query processing capabilities. Hardware progress favors in-memory technologies, as is also indicated by the many start-up companies developing OLTP main-memory databases, such as VoltDB, Clustrix, Akiban, DBshards, NimbusDB, ScaleDB, Lightwolf, and ElectronDB.

To assess the performance of a hybrid database workload consisting of OLTP and BI/OLAP processing, we propose a new OLTP&OLAP benchmark that combines the transaction processing functionality of the TPC-C benchmark with the query suite of the TPC-H benchmark in one mixed workload. Based on this benchmark we substantiate the claim that it is indeed possible to architect a hybrid system that can achieve the transactional throughput rates of dedicated in-memory OLTP systems and, in parallel, execute a BI workload on the same data at the same performance as dedicated OLAP systems, such as in-memory column stores.

2 Architecture Proposals

We will survey different architecture proposals for building such an operational store for real-time business intelligence on a high-performance transaction processing system.

2.1 Update Staging

Many read optimized database systems apply some kind of update staging as update in place is too costly. Thereby, updates (including inserts, deletes) are buffered in a so-called *Delta* and are only periodically merged with the *main* read optimized database – cf. Figure 2. Such a deferred update/insert approach is typical for compressed column store databases [HZN$^+$10a]. The deferred update mechanism is also advocated by SAP engineers to accommodate transactions on their column store T-REX (BWA) [KGT$^+$10]. The Delta serves as an overlay for the OLTP transactions to make sure that they read the most current version of any updated object. The OLAP queries are performed against the transaction consistent read-optimized *main* database, which corresponds to a snapshot of the database. The advantage of this approach is that the *main* database can be optimized for read-only accesses, e.g., in a sorted, partitioned and/or compressed column format [BHF09]. The problematic issue is the merge of the Delta into the *main* database which, according to [KGT$^+$10], requires a time- and space-consuming reorganization of the database.

The Delta acts as an "overlay" for the main database as it collects all updates and has to be read by the OLTP transactions. Therefore, point-wise and scan-based access to the entire database (main including the delta) has to be supported efficiently. An easy implementytion would be to maintain a list (e.g., implemented as a bit map) to identify invalidated objects of the main database that have a more current counter part in the Delta [ASJK11]. However, this slows down the scan performance severely as every object access results in a branch. In the context of the VectorWise project the positional trees were [HZN$^+$10b] were developed which allow fast scan (at clock speed) in between positions of invalidated objects.

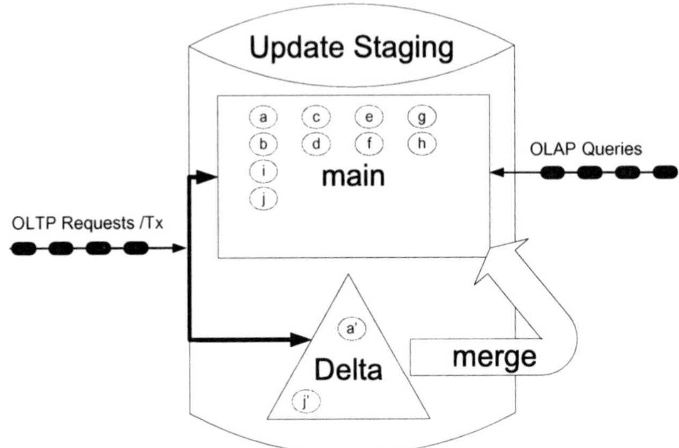

Fig. 2. Staging the Updates from a OLTP-Maintained Delta to the Read-Optimized *main* Database

2.2 Mixed Workload Management

A large body of work exists in this area that strives to optimize the workload mix in order to accomodate transactions and queries in the same system. Basically, the approach consists of an admission control scheme to prevent the database system from resource contention. [KKW+09, TBA10]. One of the most important paramters to tune the effective workload processing is the MPL [ASB10, SHBI+06]. By taking the service level agreement for the different service classes into account, the workload management tries to satisfy all objectives – as long as resources suffice. In commercial systems this is typically achieved by statically determining priorities for different service types, e.g., OLTP or OLAP [Com07]. A more dynamic quality of service model was developed in [GKS+08]

2.3 Continuous Warehouse Refreshing

In this approach the separation between OLTP and OLAP databases is preserved; however the OLTP updates are continuously transferred to the data warehouse. Instead of using periodic data extraction tasks the changes to the operational database are continually captured. In order to minimize the additional load of the operational OLTP system the change capturing can be performed via the redo log (sometimes referred to as log sniffing), as exemplified by the Oracle Change Data Capture system [Ora07].

The continuous transferral of all changes from the operational system induces basically the same update load on the DW as on the OLTP system. There is however an advantage: The DW schema can be optimized for the query processing. But keeping up with the transaction throughput may neceesitate to find a tradeoff between OLAP and OLTP optimized schema design.

2.4 Versioning of the Transactional Data

Already in the early Nineties the Postgres designers proposed to version all database objects [SRH90]. Thereby, the objects would never be updated in place; rather new

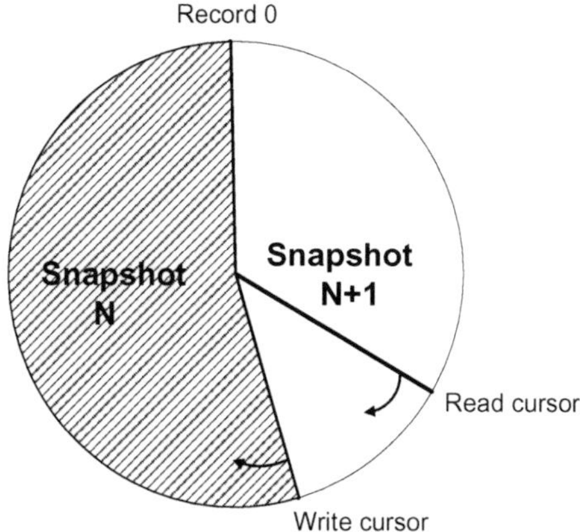

Fig. 3. Crescando Cyclic Scan Processing

versions were created. This versioning allows time travel queries as well as separating queries from update transactions by executing queries on snapshots that can be determined by comparing the version numbers with the query's initiation time stamp. Versioning data was recently employed in the context of RDF data management to realize serializability [NW10].

2.5 Batch Processing

Crescando is a special purpose information system that applies a particular approach to create transaction consistent snapshots by batching the updates and simple queries. The batching allows to leverage cooperative scans of the entire database. This approach can intuitively be viewed as a repeating circular scan of the database. In each cycle all the updates and reads collected during the previous phase (cycle) are executed. This is visualized in Figure 3.

The update/read operation processing is optimized by performing a query/data join as devised for data stream processing. Instead of indexing the data, the query predicates (of the read and update operations) are indexed to associate the records during the circular scan to the matching operations. The updates are applied first, before the read cursor associates the records to the queries. Furthermore, updates have to be applied in the given order to preserve serializability.

2.6 Shadow Pages in a Disk-Based DBMS

In the early ages of relational database technology Raymond Lorie [Lor77] invented the shadow paging concept for checkpointing a disk-based database system. The basic concept is shown in Figure 4. It relies on maintaining two page tables within the database management system: one current page table V1 that is used to translate page numbers to disk blocks and an additional shadow page table V0 that lags behind. Periodically, the shadow page table is updated to create a new (more current) consistent shadow

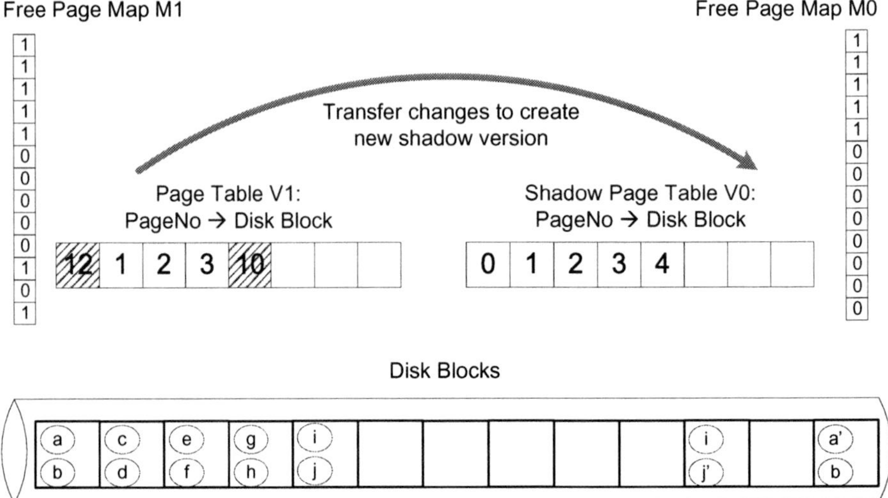

Fig. 4. Shadowed Disk Pages

snapshot of the database. It is important to note that the DBMS page tables are maintained in addition to the operating system's page table that controls the virtual memory address transformations, on which HyPer's snapshot mechanism relies (cf. Section 3).

Unfortunately, for disk-based DBMSs, the shadow page concept proved to be prohibitively inefficient because it destroys the clustering. This is exemplified in the figure as the originally contiguous object sequence *a, b, c, d, e, f, g, h, i, j* becomes torn apart after some of the objects (e.g., *a* and *j*) are updated and therefore copied to other, non-contiguous disk blocks. In addition, the software controlled page table shadowing incurs a severe maintenance overhead as every modifying access has to verify whether or not the affected disk block has already been replicated (indicated by the shaded entry in the page table) or not. Also the free page management needs to be controlled by two free page maps M1 and M0.

Originally the shadow page mechanism was proposed for checkpointing a database, that is, to recover a database to the consistent shadowed state. However, the shadowed state could also be used for to separate complex OLAP query processing from the transaction processing – as we propose in the HyPer architecture.

2.7 Computed Snapshots

In Oracle (and some other database systems) read-only queries are serialized via some kind of snapshot isolation [BBG+95]. These snapshots constitute the database state that existed at the time the query was started. Instead of maintaining materializations of all versions of modified objects that are needed to evaluate the various active queries the database systems temporarily undoes the modifications to roll individual objects back in time, i.e., into the state that existed right before the query started. Obviously, this reduces the conflict rates between read-only queries and update transactions because the queries need not acquire read locks – but at the cost of rolling back the modified objects.

2.8 Reduced Isolation Levels

If an application can tolerate weaker consistency levels of the queried objects it is also possible to execute queries in the *read committed* or even *read uncommitted* (dirty read) SQL isolation level in order to avoid the negative synchronization interference between transactional and query processing. While this approach obviates the need for long-lasting locks, it still requires latching (short duration locking) for synchronizing the access to physical data structure (e.g., pages, idexes, etc.) between concurrent threads.

3 HyPer: Virtual Memory Snapshots

We have developed a novel hybrid OLTP&OLAP database system based on snapshotting transactional data via the virtual memory management of the operating system [KN11]. In this architecture the OLTP process "owns" the database and periodically (e.g., in the order of seconds or minutes) forks an OLAP process. This OLAP process constitutes a fresh transaction consistent snapshot of the database. Thereby, we exploit the operating systems functionality to create virtual memory snapshots for new, duplicated processes. In Unix, for example, this is done by creating a child process of the OLTP process via the `fork()` system call. One possibility to guarantee transactional consistency is to `fork()` only after quiescing the transaction processing. Actually, this constraint can be relaxed by utilizing the undo log (that is anyway maintained in-memory for all running transactions) to convert an action consistent snapshot (created in the middle of transactions) into a transaction consistent one.

The forked child process obtains an exact copy of the parent processes address space, as exemplified in Figure 5 by the overlayed page frame panel. This virtual memory snapshot that is created by the `fork()`-operation will be used for executing a session of OLAP queries – as indicated in Figure 6. These queries can be executed in parallel threads or serially, depending on the system resources or client requirements.

The snapshot stays in precisely the state that existed at the time the `fork()` took place. Fortunately, state-of-the-art operating systems do not physically copy the memory segments right away. Rather, they employ a lazy *copy-on-update* strategy – as sketched out in Figure 6. Initially, parent process (OLTP) and child process (OLAP) share the same physical memory segments by translating either virtual addresses (e.g., to object a) to the same physical main memory location. The sharing of the memory segments is highlighted in the graphics by the dotted frames. A dotted frame represents a virtual memory page that was not (yet) replicated. Only when an object, like data item a, is updated, the OS- and hardware-supported copy-on-update mechanism initiate the replication of the virtual memory page on which a resides. Thereafter, there is a new state denoted a' accessible by the OLTP-process that executes the transactions and the old state denoted a, that is accessible by the OLAP query session.

In essence, the virtual memory snapshot mechanism constitutes a OS/hardware supported shadow paging mechanism as proposed decades ago for disk-based database systems [Lor77] (cf. Section 2.6). However, the original proposal incurred severe costs as it had to be software-controlled and it destroyed the clustering on disk. Neither of these drawbacks occurs in the virtual memory snapshotting as clustering across RAM pages is not an issue. Furthermore, the sharing of pages and the necessary copy-on-update/write

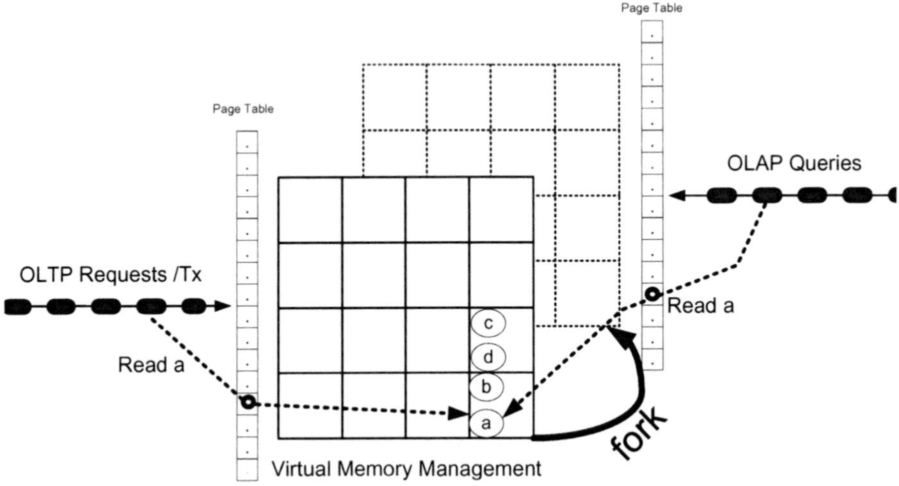

Fig. 5. Forking a New Virtual Memory Snapshot

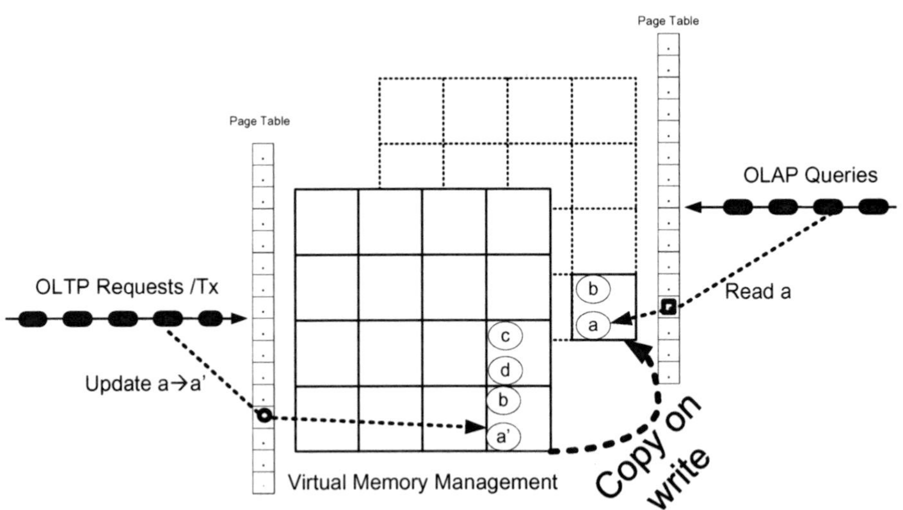

Fig. 6. Maintaining the New Snapshot: Copy on Write

is managed by the operating system with effective hardware support of the MMU (memory management unit) via the page table that translates VM addresses to physical pages and traps necessary replication (copy-on-write) actions. Therefore, the page replication is extremely efficiently done in 2 μs as we measured in a micro-benchmark. The hardware supported address transformation and copy-on-write initiation is carried out by the memory management unit that is sketched in Figure 7. The MMU-supported VM management not only translated VM addresses and traps necessary copy-on-write operations, it also keeps track of the page sharing in order to free VM pages that are no

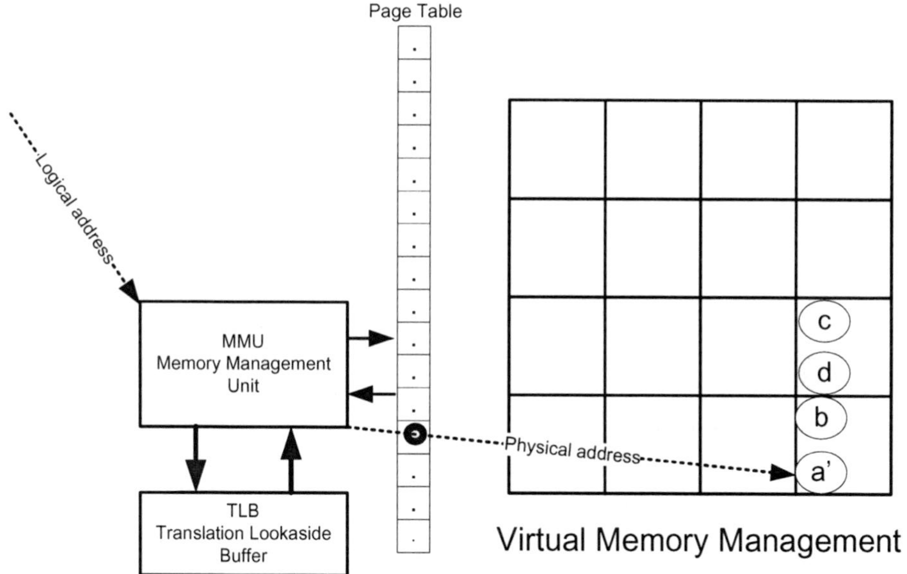

Fig. 7. Ultra Fast Address Calculation

longer needed. In the original shadowing of disk blocks this functionality had to be incorporated into the database system software – exemplified by thetwo *Free Page Maps* of Figure 4 – without hardware support.

Unlike Figure 6 suggests, the additional page is really created for the OLTP process that initiated the page change and the OLAP snapshot refers to the old page – this detail is important for estimating the space consumption if several such snapshots are created (cf. Figure 8).

HyPer adheres to the ACID paradigm for the transactional processing. The *atomicity* is guaranteed by maintaining the above mentioned undo-log in main-memory. The *durability* is achieved by efficiently writing logical redo-log records via a high-bandwidth network to a storage server and relying on group commit [JPS$^+$10]. The VM snapshot mechanism enables us to periodically write transaction consistent snapshots (mimicked as an OLAP session) to a storage server. As far as *isolation* is concerned we follow the approach pioneered in H-Store/VoltDB [HAMS08, JAM10] of lockless synchronization. Transactions, which constitute stored procedures written in a SQL-like scripting language, are executed serially on their corresponding partition [CZJM10]. If more than one partition is needed we resort to a serial (i.e., exclusive) operation mode.

So far we have sketched a database architecture utilizing two processes, one for OLTP and another one for OLAP. As the OLAP queries are *read-only* they could easily be executed in parallel in multiple threads that share the same address space. Still, we can avoid any synchronization (locking and latching) overhead as the OLAP queries do not share any mutable data structures. Modern multi-core computers which have more than ten cores can certainly yield a substantial speed up via this inter-query parallelization.

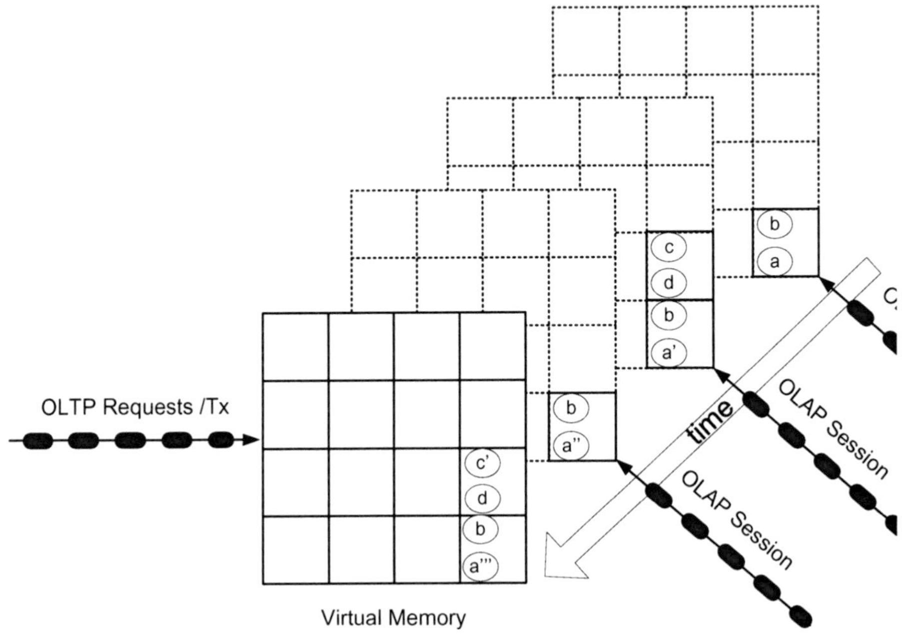

Fig. 8. Multiple OLAP Sessions at Different Points in Time

Another possibility to make good use of the multi-core servers is to create multiple snapshots that overlap in time. The HyPer architecture allows for arbitrarily current snapshots. This can simply be achieved by periodically (or on demand) `fork()`-ing a new snapshot and thus starting a new OLAP query session process. This is exemplified in Figure 8. Here we sketch the one and only OLTP process'es current database state (the front panel) and three active query session processes' snapshots – the oldest being the one in the background. The successive state changes are highlighted by the four different states of data item a (the oldest state), a', a'', and a''' (the youngest transaction consistent state). Obviously, most data items do not change in between different snapshots as we expect to create snapshots for most up-to-date querying at intervals of a few seconds – rather than minutes or hours as is the case in current separated data warehouse solutions with ETL data staging. The number of active snapshots is, in principle, not limited, as each "lives" in its own process. By adjusting the priority we can make sure that the mission critical OLTP process is always allocated a core – even if the OLAP processes are numerous and/or utilize multi-threading and thus exceed the number of cores.

A snapshot will be deleted after the last query of a session is finished. This is done by simply terminating the process that was executing the query session. It is not necessary to delete snapshots in the same order as they were created. Some snapshots may persist for a longer duration, e.g., for detailed stocktaking purposes or for archiving a snapshot. However, the memory overhead of a snapshot is proportional to the number of transactions being executed from creation of this snapshot to the time of the next younger snapshot (if it exists or to the current time). The figure exemplifies this on the data item c which is physically replicated for the "middle age" snapshot and thus shared and accessible by the oldest snapshot. Somewhat against our intuition, it is still possible to terminate the middle-aged snapshot before the oldest snapshot as the page on which c resides will be automatically detected by the OS/processor as being shared with the oldest snapshot via a reference counter associated with the physical page. Thus it survives the termination of the middle-aged snapshot – unlike the page on which a' resides which is freed upon termination of the middle-aged snapshot process. The youngest snapshot accesses the state c' that is contained in the current OLTP process'es address space.

4 OLTP&OLAP Benchmark: TPC-CH

We propose a new benchmark we call TPC-CH to denote that it is a "merge" of the two standard TPC benchmarks (`www.tpc.org`): The TPC-C benchmark was designed to evaluate OLTP database system performance and the TPC-H benchmark for analyzing OLAP query performance. Both benchmarks "simulate" a sales order processing (order entry, payment, delivery) system of a merchandising company. The benchmark constitutes the core functionality of such a commercial merchandiser like Amazon.

4.1 Benchmark Schema and Workload

The database schema of the TPC-CH benchmark is shown in Figure 9 as an Entity-Relationship-Diagram with cardinality indications of the entities and the (min,max)-notation to specify the cardinalities of the relationships. The cardinalities correspond

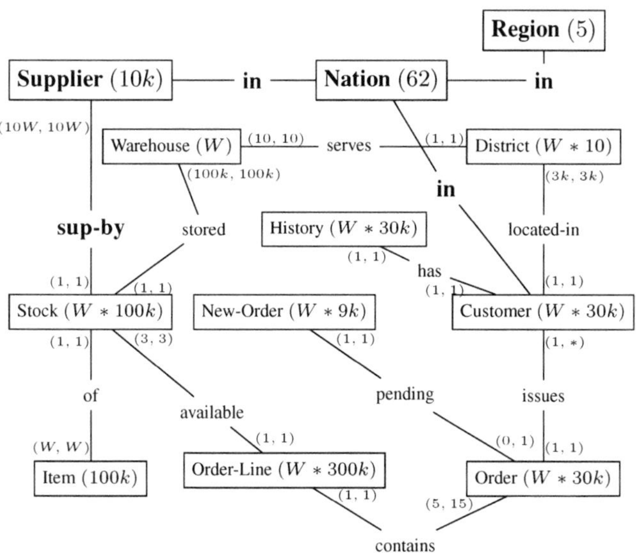

Fig. 9. Entity-Relationship-Diagram of the TPC-C&H Database

to the initial state of the database when the TPC-C benchmark is started and increase (in particular, in number of Orders and Order-Lines) during the benchmark run. The initial database state can be scaled by increasing the number of Warehouses – thereby also increasing the number of Customers, Orders and Order-Lines, as each Customer has already submitted one Order with 10 Order-Lines, on average. The original TPC-C schema, that we kept entirely unchanged, consists of the 9 relations in non-bold type face.

In addition, we included three relations (highlighted in bold type face) from the TPC-H benchmark in order to be able to formulate all 22 queries of this benchmark in a meaningful way: There are 10000 **Suppliers** that are referenced via a foreign key of the *Stock* relation. Thus, there is a fixed, randomly selected Supplier per Item/Warehouse combination. The relations **Nation** and **Region** model the geographic location of Suppliers and Customers.

The TPC-C OLTP transactions include entering and delivering orders, recording payments, checking the status of orders, and monitoring the level of stock at the warehouses – cf. left-hand side of Figure 10. All these transaction, including the read-only transactions *Order-Status* and *Stock-Level* have to be executed in serializable semantics – in HyPer's case via the OLTP workload queue. We only deviate from the original TPC-C benchmark specification by abandoning the waiting time such that clients submit their transactions as fast as possible. For the comprehensive OLTP&OLAP Benchmark we adapted the 22 queries of the TPC-H benchmark for the TPC-CH schema. In the reformulation we made sure that the queries retained their semantics (from a business point of view) and their syntactical structure. The OLAP queries do not benefit from database partitioning as they all require scanning the data across all partition boundaries.

The complete TPC-CH benchmark specification can be found in [FKN11].

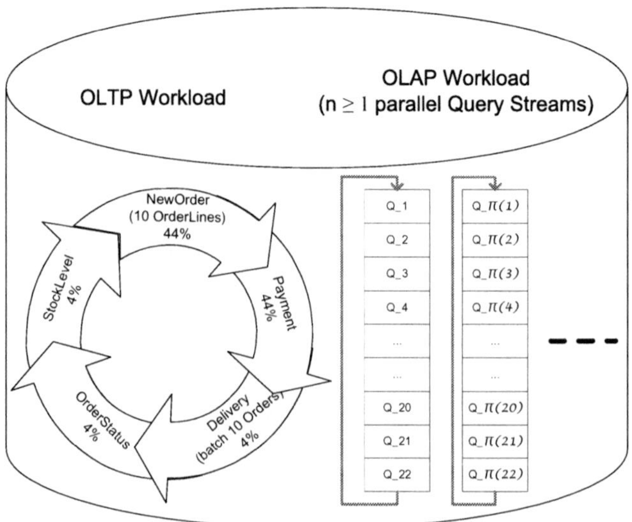

Fig. 10. Mixed OLTP&OLAP Workload Benchmark

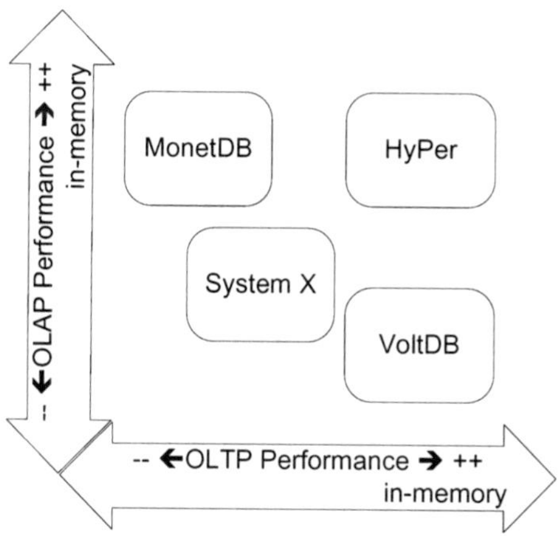

Fig. 11. Systems under Test

4.2 Performance Comparison

To demonstrate that this vision of a unified OLTP&OLAP system is feasible, we ran the benchmark on several database systems that are representatives for the various types of systems shown in Figure 11. System X stands for an "out of the box" commercial disk-based database system, to which Java clients were submitting the benchmark transaction steps and queries via JDBC.

All benchmarks were carried out on a TPC-CH-setup with 12 Warehouses. Thus, the initial database contained 360,000 Customers with 3.6 million order lines – totalling about 1 GB of net data. For reproducability reasons all HyPer query sessions were started (fork-ed) at the beginning of the benchmark (i.e., in the initial 12 Warehouse state) and the 22 queries were run in – altered, to exclude caching effects – sequence five times within each query session. Thus, each OLAP session/process was executing 110 queries sequentially. We report the median of each query's response times. These query sessions were executed in parallel to a single- or multi-threaded OLTP process – see Figure 12.

HyPer can be configured as a row store or as a column store. For OLTP we did not experience a significant performance difference; however, the OLAP query processing was significantly sped up by a column-wise storage scheme. In the future we will investigate hybrid storage schemes in our context [GKP$^+$10]. Here, we only report the OLTP and OLAP performance of pure column store configurations.

Except for VoltDB, the benchmarks were run on a commodity server, with the following specifications:

- Dual Intel X5570 Quad-Core-CPU, 8MB Cache
- 64GB RAM
- 16 300GB SAS-HD (only used for System X)
- Linux operating system RHEL 5.4
- Price: 13,886 Euros (discounted price for universities)

	System X		**HyPer** configurations				**MonetDB**	**VoltDB**
	3 query streams 25 JDBC clients		8 query sessions (streams) single threaded OLTP		3 query sessions (streams) 5 OLTP threads		no OLTP 1 query stream	no OLAP only OLTP
Query No.	OLTP throughput	Query resp. times (ms)	OLTP throughput	Query resp. times (ms)	OLTP throughput	Query resp. times (ms)	Query resp. times (ms)	results from [Vol10a]
Q1	new order: 220 tps; total: **450** tps	2466	new order: 29359 tps; total: **65269** tps	71	new order: 112217 tps; total: **249237** tps	71	63	**55000** tps on single node; **300000** tps on 6 nodes
Q2		4507		233		212	210	
Q3		1230		78		73	75	
Q4		2142		257		226	6003	
Q5		9160		1768		1564	5930	
Q6		2853		19		17	123	
Q7		17075		1611		1466	1713	
Q8		465		680		593	172	
Q9		1494		269		249	208	
Q10		11981		2490		2260	6209	
Q11		3958		38		35	35	
Q12		2919		195		170	192	
Q13		450		272		229	284	
Q14		3999		210		156	722	
Q15		4946		1002		792	533	
Q16		5125		1584		1500	3562	
Q17		2506		171		168	342	
Q18		8385		133		119	2505	
Q19		2904		219		183	1698	
Q20		2518		230		197	750	
Q21		5769		50		50	329	
Q22		6893		9		9	141	

Fig. 12. Performance Comparison: System X, HyPer OLTP&OLAP, MonetDB only OLAP, VoltDB only OLTP

The OLTP performance of VoltDB we list for comparison was not measured on our hardware but extracted from the product overview brochure [Vol10a] and discussions on their web site [Vol10b]. The VoltDB benchmark was carried out on similar hardware (dual-quad Xeon CPU Dell R610 servers). The major differences was that the HyPer benchmark was run on a single server whereas VoltDB was scaled out to 6 nodes. In addition, the HyPer benchmark was carried out with redo logging to another storage server while VoltDB was run without any logging or replication. Both, HyPer as well as VoltDB partitioned the database by Warehouse – as can be automatically derived via the Schism method [CZJM10]. Contrary to the TPC-C specification VoltDB did not execute any partition-crossing transactions, while the HyPer benchmark observed this requirement.

The performance results reveal that the hybrid OLTP&OLAP system HyPer basically achieves the same query performance as OLAP-centric systems such as MonetDB and, in parallel within the same system, retains the high transaction throughput of OLTP-centric systems, such as VoltDB's H-Store. In assessing the mixed workload (that is not feasible on VoltDB or on MonetDB) we observe a vast performance benefit from the virtual memory snapshot mechanism in comparison to the conventional disk-based System X. This performance benefit is due to HyPer's cache conscious in-memory techniques without the ballast of traditional DBMSs (like buffer management, page structuring, locking) and to the separation of transactions and queries via the VM snapshotting – even though System X ran the OLAP queries in "read committed" isolation level, which should cause less overhead than a fully versioned system (cf. Section 2.4). As HyPer's OLAP snapshots can be as current as desired by forking a new OLAP session the virtual memory snapshot approach is a promising architecture for *real-time business intelligence* systems.

5 Summary

In this paper we surveyed different approaches for building a real-time/operational business intelligence system comprising transaction and query processing. To comprehensively evaluate such emerging systems we propose the new TPC-CH benchmark that combines an OLTP and an OLAP workload in one mixed workload benchmark. Based on this benchmark we showed that it is indeed possible to architect a high performance hybrid database system (operational store) that achieves the same combined performance as high-performance in-memory OLTP systems in terms of Tx throughput and as dedicated OLAP column store systems in terms for queries.

Our HyPer architecture is based on virtual memory supported snapshots on transactional data for multiple query sessions. Thereby, the two workloads – OLTP transactions and OLAP queries – are executed on the same data without interfering with each other. The snapshot consistency and the high processing performance in terms of OLTP throughput and OLAP query response times is achieved via hardware supported copy on demand (= write) to preserve snapshot consistency. The detection of shared pages that need replication is done by the OS with MMU assistance. The concurrent transactional workload and the BI query processing use multi core architectures effectively without concurrency interference – as they are separated via the VM snapshot.

In comparison to conventional disk-based database systems we observe a performance improvement of one to two orders of magnitude. While the current HyPer prototype is a single server scale-up system, the VM snapshotting mechanism is orthogonal to a distributed architecture that scales out across a compute cluster – as VoltDB exercises.

Acknowledgment. We gratefully acknowledge the fruitful discussions about the mixed workload benchmark as part of the "Robust Query Processing" workshop at Dagstuhl castle in September 2010. We thank Florian Funke, Stefan Krompass, and Michael Seibold for helping with the performance evaluation. We acknowledge the many colleagues with whom we discussed HyPer.

References

[ASB10] Abouzour, M., Salem, K., Bumbulis, P.: Automatic Tuning of the Multiprogramming Level in Sybase SQL Anywhere. In: Proc. of the 2010 Workshop on Self-Managing Database Systems, SMDB (2010)

[ASJK11] Aulbach, S., Seibold, M., Jacobs, D., Kemper, A.: Extesibility and Data Sharing in Evolving Multi-Tenancy Dtabases. In: ICDE (2011)

[BBG+95] Berenson, H., Bernstein, P.A., Gray, J., Melton, J., O'Neil, E.J., O'Neil, P.E.: A Critique of ANSI SQL Isolation Levels. In: SIGMOD (1995)

[BHF09] Binnig, C., Hildenbrand, S., Färber, F.: Dictionary-based order-preserving string compression for main memory column stores. In: SIGMOD (2009)

[BMK09] Boncz, P.A., Manegold, S., Kersten, M.L.: Database Architecture Evolution: Mammals Flourished long before Dinosaurs became Extinct. PVLDB 2(2) (2009)

[Com07] Comeau, B.: Introduction to DB2 9.5 Workload Management. Oracle (June 2007)

[CZJM10] Curino, C., Zhang, Y., Jones, E.P.C., Madden, S.: Schism: a Workload-Driven Approach to Database Replication and Partitioning. In: VLDB 2010 (2010)

[FKN11] Funke, F., Kemper, A., Neumann, T.: Benchmarking Hybrid OLTP&OLAP Database Systems. In: The 14th BTW Conference on Database Systems for Business, Technology, and Web (BTW 2011) of the Gesellschaft für Informatik, GI (2011)

[GKP+10] Grund, M., Krüger, J., Plattner, H., Zeier, A., CudreMauroux, P., Madden, S.: HYRISE: A Main Memory Hybrid Storage Engine. PVLDB 4(2) (2010)

[GKS+08] Gmach, D., Krompass, S., Scholz, A., Wimmer, M., Kemper, A.: Adaptive quality of service management for enterprise services. ACM Trans. WEB 2(1) (2008)

[HAMS08] Harizopoulos, S., Abadi, D.J., Madden, S., Stonebraker, M.: OLTP through the looking glass, and what we found there. In: SIGMOD (2008)

[HZN+10a] Héman, S., Zukowski, M., Nes, N.J., Sidirourgos, L., Boncz, P.A.: Positional update handling in column stores. In: SIGMOD Conference, pp. 543–554 (2010)

[HZN+10b] Héman, S., Zukowski, M., Nes, N.J., Sidirourgos, L., Boncz, P.A.: Positional update handling in column stores. In: SIGMOD Conference, pp. 543–554 (2010)

[JAM10] Jones, E.P.C., Abadi, D.J., Madden, S.: Low overhead concurrency control for partitioned main memory databases. In: SIGMOD (2010)

[JPS+10] Johnson, R., Pandis, I., Stoica, R., Athanassoulis, M., Ailamaki, A.: Aether: A scalable approach to logging. In: VLDB (2010)

[KGT+10] Krueger, J., Grund, M., Tinnefeld, C., Plattner, H., Zeier, A., Faerber, F.: Optimizing write performance for read optimized databases. In: Kitagawa, H., Ishikawa, Y., Li, Q., Watanabe, C. (eds.) DASFAA 2010. LNCS, vol. 5982, pp. 291–305. Springer, Heidelberg (2010)

[KKN+08] Kallman, R., Kimura, H., Natkins, J., Pavlo, A., Rasin, A., Zdonik, S.B., Jones, E.P.C., Madden, S., Stonebraker, M., Zhang, Y., Hugg, J., Abadi, D.J.: H-Store: a high-performance, distributed main memory transaction processing system. PVLDB 1(2) (2008)

[KKW+09] Krompass, S., Kuno, H.A., Wiener, J.L., Wilkinson, K., Dayal, U., Kemper, A.: A Testbed for Managing Dynamic Mixed Workloads. PVLDB 2(2) (2009)

[KN11] Kemper, A., Neumann, T.: HyPer: A Hybrid OLTP&OLAP Main Memory Database System Based on Virtual Memory Snapshots. In: ICDE (2011)

[Lor77] Lorie, R.A.: Physical Integrity in a Large Segmented Database. TODS 2(1) (1977)

[NW10] Neumann, T., Weikum, G.: x-RDF-3X: Fast Querying, High Update Rates, and Consistency for RDF Databases. In: VLDB (2010)

[OAE+09] Ousterhout, J.K., Agrawal, P., Erickson, D., Kozyrakis, C., Leverich, J., Mazières, D., Mitra, S., Narayanan, A., Parulkar, G.M., Rosenblum, M., Rumble, S.M., Stratmann, E., Stutsman, R.: The case for RAMClouds: scalable high-performance storage entirely in DRAM. Operating Systems Review 43(4) (2009)

[Ora07] Oracle. Change Data Capture (2007), `http://download.oracle.com/docs/cd/B28359_01/server.111/b28313/cdc.htm`

[Pla09] Plattner, H.: A common database approach for OLTP and OLAP using an in-memory column database. In: SIGMOD (2009)

[SHBI+06] Schroeder, B., Harchol-Balter, M., Iyengar, A., Nahum, E.M., Wierman, A.: How to Determine a Good Multi-Programming Level for External Scheduling. In: ICDE, p. 60 (2006)

[SRH90] Stonebraker, M., Rowe, L.A., Hirohama, M.: The Implementation of Postgres. IEEE Trans. Knowl. Data Eng. 2(1), 125–142 (1990)

[TBA10] Tozer, S., Brecht, T., Aboulnaga, A.: Q-Cop: Avoiding bad query mixes to minimize client timeouts under heavy loads. In: ICDE, pp. 397–408 (2010)

[Vol10a] VoltDB. Overview (March 2010), `http://www.voltdb.com/_pdf/VoltDBOverview.pdf`

[Vol10b] VoltDB. VoltDB TPC-C-like Benchmark Comparison-Benchmark Description (May 2010), `https://community.voltdb.com/node/134`

Insight into Events: Event and Data Management for the Extended Enterprise

Julio Navas

SAP France, 157-159 rue Anatole France,
92309 Levallois-Perret, France
Julio.Navas@sap.com

Abstract. This paper describes the methodology and implementation of an event management system, called Event Insight, for highly distributed systems, which was built by SAP to solve the scalability and reliability problems faced by SAP customers in industries such as logistics, supply-chain, oil and gas, and consumer product goods. The core of the approach integrates three main technologies together: event federation, an event processing network, and complex event processing. This paper will use a high-level motivating example from the oil and gas industry to illustrate the use of the technology.

Keywords: Wide-Area Event Management, Sensor Networks, Distributed Event Management.

1 Introduction

Interactions with SAP customers show that new problems have arisen as a result of the success of enterprise systems. The rapid decrease in the cost and size of data communications hardware and various sensor technologies offers to support a wealth of new businesses, loosely termed "sensor networks" [1][2]. It is common for customers to have 10's, 100's, or even 1000's of data sources throughout their IT landscape. Yet these customers have a need for a holistic operational view across all of these data sources.

New applications have been proposed in areas including intelligent highways, power grid management, intelligent battlefields, and remote product service and maintenance. Although the applications are varied, they share common features such as relatively large number of data sources (typically on the order of 10^5 or more) and relatively volatile data and data organization.

Most application-level tools wish to treat such a collection of data as a traditional database, using well-known query languages to access the data. In the state-of-the-art of commercial systems, the solution to similar problems is to use a centralized database (known as an operational data store), and collect the data as fast as possible, either through polling or event-driven reporting. Applications then act on the database in the traditional way.

The operational data generated by these systems, by partner company enterprise systems, and by complementary data systems, creates situations where it is not possible to insert this information into a central database in a timely manner. Worse,

M. Castellanos, U. Dayal, and V. Markl (Eds.): BIRTE 2010, LNBIP 84, pp. 24–35, 2011.

in a world where 73% of companies out-source significant parts of their business process, much of the operational data is not even directly available. The databases themselves, and especially their data communications channels, become bottlenecks that prevent the system from achieving these scales. Moreover, such databases represent critical failure points, and also introduce latency that may be relevant in real-time applications. A system is needed which is highly scalable, offers no critical failure points, and lets data flow from the source to the requestor as rapidly as possible. One research project addressing this space is COUGAR [3], but this system assumes a centralized index of all data sources, which does not address our scalability or critical failure point requirements.

At SAP, we see a great future potential in developing technology that will satisfy these very challenging constraints. A motivating example from the oil and gas industry will serve as a guide for this paper, as we show examples from this domain to illustrate how our system operates. Section 3 describes this example and Section 5 describes how EI would be applied to it. Section 4 describes the technology approach taken by SAP's Event Insight. Our possible future directions are described in Section 6.

2 Goals

As a result of interactions with customers, the following software requirements were deemed necessary (See Fig. 1):

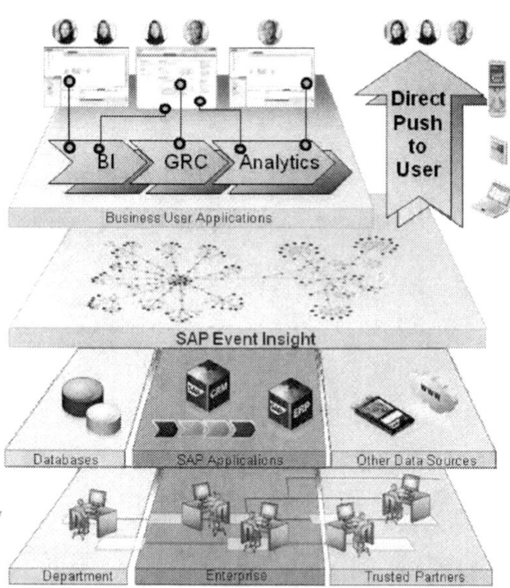

Fig. 1. SAP Event Insight - Solution Overview

- **Real-time Push of Information to Business Users** - Events across high volumes and distributions of data in "internet time." For example, up to 30,000 event correlations per second.

- **Cross-enterprise Automation** - Automate the process of resolving new event requests to reduce the time-to-value for a new event question from the current industry standard of 5-6 person-weeks per question.
- **System Scaling** - Throughput would be independent of data volume, quantity, and distribution pattern. For example, 2000 tier-one suppliers and 30,000 tier-two suppliers.
- **Manage the data "in place"** - But easily allow the flexible and ad hoc movement of data when necessary
- **Allow local control over data administration** - But easily enable participation in broader data footprint of "integrated enterprise"
- **Layer on top of Existing Landscape** - Within and across enterprises through standards already in place

3 Motivating Example in the Oil and Gas Industry

Fig. 2 shows an example of the type of application that we support. This example is a generalization of the types of problems faced by customers in the oil & gas industry and is similar to the types of problems encountered in other verticals as well. The main problems are:

- **Canonical Data Model** - Each oil rig is a custom process factory implementation with each having custom data models and tag names. So, it is not possible to do an apples-to-apples comparison between oil rigs.

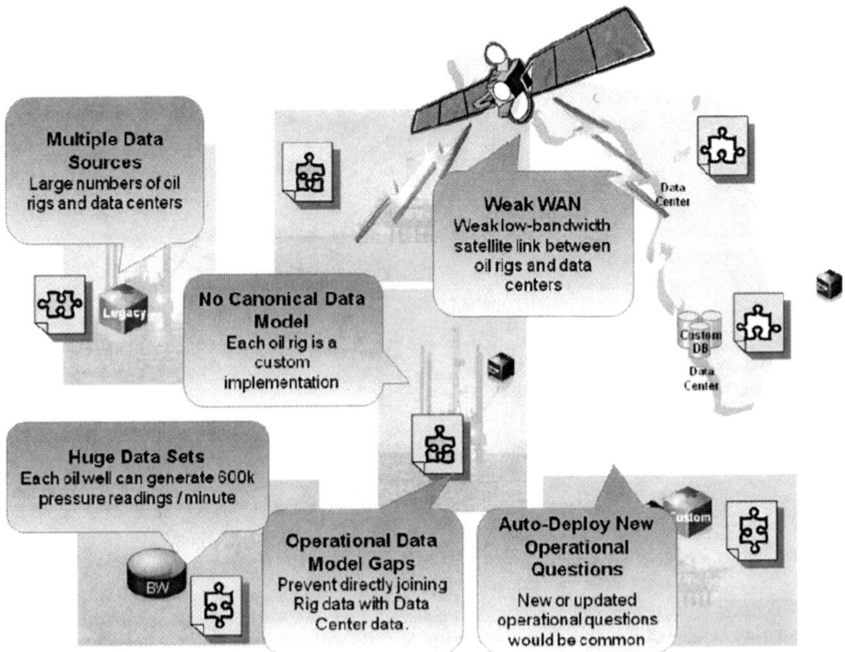

Fig. 2. Event Management Issues Encountered in the Oil & Gas Industry

- **Scale to large numbers of oil rigs (both on land an in the ocean) and data centers** – Because of the remote locations of oil rigs, weak low-bandwidth connections (such as satellite links) between oil rigs and data centers are common. Oil companies typically have 100's of oil rigs both on land and in the ocean and would want to globally deploy any resulting solution.
- **Automated Deployment of New Operational Questions** – Each oil well can generate approximately 600,000 pressure readings per minute. This quantity of data is too large to fit through the satellite link. For the data to be easily consumed by business users, the sensor data from the oil rigs needs to be enriched with the data from the enterprise systems that are located in the data centers. New or updated operational questions would be common and would occur at least once a week. All of the experts would be located at the data centers on the mainland.
- **Correlate oil rig data with enterprise data at the data centers** - It is not possible to directly join the tag data from the oil rigs with the data in enterprise systems in the data center because there is a translation gap in the data model between the oil rigs and the data centers. Oil companies want to be able to walk the equipment hierarchy from the architectural documents in enterprise system to the tag-level information.

4 The Event Insight Approach

Event Insight (EI) is designed to be a horizontal event enabling solution for all industries and companies that have a need for a global and unified view into their operational enterprise data no matter how widely distributed. EI integrates three key technologies (See Fig. 3):

- Event Federation
- Event Processing Network
- Complex Event Processing (CEP)

Since EI is meant to answer event-based operational questions in real-time or near-real-time, it needs to correlate raw operational data on-the-fly. Customer interviews indicate that within 2-3 years, it will be necessary to perform up to 30,000 event correlations per second and beyond. Therefore, EI chose to use a third-party CEP engine that can handle huge volumes of data streams in real-time. Since a third-party CEP engine is used, it will not be described here in this paper.

Currently, a major impediment to eventing systems is the large amount of time required to program the logic behind each operational question. In other words, not only do users need to specify *what* they want, they also need on average 5-6 weeks of programming to specify *how* to go about answering the question (See Fig. 4).

EI is therefore designed with federation and streaming database principles in mind so that a user need only specify *what* they want and EI automatically determines *how* to go about answering the question. This use of federation techniques for events results in the value proposition graph of Fig. 5. Previously, a human being needed to program both the *how* for every operational question and for every data source.

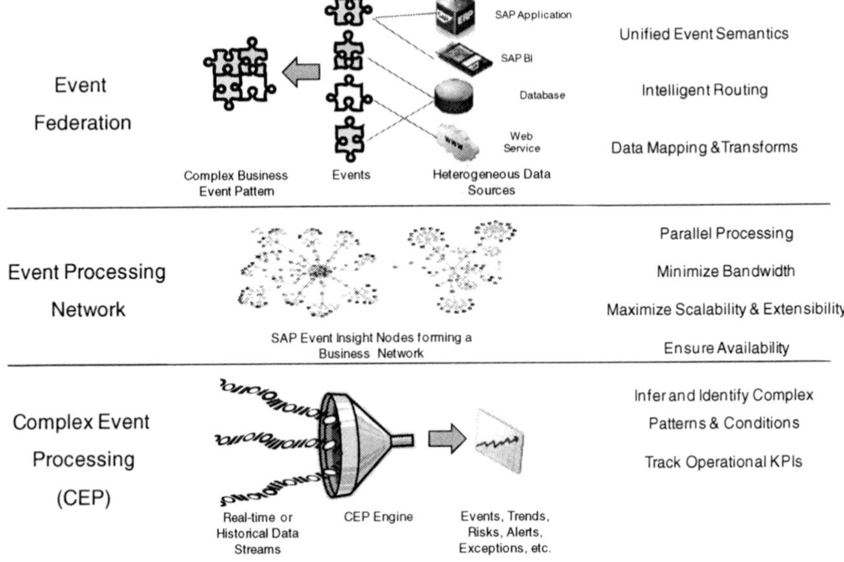

Fig. 3. Key Technologies for Event Insight

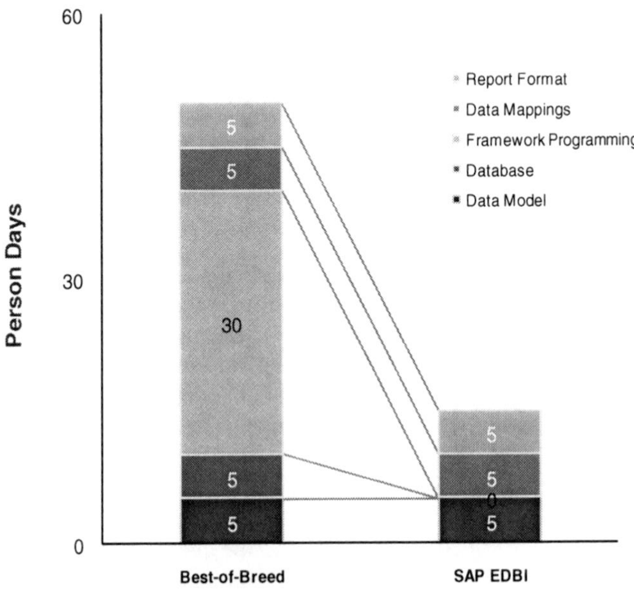

Fig. 4. Operational report creation assuming one operational query and four data sources

This resulted in a cost that curves upward very quickly. By automating *how* the query will be executed, EI reduces the cost to just the time needed to connect and define each data source, which is linear. In other words, the more questions or data sources that are needed for a particular project, the greater the difference between the two lines and, therefore, the greater the value that EI delivers. Finally, another one of the federation principles that EI uses is the abstraction of data organization and formats through the use of a single normalized and global view into all of the operational data.

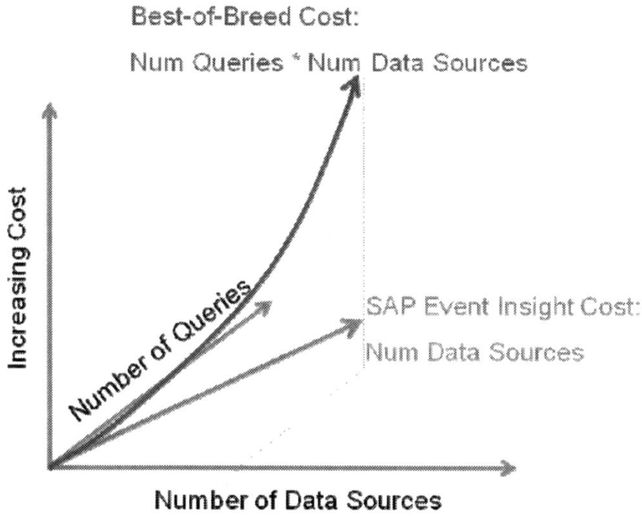

Fig. 5. Relative Implementation Costs when Scaling Up

The raw information that EI needs to correlate is often found scattered over multiple enterprise systems and across multiple locations. Customer interviews have shown that the number of systems could be as high today as 3000+ enterprise systems. Since 73% of companies out-source major portions of their business process these days, oftentimes, the operational information is also scattered across multiple companies. These partner companies form a value chain with multiple tiers. Customer interviews indicate that these tiers can be as large as 2000 companies in tier 1 and 25,000 companies in tier 2. As a result, in many customer instances, this raw operational data is too voluminous to be centralized. Therefore, EI is designed to be able to operate in a distributed manner and as close as possible to the systems of record themselves. Also, EI is designed to scale to very large numbers of servers, locations, and companies and allow them to operate in an uncoordinated and decentralized manner. It accomplishes this through the use of a publish-and-subscribe messaging layer.

EI needs to effectively layer on top of an existing enterprise landscape. However, customer interviews show that all of these potentially thousands of enterprise systems can be comprised of SAP systems, competitor offerings, and custom-built applications. Therefore, EI is designed to operate across a heterogeneous landscape.

Finally, EI is meant to be used in an application environment. Therefore, EI uses a publish-and-subscribe paradigm with standard application APIs.

4.1 Federated Event Query Processing

Event Query Planning. When a client submits an event query for processing, an execution plan will first be created. The event query will be analyzed, optimized, and federated into simpler fragments composed of individual raw event types and tables. The techniques used are similar to traditional algorithms for distributed joins as described in [4]. EI will use the global⇔local mapping information to determine what transformations need to be performed. It will use the index information within the Event Processing Network to determine whether it needs to execute the event query (or fragments) remotely. For each event query, there will be one master coordinator and possibly one or more slave servers. See Fig. 6.

The basic concept of event query parallelization assumes that a given event query can be decomposed into a hierarchical Abstract Syntax Tree (AST). The AST can be further decomposed into a set of query fragments. Each query fragment would contain a subset of the AST with instructions to the slave servers to execute that piece of the AST in parallel or in series depending on the flow of data within the AST. Note that currently the Event Insight product uses only two levels of execution – a single master and a set of slaves. However, theoretically, multiple levels of execution are possible.

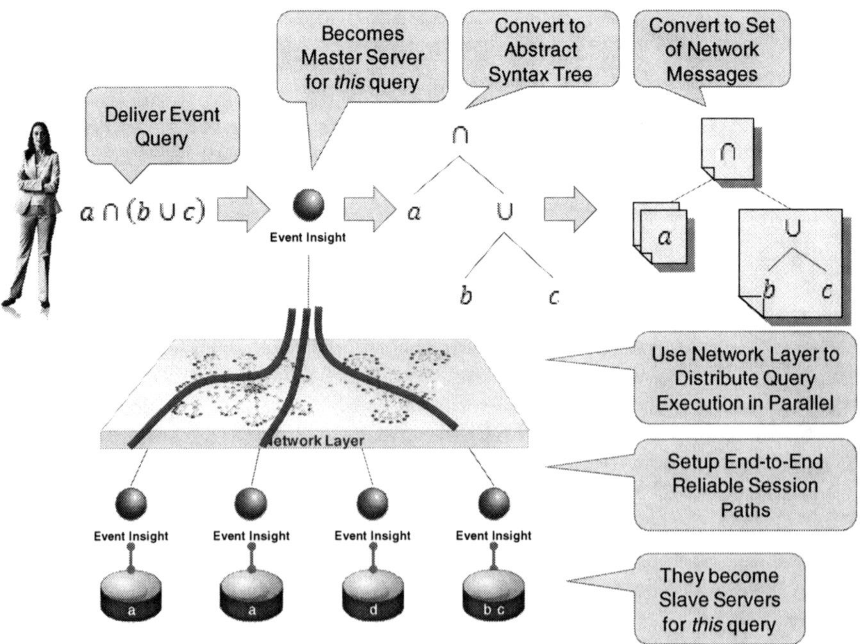

Fig. 6. Process for Event Planning and Execution

Event Query Execution. Once the event query plan is finalized, EI will setup the paths down which the event query and results sets will flow. The query plan will be deployed amongst the underlying Input Adapters, Complex Event Processing engines, and remote EI servers. If EI detects that multiple users who have equivalent access rights are asking the same question, then stream sharing will be used and their query execution will be joined together.

All event queries are executed in a publish-and-subscribe manner. When the information comes from a data source, the data will be transformed from that data source's local schema to the normalized global schema. The event query will be executed continuously until the user specifically unsubscribes.

4.2 Event Processing Network

An overlay network layer is used to distribute the query fragments from the master to the set of slave servers and reliable session paths are created between the master and slave servers for the efficient flow of the query fragments downstream and the events, data, and intermediate results upstream. As the query fragments are processed by the slave servers upon the event streams and data, intermediate results are pushed upstream to the master server where the final operations and joins take place. Final results are then streamed out of the master server.

An Event Federation Grid will be used to achieve fast performance. Here we assume that the data sources will be distributed in a disjoint manner between several EI servers. These servers may or may not be in different locations.

Once the user defines the specific complex event pattern for the business event he wishes to receive, EI will analyze that event and attempt to break it up into smaller and simpler pattern fragments. If more than one data source applies to an event pattern fragment, then copies of that fragment would be sent to all EI servers that are connected to the applicable data sources and executed in parallel. Note that this process may be recursive. Event pattern fragments themselves may be broken up into even simpler patterns and also executed in parallel.

When the fragment's pattern is matched by the local data, then the result would be sent to the first EI server. This server would collate the responses from the various fragments and perform any last-minute calculations, joins, or functions. If, after all this, the server detects that the original event pattern has been matched, then the response would be forwarded to the user.

Forwarding Between Servers. EI uses a novel network routing protocol as the basis for its Event Processing Network. This is a one-to-many network routing protocol and uses techniques derived from IP-multicast [5]. In the simple case of a flat network, each EI server's routing component will have a routing table entry for each EI server in the network. Each entry will then contain information on a destination's event and data content, IP address, and the shortest path to the destination. In the case of a large network of servers or of a multitude of administrative domains, hierarchical routing with an unlimited number of hierarchy levels is also possible.

The destination for a message is defined as the event or data content that is sought. When forwarding a message, an EI router uses its routing table information to determine the specific final destinations that contain that event or data content and then forwards the message on the shortest path to those destinations. Because the destinations for a message are described using event or data content, this allows for a decoupling of event consumers and event producers, which, in turn, allows for new destinations, locations, or companies, to be added quickly in an uncoordinated fashion and without requiring that the system by reprogrammed in any way.

Once a message has been forwarded all of the way from the sender to all of the destinations, the routers will have created a one-to-many shortest-path routing tree with the *root* at the sender and the *leaves* at all of the destinations. This routing tree is called a session and soft-state at each router (in the form of a routing cache) is used to maintain and manage a record of this session.

Because probabilistic equations are used for the destination indexing for engineering trade-off reasons, false positives may result during the forwarding phase. Final checks at the destinations are performed and, if false positives are detected, those routing paths may be pruned as a result.

4.3 OSGI Framework

EI is based on the OSGI Framework[6]. This framework allows for all EI servers in multiple locations within an enterprise to be managed from a single Administration Console. All Java server and UI side functionality is packaged into bundles and is managed by a Bundle Manager at each physical server. Furthermore, all bundles can be pre-loaded into a Bundle Repository and then distributed to all of the EI servers throughout an enterprise.

Since EI management is based on OSGI, this allows for low TCO because only the bundles that are required for a particular location need to be installed. When an updated bundle is available, it can simply be loaded into the Bundle Repository and, from there, pushed to all EI server installations that require it.

Bundle Repository. Each location does not need a full copy of all of the components of EI. An administrator would push only the necessary components from the Bundle Repository to the different locations. Note that a copy of the Bundle Manager must be installed at each location in order to manage the local components.

In a multiple location scenario, the individual components are designed to automatically discover each other and establish connections between each other. However, the servers need to be on the same LAN subnet in order for the individual components to find each other. Otherwise, they must be specifically configured to connect to each other.

Input and Output Adapter Frameworks. The Input and Output Adapter Framework is designed to abstract away both the underlying data sources as well as the destination sinks. See Fig. 7. Each adapter presents the same manager API internally and registers with the EI Server so that it knows about them. Input Adapters can be configured as either event sources or historical data sources. The framework is designed as a Software Development Kit so that new adapters can be created in a straightforward manner. Adapters have a filtering capability that can be configured on a per-event-query basis.

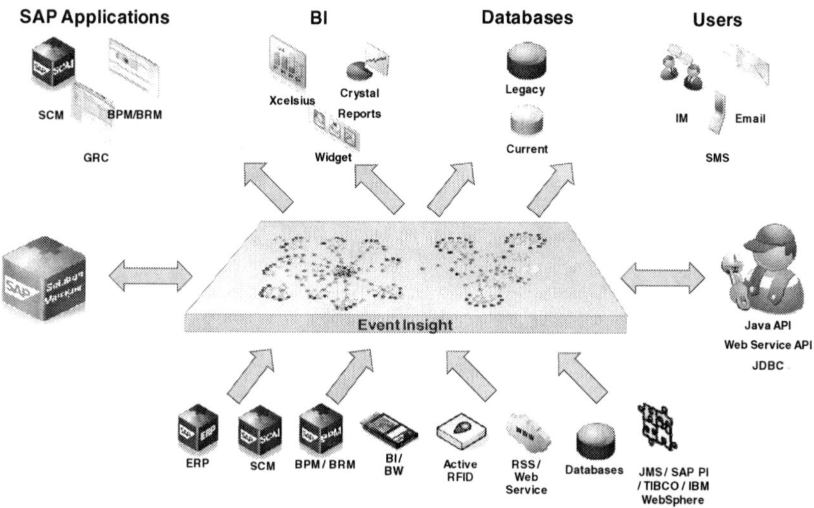

Fig. 7. Input and Output Adapter Frameworks

5 Application of Event Insight to the Oil and Gas Example

Let's revisit the motivating example of the customer in the oil & gas industry. Here is how EI would be applied to this problem:

- **Canonical Data Model** - Use the EI global schema to have a virtual single view across all data sources. This enables standard comparisons, KPIs, and SLAs across all locations and data sources.
- **Scale to large numbers of oil rigs and data centers** - Because of the weak satellite link, central processing is not possible. Deploy multiple EI servers – at least one per oil rig and data center. Use the EI Event Processing Network to tie them all together into a single system. Then make use of EI's OSGi-based platform to centrally deploy, configure, monitor, and maintain EI by the experts at the data centers.
- **Automated Deployment of New Operational Questions** - Use EI's event federation and parallel processing capability to automatically split up a new operational question into multiple fragments and push these fragments down to the EI servers on the oil rigs for local processing. Only result sets would be sent from the oil rigs back to the data centers over the satellite link. Use the CEP engine at each server to be able to handle the high volumes of event traffic from the oil well pressure readings.
- **Correlate oil rig data with SAP data at the data centers** - As part of our global schema, we created a translation table between the tag fields at the oil rigs and the data model in the enterprise systems. This allows us to correlate and integrate data from the architectural document level down to the tag level and to be able to show both together.

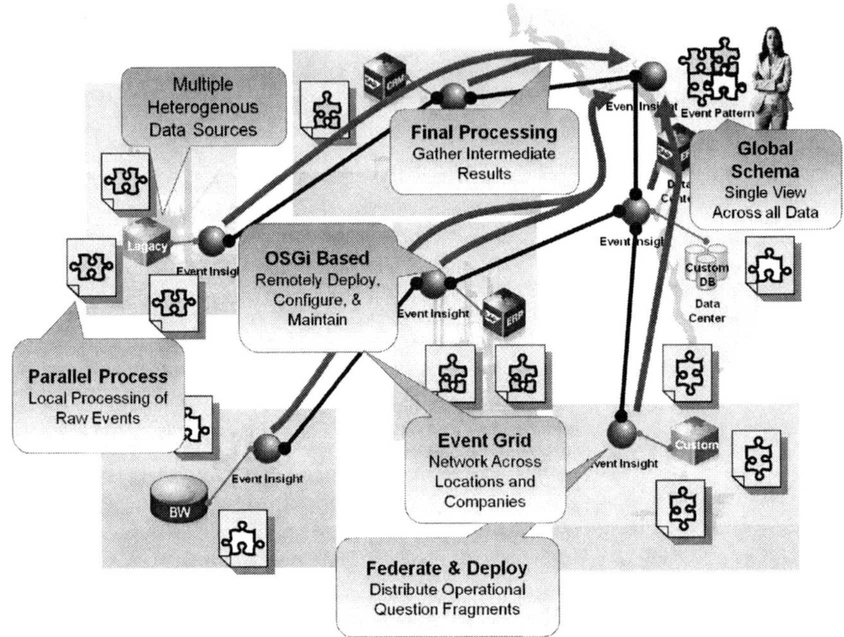

Fig. 8. Federated Parallel Execution

6 Possible Future Directions

SAP continues to extend EI into nearby technology realms. Customer co-innovation projects are underway that push EI onto embedded devices and onto the network cloud.

The embeddable version of EI is meant to be run on small resource-poor devices with no dependencies on external libraries except for a Java run-time engine. Envisioned uses include mobile applications as well as on hardened devices for industrial uses. Typical deployment size for the prototype system is about 400KB. The smallest deployment has been 140KB on an Android Smartphone.

The cloud-based version of EI is meant to achieve a cloud-based cluster scalability capability. It would utilize dynamic auto-deployment based on measured workload. The prototype can already dynamically deploy, control, and scale up and down multiple EI instances in the cloud. The Event Processing Network automatically ties all of the EI instances together into a single system. The prototype has been executed simultaneously across the American and European cloud data centers.

References

1. Estrin, D., Govindan, R., Heidemann, J., Kumar, S.: Next Century Challenges: Scalable Coordination in Sensor Networks. In: ACM/IEEE Intl. Conf. on Mobile Computing and Networking, ACM MobiCom 1999, Seattle (1999)
2. Kahn, J., Katz, R., Pister, K.: Mobile Networking for Smart Dust. In: ACM/IEEE Intl. Conf. on Mobile Computing and Networking, ACM MobiCom 1999, Seattle (1999)

3. Bonnet, P., Gehrke, J., Seshadri, P.: Towards Sensor Database Systems. In: 2nd International Conference on Mobile Data Management, Hong Kong (2001)
4. Ozsu, M., Valuriez, P.: Principles of Distributed Database Systems. Prentice Hall, Englewood Cliffs (1999)
5. Deering, S.: Multicast Routing in a Datagram Internetwork, Stanford Technical Report, STAN-CS-92-1415, Department of Computer Science, Stanford University (1991)
6. OSGI Service Platform Specification R4, http://www.osgi.org/

Building Enterprise Class Real-Time Energy Efficient Decision Support Systems

Meikel Poess[1] and Raghunath Nambiar[2]

[1] Oracle Corporation, 500 Oracle Pkwy, Redwood Shores, CA 94065, USA
meikel.poess@oracle.com
[2] Cisco Systems, Inc., 3800 Zanker Road, San Jose, CA 95134, USA
rnambiar@cisco.com

Abstract. In today's highly competitive marketplace, companies have an insatiable need for up-to-the-second information about their business' operational state, while generating Terabytes of data per day [2]. The ability to convert this data into meaningful business information in a timely, cost effective manner is critical to their competitiveness. For many, it is no longer acceptable to move operational data into specialized analytical tools because of the delay this additional step would take. In certain cases they prefer to directly run queries on their operational data. To keep the response time of these queries low while data volume increases, IT departments are forced to buy faster processors or increase the number of processors per system. At the same time they need to scale the I/O subsystem to keep their systems balanced. While processor performance has been doubling every two years in accordance with Moore's Law, I/O performance is lagging far behind. As a consequence, storage subsystems not only have to cope with the increase in data capacity, but, foremost, with the increase in I/O throughput demand, which is often limited by the disk drive performance and the wire bandwidth between the server and storage.

A solution to this problem is to scale the I/O subsystem for capacity and to cache the database in main memory for performance. This approach not only reduces the I/O requirements, but also significantly reduces power consumption. As the database is physically located on durable media just like traditional databases, all ACID requirements are met.

While such an in-memory solution is feasible today for small data amounts using custom built systems, such a solution seems unfeasible for Multi-Terabyte systems running main-stream relational database management systems (RDBMS) simply because today's systems use CPUs with built-in memory controllers that support only a limited number of memory channels per CPU. In this paper we discuss the viability of building an enterprise class real-time Multi-Terabyte decision support infrastructure by combining the power of Oracle's RDBMS technologies and Cisco's extended memory technology [4]. We believe that Oracle and Cisco combined can deliver effective enterprise class real-time data warehouse infrastructure can deliver value by helping companies to respond to competitive pressures and new opportunities.

Keywords: Real-Time Decision Support Systems, Lessons learned from large practical applications of real-time Business Intelligence, Industrial experience and challenges.

M. Castellanos, U. Dayal, and V. Markl (Eds.): BIRTE 2010, LNBIP 84, pp. 36–51, 2011.

1 Introduction

In today's highly competitive marketplace, companies have an insatiable need for up-to-the-second information about their business' operational state, while generating Terabytes of data per day [2]. The ability to convert this data into meaningful business information in a timely, cost effective manner is critical to the competitiveness of such businesses. For many, it is no longer acceptable to move operational data into specialized tools just because of the latency of performing this additional step. In many cases they want to directly run queries on their operational data. To keep the response time of these queries low while data is increasing they are forced to increase their systems' compute capability by buying faster processors or increasing the number of processors either in a scale up or scale out way.

As can be observed in TPC-H benchmark publications, enterprise data warehouses are built using large Symmetric Multiprocessor Systems (SMP) or clusters of industry standard servers that are connected to a Storage Area Network (SAN) or Direct Attached Storage (DAS). In both cases, because of the increase in CPU performance, the largest single performance bottleneck is the I/O bandwidth. As has been demonstrated in the Standard Performance Evaluation Corporation benchmarks (SPEC), processor performance has been doubling every two years in accordance with Moore's Law. Contrary, disk performance is lagging far behind. As a consequence, storage subsystems not only have to cope with the increase in data capacity, but, foremost, with the increase in I/O throughput demand, which is often limited by the disk drive performance and the wire bandwidth between the server and storage. Hence, customers are forced to increase the number of spindles and controllers to achieve higher I/O performance. In many cases they are running into bandwidth limitations between the database servers and storage subsystems. Similar trends can be observed in industry standard benchmark publications like TPC-H, which is widely adapted in the industry as the landmark for decision support performance and the showcase for emerging technology. For instance, between 2003 and 2010 the maximum number of processors used in 1 Terabyte TPC-H publications increased from 12 to 64. More dramatic, the maximum number of processor cores [21] of publications increased from 16 to 512. At the same time the number of disk drives per processor increased from 10 in 2003 to 40 in 2010.

High I/O bandwidth comes with a very steep cost factor, both in terms of hardware cost as well as energy cost. In today's competitive environment it is not uncommon for a customer to ask for a system to be able to scan 10TBytes[1] of active data in one minute. Such a configuration would require an I/O bandwidth of 166 Gbytes[2] per second, that is, about 530 4 Gbit Fibre Channel SAN connections and over 2266 disk drives, assuming an average 75MBytes[3]/s scan rate per disk with large random I/Os. Not counting the cooling cost, such an I/O subsystem would consume about 34 kW[4]. Assuming $0.11 per kWh the power to operate this I/O subsystem 24 by 7 would cost about $32,313 per year.

---

[1] TBytes=1024*1024*1024*1024 bytes.

[2] GBytes=1024*1024*1024 bytes.

[3] Mbytes=1024*1024.

[4] Using [8] to estimate the power consumption.

At the same rate as CPU performance has been increasing, memory DIMM capacity has been increasing and memory DIMM cost has been decreasing steadily. Memory DIMM capacity has increased from 256 Mbytes per DIMM in 2000 to 16 Gbytes per DIMM today. This trend is expected to continue and will lead to a 32 Gbytes per DIMM capacity by end of this year. In the same time window the cost per memory DIMM ($/Gbytes) has decreased from $5000 to less than $150.

As a consequence, new technologies for decisions support systems have emerged that take advantage of this trend. These technologies achieve extremely high performance by keeping the active data portion of a decision support system in memory. While traditional TPC-H systems configure about 25% of the TPC-H database size for main memory, recent publications configure up to 288% of the TPC-H database size for main memory [16]. At the same time they are able to substitute large, fast I/O subsystems with low cost, low performing I/O subsystems. In TPC-H benchmark publications performance of these types of configurations has dwarfed traditional approaches by factors of 10. History has shown that ground braking technologies were first demonstrated by TPC-H publications and later widely adapted by the industry. The authors predict that very large memory systems will be a viable solution for high performance decision support systems in the near future. A side effect of this trend is an increased energy efficiency of such configurations.

In this paper we discuss building enterprise class real-time data warehouse infrastructure by combining the massive scale-out and in-memory capabilities of Oracle database technologies and Cisco System's extended memory technology [4]. Oracle's massive scale-out capability enables clustering large number of servers while allowing concurrent access to one database. In-Memory database cache option delivers a real-time, dynamic, updatable cache for frequently accessed data in the Oracle Database. This has been demonstrated in recent benchmark result [15]. Caching performance-critical subsets of a database in main memory dramatically reduces the I/O bandwidth requirements and increases throughput significantly by relying on memory-optimized algorithms. For performance-critical applications in industries such as communications, financial services, and defense, the Oracle in-memory database cache option delivers application response times in sub-seconds by bringing the frequently accessed data closer to the application. To enable real-time decision support systems in-memory, systems need to accommodate large amounts of memory into individual servers. Cisco's extended memory provides more than twice as much industry-standard memory (384 Gbytes) as traditional two-socket servers, increasing performance and capacity for demanding workloads [4].

At the same time in-memory decision support system increase performance they decrease energy cost by omitting energy-hungry storage subsystems. Using the TPC-H benchmark model we conduct an analysis on performance, energy cost and energy efficiency of such configurations compared to traditional disk I/O based configurations.

The remainder of the paper is organized as follows. Section 2 introduces necessary details about the TPC-H benchmark, especially its performance metric. It furthers demonstrates that technology trends used in TPC-H benchmarks are precursors for customer deployments. Section 3 analyzes the energy consumption of large scale TPC-H systems. It uses the accepted name plate energy estimation, published in [8]. Section 4 introduces a simple mathematical model that shows how TPC-H benchmark systems scale with the number of processors. Based on this model Section 4 sizes systems to run large scale decision support systems that achieve real-time performance. Two types of systems are showcased: systems relying on disks to achieve low query elapsed time and high performance (traditional approach) and systems using large amounts of memory to achieve low query elapsed time and high performance (in-memory approach). Performance and energy consumption are shown for both, the traditional and in-memory solutions, followed by a demonstration on how such configurations can be built realistically using currently available technologies.

2 TPC-H and Industry Trends

TPC-H is a well known industry standard benchmark to measure performance of decision support systems. It models the decision support area where business trends are computed and refined data are produced to support the making of sound business decisions. It reduces the diversity of operations found in a typical decision support application, while retaining the application's essential performance characteristics, namely the level of system utilization and the complexity of operations when the system is utilized by a single user and multiple users concurrently. At its core TPC-H executes 22 business queries and concurrent data modifications, which are designed to exercise system functionalities in a manner representative of complex decision support applications. These queries have been given a realistic context, portraying the activity of a wholesale supplier to help the audience relate intuitively to the components of the benchmarks. TPC-H unifies single and multi-user performance into a single metric. The size of the dataset in Gbytes is indicated by the scale factor (SF). For a given scale factor this metric is computed as the geometric mean of single and multi-user performances in the following way:

$$QphH@SF = \sqrt{SingleUserPerformance@SF * MultiUserPerformance@SF} \tag{1}$$

This metric is also referred to as the *primary performance metric*. The single- user performance is calculated as the geometric mean of the elapsed times of all 22 queries and two update operations uf1 and uf2. t_{q0i} indicates the query elapsed time of query i as measured during the single user run with i∈ [1,2,..22]. t_{u0i} indicates the elapsed time of update function i as measured during the single user run with i∈ [1,2]. It is computed in the following way:

$$SingleUserPerformance@SF = \frac{SF * 3600}{\sqrt[24]{\prod_{i=1}^{22} t_{q0i} * \prod_{i=1}^{2} t_{u0i}}} \tag{2}$$

The multi-user performance is calculated as the arithmetic mean of the elapsed times of queries and updates run consecutively by multiple users. The number of concurrent users of the benchmark is indicated by S..

$$MultiUserPerformance@SF = \frac{3600 * 22 * S * SF}{\max_{s\in[1,2,..S]} \left(\sum_{ix=1}^{22} t_{qsi} + \sum_{i=1}^{2} t_{usi}\right)} \tag{3}$$

The resulting primary metric expresses the number of queries a system can perform per hour (QphH) in the presents of updates. The use of the geometric mean of the single-user test guarantees that short and long running queries are weighted equally and, consequently, optimized equally. Please note that both the single-user and multi-user performance metrics are normalized by scale factor (SF). Assuming that on a given system the query and update times scale linearly with scale factors, the QphH numbers that are achieved by this system running two different scale factors are identical. However, the actual query elapsed times increase according to the scale factor. This is done for marketing reasons. If the metrics were not normalized, small systems running on small scale factors would get about the same performance as large systems running on large scale factors.

In the context of real-time decision support systems the TPC-H metric is deceiving because a high QphH@SF indicates high query per hour performance since QphH@SF is multiplied by the scale factor. In order to demonstrate the real query per hour metric, we introduce a non-normalized version of the TPC-H primary metric [Qph] for our subsequent analysis. We define this non-normalized version of the TPC-H benchmark as:

$$QpH = \sqrt{SingleUserPerformance * MultiUserPerformance} \tag{4}$$

$$SingleUserPerformance = \frac{3600}{\sqrt[24]{\prod_{i=1}^{22} t_{q0i} * \prod_{i=1}^{2} t_{u0i}}} \tag{5}$$

$$MultiUserPerformance = \frac{3600 * 22 * S}{\max_{s\in[1,2,..S]} \left(\sum_{ix=1}^{22} t_{qsi} + \sum_{i=1}^{2} t_{usi}\right)} \tag{6}$$

For a detailed description of the TPC-H benchmark, its dataset and query workload, please refer to [6].

Even though the TPC-H benchmark lacks some aspects of modern decision support systems [6][11], the author's observation is that many businesses can relate the TPC-H workload to their own business, and that key technologies advances, which demonstrated performance gains in TPC-H benchmark publications, have been later adapted by the industry in implementing main stream decision support systems.

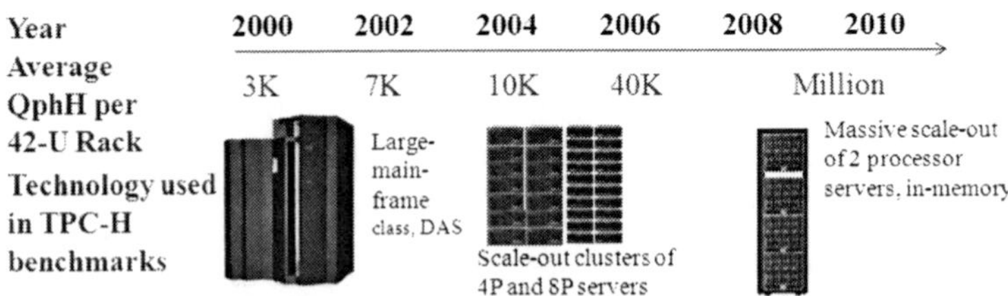

Fig. 1. Comparison of TPC-H Performance Trends to Industry Innovations

Figure 1 correlates key industry technologies with TPC-H performance. In the early 2000's, the TPC-H leadership was dominated by large SMP systems using Direct Attach Storage (DAS) systems delivering an average of 3000 QphH per 40U-rack. By 2005 the industry observed a shift towards scale-out cluster attached Storage Area Networks leading the TPC-H benchmarks. Scale-out cluster and SAN were widely adapted by the industry due to the performance, scalability and high-availability it offered [9]. Many of the industry's leading data warehouses ran on such configurations.

For instance, Amazon.com's online recommendation system is fed by an industry standard Grid data warehouse [2]. Another example is eBay's Greenpulm data warehouse holding over 6.5 petabyte of user data. Its implementation uses a cluster of 96 servers [5]. Later in the decade an influx of TPC-H benchmark has been observed on massive scale-out clusters that supported large aggregate memory capacity delivering over a Million queries-per hour per 42-u rack. In some cases, large numbers of nodes were clustered to achieve the desired memory capacity.

3 In-Memory TPC-H

TPC-H benchmark publications are grouped according to a number called the scale factor (SF). The scale factor determines the size of the raw data outside the database, e.g. SF=1000 means that the sum of all base tables equals 1 Tbyte. It must be chosen from the following set of discrete values: 100, 300, 1000, 3000, 10000, 30000 and 100000. An often asked question is the relevance of these discrete values. Rather than interpreting them as the database size, they should be viewed as the active dataset of a decision support system at peak load. Although each query only reads a portion of the entire database, the aggregate data that is read by all queries running during the benchmark execution equals the entire data set. The insert and delete operations that are executed as part of the benchmark execution do not cause the overall amount of data to grow, i.e. the amount of data inserted equals the amount of data deleted. This means that in order to keep a TPC-H database in memory, one needs to provision memory to keep an amount of data in memory that is roughly identical to the scale factor, plus the memory needed for any additional indexes and metadata. This is an upper boundary of the amount of memory needed to run in-memory. The actual amount of memory that is required depends on many factors such as the internal data representation within a database management system (DBMS), the amount of metadata required, number and type of indexes, compression etc. For instance, using the standard Deflate algorithm the size of a TPC-H database can be reduced to 29%.

Because the amount of memory needed to store a TPC-H database in memory depends on the DBMS and its configuration the TPC cannot label a benchmark result in-memory. However, the TPC reacted on the fact that more results use very large memory by mandating the disclosure of a memory to database size percentage. It is computed by multiplying by 100 the total memory size priced on the SUT and dividing this number by the size chosen for the test database. The ratio must be disclosed to the nearest 1/10th, rounded up. For example, a system configured with 256 Gbytes of memory for a 1000 SF test database has a memory to database size percentage of 25.6%.

Figure 2 shows all scale factor 1000 TPC-H results that were published since 2003. The triangles represent results that use up to 512 Gbytes of main memory (=72 results) while the squares represent results that use 768 Gbytes and more of main memory (=5 results[5]). We divide the results in these two groups because it is our believe that the results using up to 512 Gbytes (52.2% memory to database size percentage) of main memory can be considered "traditional" results in the sense that they relied

[5] Result IDs:110041101[16], 109060301[15], 108060302[14], 107121001[13], 107102903 [19].

mostly on disk I/O to achieve high performance, while results that use 768 Gbytes (76.8% memory to database size percentage) or more can be considered in-memory results. The average memory to database size percentage of all in-memory results at scale factor 1000 is 182.4%.

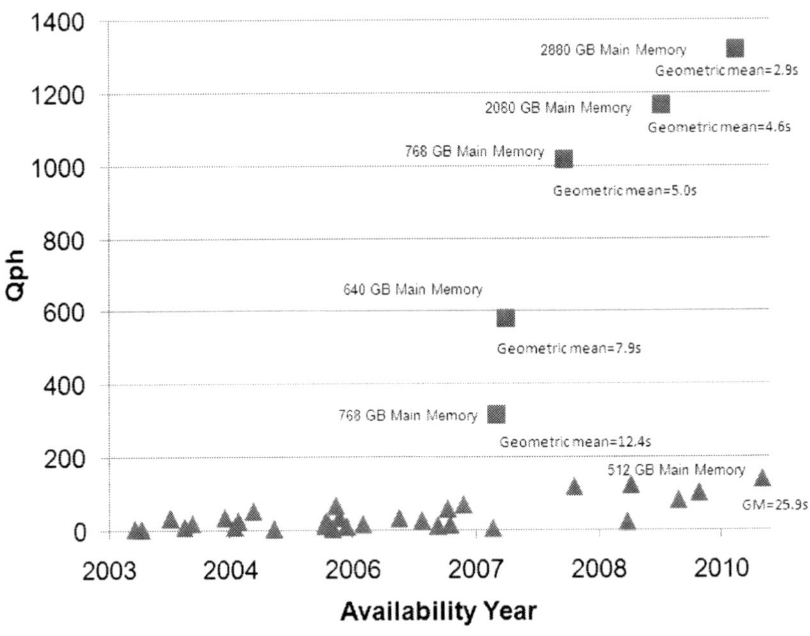

Fig. 2. Performance TPC-H Results at Scale Factor 1000

Achieving high performance by keeping the entire database in main memory is not a new concept. However, until recently it has not been practical mainly due to the limited capacity and higher cost of memory DIMMS. In recent year the industry has observed significant increase in the number of memory DIMMs that fit into industry standard servers and an increase in the capacity per memory DIMMs. These two factors combined with the massive scale-out capabilities of mainstream and startup databases led to the use of in-memory TPC-H solutions. On average in-memory results achieved 14.2 times the performance[6] of traditional results in 2007, 8.6 times in 2008, 15.3 times in 2009 and 10.8 times in 2010. The same trend can be observed in the geometric mean of single-user queries. The current leader, at scale factor 1000, configured 2.8 Tbytes of main memory and achieved 1317 Qph and a geometric mean of the single-user queries of 2.9s. The highest performing traditional result configured 384 Gbytes of main memory and achieved 102,7 Qph and a geometric mean of the single-user queries of 33.2s. The following graph clearly shows that since its introduction in-memory configurations increased the TPC-H metric significantly.

[6] Performance as measured by QphH.

The reason for this is two-fold; firstly, large-memory configurations substitute slow disk I/O with fast memory I/O. As a consequence processors are utilized better and performance per processor increases. Figure 3 shows the average per processor performance of traditional and in-memory TPC-H results. Per processor performance of traditional TPC-H publications increased from 3601 QphH to 10779 QphH in 2010, while per processor performance of in-memory results increased from 5274 QphH to 16461 QphH in 2010.

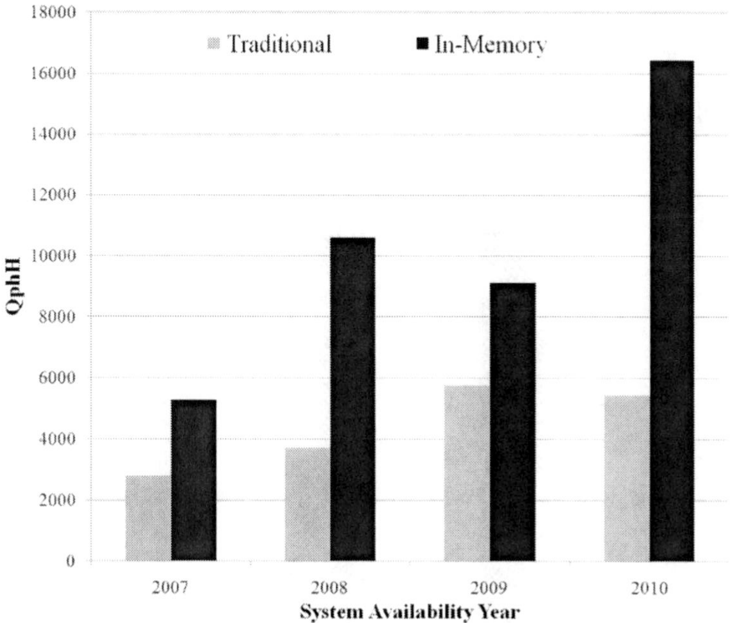

Fig. 3. Per Processor Performance TPC-H

The second reason for the enormous increase in TPC-H performance is reduced benchmarking cost of in-memory results. In-memory solutions make it cost prohibitive to publish benchmarks with a very large number of CPUs. In traditional, disk-based TPC-H publications the number of spindles needed to saturate one CPU can be as high as 36. At this processor to disk ratio a 128 processor publication would need 4608 disk drives, disk enclosures, cables and power supplies.

4 How In-Memory Systems Reduce Energy Consumption

Recent studies have shown that I/O subsystems are by far the largest energy consumers in large, modern computer systems [8][10][12]. Using the power estimation model defined in [8], Figure 4 shows the power consumption of key components of typical decision support systems t based on TPC-H workload at scale factors 100, 300 and 1000 using x86 based servers for a seven year period. The study distinguishes between three different types of benchmark configurations, also referred to as System Under Test (SUT):

Type 1: The most traditional type of SUT comprises of one or more servers with multiple CPUs, small main memory to database size ratio, typically less than 20 percent, and one or more HBAs (controllers). These systems are either directly attached to a storage subsystem or, in case of clustered systems, funnelled through one or multiple switches. The disk subsystem is comprised of multiple disk enclosures and usually many hard disk drives. 71 percent of the sample set uses this type of configuration.

Type 2: The second most common type of system used in TPC-H publications uses only internal controllers and disks to host the database. The servers look similar to the first configuration type. 23 percent of the sample set uses this type of configuration.

Type 3: In the last few years, benchmark publications emerged that use servers with a main memory to database size ratio of more than 50 percent. These systems use no or very small storage systems. Six percent of the sample set fall in this category.

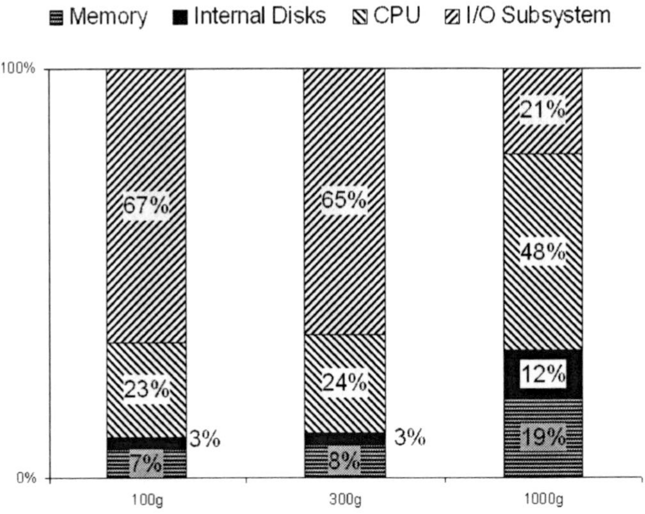

Fig. 4. Average Power Consumption of Key TPC-H Components

Figure 4 shows the power consumption of key components used in TPC-H benchmarks as a percent of the overall power consumption of the system. The percentages shown are based on the average power consumption of all benchmark results considered for each scale factor. The power consumption distribution across the different components is very similar for scale factors 100 and 300. Power consumption of systems used to publish results for scale factors 100 and 300 is dominated by the I/O subsystem. For both scale factors, about 66 percent of all power is consumed in the I/O subsystem. The second-largest power consumers are the CPUs. Power consumption (TDP) per CPU of the 78 results considered varies from 50W to 165W. Scale factor 100 and 300 results indicate that about 23 percent of all power is consumed by the CPUs. The third largest power consumer is the memory. About seven percent of all power for scale factor 100 and 300 results is consumed by memory. Internal disks play a smaller role for scale factors 100 and 300. Only three percent of all power is consumed by internal disks. The governing power consumer in the 1000 scale factor category is the CPU rather than the I/O subsystem. Forty-eight percent of all power is consumed by the CPUs, while 21 percent of power is consumed in the I/O subsystem. Memory takes the third spot with 19 percent and internal disks take the last spot with 12 percent.

The difference between the power distribution of the smaller scale factors of 100 and 300 compared to the larger scale factor of 1000 seems to be related to a recent development using large memory systems rather than large I/O systems. This development has two significant effects: higher performance and lower power consumption. Both effects are beneficial for customers as they can achieve their performance goal and still spend less on system power. With the introduction of the energy metric in TPC benchmarks, combined with the industry demand for energy efficiency, we anticipate that the vendors further focus on TPC-H benchmarks using very large memory.

5 Building Large Scale Real-Time Decision Support Systems

Two of the key characteristics of real-time decision support systems are real-time information delivery and real-time data analysis [2]. That is, real-time decision support systems enable the processing of information about business operations as they occur. There are two performance aspects to achieve this, namely Access Latency and Processing Latency. *Access Latency* is the latency time it takes to access the data by the decision support system. This can be achieved by moving operational data to the decision support system on a near real-time basis, or directly running queries on the operational database. In this section we concentrate on systems directly running queries on the operational database. *Processing Latency* is the time it takes to process raw data into information relevant to the business. This requires high compute power, low latency and high bandwidth servers combined with the query processing capabilities of a scalable database engine.

Let us first define what we consider real-time decision support performance in the context of TPC-H benchmark results. The average queries per hour (Qph) per processor core of the five in memory results published at scale factor 1000 is 2.5. Assuming that the average query elapsed time in a real-time decision support system is 10s, the system must achieve a Qph performance of less or equal to 360. On large data sets this can only be achieved by vastly increasing the number of processors. And, in order to keep the system balanced, it also means to scale all other components of a typical TPC-H system. In the next section we introduce a simple model how the components of TPC-H systems can be scaled to achieve a target performance.

5.1 Scaling Systems to Achieve High Performance

The design of a balanced TPC-H system requires that all of its components to be sized harmoniously. The major components that need to be scaled correctly for a balanced TPC-H system are: *processor; memory; storage arrays, I/O Channels and disks*. One can pick any of the components above and derive the size of any other components from it. In our experience, systems are usually sized around the number and speed of their processors. Of course the ratio at which the various components need to be scaled depends highly on the system's hardware and software. We develop a very simple model based on average component ratios of recent, x86 based TPC-H results. The following Table 1 lists all components that are relevant to a typical TPC-H system including the formulas how to scale the component based on a system with *c* cores.

Table 1. TPC-H Scaling Assumptions

Component	Calculation
Qph per processor core per Tbyte DBsize	$Qph_{Core} = \frac{5*Qph*Tbytes}{2}$
Number of cores required P Qph	$Num_{Cores} = \frac{P*SF}{Qph_{Core}}$
I/O capability per single drive	$IO_{disk} = 75\frac{MB}{s}$
I/O capability per single I/O Channel	$IO_{Channel} = 320\frac{MB}{s}$
I/O Channel connections per disk array	$IOC_{Array} = 4$
Size memory DIMM	$Size_{DIMM} = 8\ GB$
Size disk	$Size_{Disk} = 2\ TB$
Memory per Tbytes of database for in-memory	$TB_{SF} = 1.824 = \frac{1824}{1000}$
Cores per server	$Cores_{Server} = 16$
I/O required per core	$IO_{core} = 300\ MB$
I/O bandwidth required	$IO_{total} = c * IO_{core} = c * 300\frac{MB}{s}$
Number of external disks	$Nm_{Edisks} = \frac{IO_{total}}{IO_{disk}} = c * 4$
Number of I/O Channel connectors	$Nm_{Channels} = \frac{IO_{total}}{IO_{Channel}} = c * 0.9375$
Number of storage arrays	$Nm_{Arrays} = Nm_{FC} * IOC_{Array}$
Memory DIMMs (in-memory)	$Nm_{DIMMs} = \frac{SF}{TB_{SF}} = \frac{SF}{\frac{1824}{1000}} = SF * \frac{1000}{1824}$
Memory DIMMs (traditional)	$Nm_{DIMMs} = SF * 0.25$
Number of servers	$Nm_{Server} = \frac{Nm_{Cores}}{Cores_{Server}}$
Number of internal disks	$Nm_{IDisks} = Nm_{Server} * 2$

Using the above formula we can now compute the number of major components of a TPC-H system that is scaled to achieve *P* Qph. These numbers can directly be fed into the model developed in [8]

$$NumberServers = \frac{\frac{P*SF}{Qph_{Core}}}{16} = \frac{\frac{P*SF}{\frac{5}{2}}}{16} = \frac{\frac{P*SF*2}{5}}{16} = \frac{P*SF*2}{5*16} = \frac{P*SF}{40} \quad (7)$$

$$Memory = SF * \frac{1000}{1824} \quad (8)$$

$$Storage\ Arrays = Nm_{FC} * FC_{Array} = \frac{IO_{total}}{IO_{FC}} * 4 = \frac{c*IO_{disk}}{320\frac{MB}{s}} * 4 = \frac{c*300\frac{MB}{s}}{80\frac{MB}{s}} = \frac{30}{8} * c \quad (9)$$

$$IO\ Channels = \frac{IO_{total}}{IO_{Channel}} = \frac{c * IO_{core}}{320\frac{MB}{s}} = \frac{c * 300\frac{MB}{s}}{320\frac{MB}{s}} = \frac{30}{32} * c \quad (10)$$

$$Disks = \frac{IO_{total}}{IO_{Disk}} = \frac{c * IO_{core}}{75\frac{MB}{s}} = \frac{c * 300\frac{MB}{s}}{75\frac{MB}{s}} = 4 * c \quad (11)$$

5.2 Building Large Scale Real-Time Decision Support Systems Using Traditional Configurations

Using the model discussed above, this section illustrates four traditional real-time decision support configurations. Table 2 shows the number of processor cores, I/O bandwidth in Gbytes/s, number of external disks, number of 8 Gbyte memory DIMMS, number of servers and number of disk arrays required to achieve 360 Qph for database sizes ranging from 4 to 32 Tbytes. For example, it would take 576 processor cores to achieve 360 QpH for a database with 4 Tbytes of raw data. The necessary I/O bandwidth of 168.8 Gbytes/s requires an external storage subsystem with 2304 external disk drives and 135 disk arrays. Based on these numbers we estimate the power consumption of the system using the power estimation model developed in [8]. This system would consume 24.99 kWh. Assuming 10 cents per kWh the yearly energy consumption would cost $21,889.

Table 2. Sizing and power consumption for traditional configurations

Size in Tbytes	Required to achieve 360 Qph						Power Consumption [kWh][7]
	Number Cores	I/O in Gbytes per second	Number External disk drives	Number Memory DIMMS[8]	Number Servers	Number Disk Arrays	
4	576	168.8	2,304	108	36	135	49.03
8	1,152	337.5	4,608	216	72	270	98.06
16	2,304	675	9,216	432	144	540	196.11
32	4,608	1350	18,432	864	288	1,080	392.23

5.3 Building Large Scale Real-Time Decision Support Systems Using In-Memory Configurations

Let us have a look at building similar capacity configurations as those described in Table 2 using in-memory systems. Table 3 displays how in-memory systems would need to be scaled assuming an average main memory to database size ratio of 182.4% as reported in Section 2. The Energy consumption in the last column was stimated

[7] Estimated using the power consumption model developed in [8].

[8] Assuming 8 Gbyte memory DIMMS.

using the power consumption model developed in [8]. For a 4 Tbyte scale factor database the system needs to be configured with 7.5 Tbytes of main memory and requires 972 8 Gbyte DIMMs. The number of servers required is identical to those in the traditional configuration, which brings the memory required per server to 216 Gbytes. The power consumption of the in-memory configuration is about half of the power consumption of the traditional system. The database is assumed to be built on a RAID protected storage system to hold the database on durable media. The traditional system uses 49.03 kWh while the in-memory system uses 24.99 kWh.

Table 3. Sizing and power consumption for in- memory based configurations

	Required to achieve 360 Qph						Energy Con- sumption [kWh]
Size in Tbytes	**Number Cores**	**I/O in Gbytes per second**	**Number External disk drives**	**Number Memory DIMMS**	**Number Servers**	**Number Disk Arrays**	
4	576	168.8	0	972	36	0	24.99
8	1,152	337.5	0	1944	72	0	49.98
16	2,304	675	0	3888	144	0	99.95
32	4,608	1350	0	7776	288	0	199.9

To demonstrate the large difference in power consumption of traditional and in-memory systems, Figure 5 plots the energy consumption columns of Tables 3 and 4.

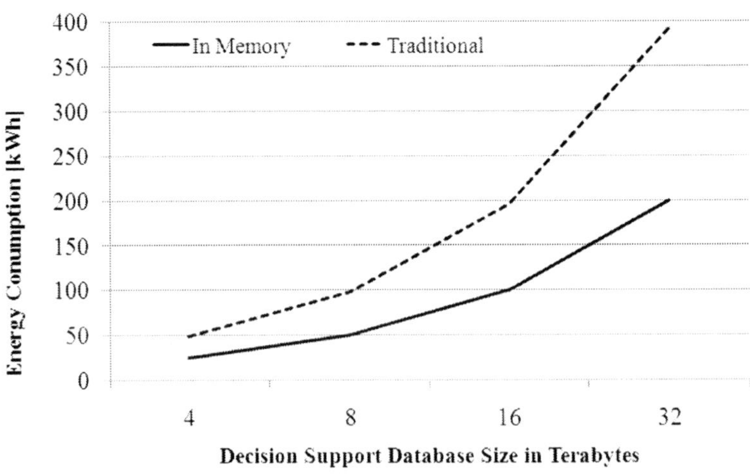

Fig. 5. Energy consumption of traditional and in-memory decision support system

5.4 Case Study: Building Large Scale Real-Time Decision Support Systems Using Cisco Unified Computing System

In this section we look at the viability of large scale real-time decision support systems based on the model discussed in Section 5.2 using Cisco Unified Computing

System, a standard-based datacenter platform. Cisco Unified Computing System integrates large number of compute nodes, connectivity and storage access resources in a single management domain.

From a high-level perspective, the Unified Computing System consists of UCS 5100 Series Blade Server Chassis, UCS 6100 Series Fabric Interconnects and UCS B-Series Blade Servers. The UCS Manager, embedded in the fabric interconnects, enables centralized management of all components including chassis, interconnects and blade servers. One of the key technologies used in Unified Computing System is the unified fabric technology. Where traditional compute environments have many parallel networks: for user connectivity; for storage access; for management; and for server clustering, the unified fabric technology consolidates these different types of network traffic onto a single general-purpose network fabric, optimized for performance and availability. This consolidation greatly simplifies the infrastructure for massive scale-out configurations.

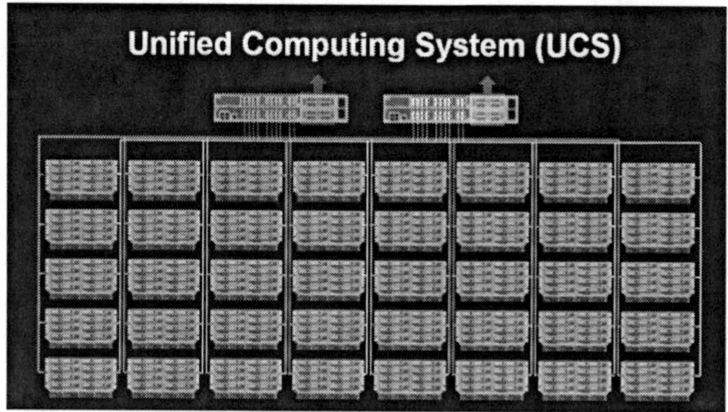

Fig. 6. Cisco Unified Computing System

The current generation of Unified Computing System supports 40 blade server chassis and up to 320 half-width blades or 160 full-width blades as depicted in Figure 6.

As an example we look at a UCS system with 40 UCS 5108 Chassis, populated with 160 UCS B250 M2 blade servers (full-width). Each server equipped with 2 sockets/12 cores and 384 GBytes main memory. It creates a powerful decision support system with a total of 1920 processor cores. Based on the model described in section 5.2 such a system supports a real-time decision support system of 13.3 Tbytes:

$$\frac{Qph_{Core} * 1920\ cores}{DBsize} = 360\ Qph \Leftrightarrow DBsize = \frac{\frac{5}{2}\frac{Qph * Tbytes}{core} * 1920\ core}{360\ Qph} \Leftrightarrow DBsize = 13.3\ Tbytes.$$

To host a 13.3 TByte in-memory decision support system, the system needs to have $13.3 * 1.824 = 24.25\ Tbytes$ of main memory, i.e. 152 Gbytes per server (rounded to 160 Gbytes/server with 8 Gbyte DIMMs). The power estimation model, developed in [8] suggests that such a system has a power footprint of 82 kW. A traditional disk drive based configuration of similar performance requires over 7,600 disk drives. Applying the same power model on such a system estimates its power consumption to 163 kW, about two times than the in-memory configuration. Assuming an operational model of 24x7 365 days and an average commercial price per kWh of 12.54 cents in the state of California for 2008 [1] the difference in annual power consumption between traditional configuration and in-memory configuration is $89,348.

To show that the power consumption numbers computed with [8] computes correct results we verify the number model is verified against UCS Power Calculator [3], a generally available power estimation tool. The power footprint of a fully populated Unified Computing System, comparable to the example above, with 40x UCS 5108 Blade Server Chassis, 160 x UCS B250 M2 blade server populated two Intel Xeon E5640 (2.66 GHz) processors, 160 GByte memory (total of 1920 processor cores and 25.24 TB memory), two UCS M81KR VIC Adapters and two internal 300 GByte 10K rpm disk drives are listed in Table 5. The power consumption estimates for idle power, power at 50% load and peak load are 30.6 kW, 56.8 kW and 83.7 kW respectively. The power consumption estimate at peak load is within 1% of the estimate from the model discussed in the paper.

Table 5. Estimates using UCS Power Calculator

	Power (kW)
Idle power (kW)	30.6
50% load power (kW)	56.8
Peak power (kW)	83.7

The number of servers supported in Unified Computing System is expected to double in the near future while the number of processor cores per server and memory capacity are also expected to increase. This enables Unified Computing System to meet future demands for larger and high performance decision support systems.

6 Conclusion

Many businesses are demanding real-time data warehouse performance. In this paper we introduced a capacity and performance model for real-time decision support systems. The model suggests that very large memory based decision support systems can offer lower cost and power footprints than traditional disk drive based solutions.

Acknowledgements. The authors thank Satinder Sethi and Ray Glasstone for their support in writing this paper, and Roy Zeighami and Jason Ding for their valuable comments and feedback.

References

1. Average Commercial Price of Electricity by State, `http://www.eia.doe.gov/cneaf/electricty/epa/fig7p6.html`
2. Azvine, B., Cui, Z., Nauck, D., Majeed, B.A.: Real Time Business Intelligence for the Adaptive Enterprise. CEC/EEE 29 (2006)
3. Cisco UCS Power Calculator, `http://www.cisco.com/assets/cdc_content_elements/flash/dataCenter/cisco_ucs_power_calculator/`

4. Cisco Unified Computing System Extended Memory Technology, http://www.cisco.com/en/US/prod/collateral/ps10265/ps10280/ps10300/white_paper_c11-525300.htmlhttp://www.cisco.com/en/US/prod/collateral/ps10265/ps10280/ps10300/white_paper_c11-525300.html
5. Monash Research, eBays two enormous data warehouses, http://www.dbms2.com/2009/04/30/ebays-two-enormous-data-warehouses/
6. Poess, M., Floyd, C.: New TPC Benchmarks for Decision Support and Web Commerce. SIGMOD Record 29(4), 64–71 (2000)
7. Poess, M., Nambiar, R.O., Vaid, K., Stephens, J.M., Huppler, K., Haines, E.: Energy Benchmarks: A Detailed Analysis. eE-Energy, 131–140 (2010)
8. Poess, M., Nambiar, R.O.: A Power Consumption Analysis of Decision Support Systems. In: WOSP/SIPEW 2010, pp. 147–152 (2010)
9. Poess, M., Nambiar, R.O.: Large Scale Data Warehouses on Grid: Oracle Database 10g and HP ProLiant Systems. In: VLDB 2005, pp. 1055–1066 (2005)
10. Poess, M., Nambiar, R.O.: Tuning Servers, Storage and Databases for Energy Efficient Data Warehouses. In: ICDE 2010 (2010)
11. Poess, M., Nambiar, R.O., Walrath, D.: Why You Should Run TPC-DS: A Workload Analysis. In: VLDB 2007, pp. 1138–1149 (2007)
12. Poess, M., Nambiar, R.O.: Energy cost, the key challenge of today's data centers: a power consumption analysis of TPC-C results. PVLDB 1(2), 1229–1240 (2008)
13. TPC-H Result: 107121001, http://www.tpc.org/tpch/results/tpch_result_detail.asp?id=107121001
14. TPC-H Result: 108060302, http://www.tpc.org/tpch/results/tpch_result_detail.asp?id=108060302
15. TPC-H Result: 109060301, http://www.tpc.org/tpch/results/tpch_result_detail.asp?id=109060301
16. TPC-H Result: 110041101 http://www.tpc.org/tpch/results/tpch_result_detail.asp?id=110041101
17. TPC-H Result, http://www.tpc.org/tpch/results/tpch_result_detail.asp?id=110041101
18. TPC-H Result, http://www.tpc.org/tpch/results/tpch_result_detail.asp?id=109060301
19. TPC-H Result: 107102903, http://www.tpc.org/tpch/results/tpch_result_detail.asp?id=107102903
20. TPC-H Specification, http://www.tpc.org/tpch/default.asp
21. Wikipedia definition: processor core, http://en.wikipedia.org/wiki/Processor_core

Data Quality Is Context Dependent*

Leopoldo Bertossi[1,**], Flavio Rizzolo[1,***], and Lei Jiang[2]

[1] Carleton University, Ottawa, Canada
{bertossi,flavio}@scs.carleton.ca
[2] University of Toronto, Toronto, Canada
leijiang@cs.toronto.edu

Abstract. We motivate, formalize and investigate the notions of data quality assessment and data quality query answering as context dependent activities. Contexts for the assessment and usage of a data source at hand are modeled as collections of external databases, that can be materialized or virtual, and mappings within the collections and with the data source at hand. In this way, the context becomes "the complement" of the data source wrt a data integration system. The proposed model allows for natural extensions, like considering data quality predicates, and even more expressive ontologies for data quality assessment.

1 Introduction

The assessment of the quality of a data source is context dependent, i.e. the notions of "good" or "poor" data cannot be separated from the context in which the data is produced or used. For instance, the data about yearly sales of a product with seasonal variations might be considered quality data by a business analyst assessing the yearly revenue of a product. However, the same data may not be good enough for a warehouse manager who is trying to estimate the orders for next month.

In addition, data quality is related to the discrepancy between the actual stored values and the "real" values that were supposed or expected to be stored. For instance, if a temperature measurement is taken with a faulty thermometer, the stored value (the measurement) would differ from the right value (the actual temperature), which was the one supposed to be stored. This is an example of *semantically inaccurate data* [3].

Furthermore, another type of semantic discrepancy occurs when *senses or meanings* attributed by the different agents to the actual values in the database disagree [19], as shown in the Example 1. In this paper, we focus on data quality (DQ) problems caused by this type of semantic discrepancy.

Example 1. Tom is a patient in a hospital. Several times a day his temperature is measured and recorded by a nurse. His doctor, John, wants to see Tom's

* Research funded by the NSERC Strategic Network on BI (BIN, ADC05) and NSERC/IBM CRDPJ/371084-2008.

** Faculty Fellow of the IBM CAS.

*** Also affiliated to University of Ottawa.

M. Castellanos, U. Dayal, and V. Markl (Eds.): BIRTE 2010, LNBIP 84, pp. 52–67, 2011.

Table 1.

TempNoon

	Patient	Value	Time	Date
1	Tom Waits	38.5	11:45	Sep/5
2	Tom Waits	38.2	12:10	Sep/5
3	Tom Waits	38.1	11:50	Sep/6
4	Tom Waits	38.0	12:15	Sep/6
5	Tom Waits	37.9	12:15	Sep/7

Table 2.

TempNoon

	Patient	Value	Time	Date
1	Tom Waits	38.5	11:45	Sep/5
2	Tom Waits	38.0	12:15	Sep/6
3	Tom Waits	37.9	12:15	Sep/7

Table 3.

S (shift)

	Date	Shift	Nurse
1	Sep/5	morning	Susan
2	Sep/5	afternoon	Cathy
3	Sep/5	night	Joan
4	Sep/6	morning	Helen
5	Sep/6	afternoon	Cathy
6	Sep/6	night	Cathy
7	Sep/7	morning	Susan
8	Sep/7	afternoon	Susan
9	Sep/7	night	Joan

Table 4.

C (certification)

	Name	Year
1	Ann	2003
2	Cathy	2009
3	Irene	2000
4	Nancy	1995
5	Susan	1996

Table 5.

T (type)

	Nurse	Date	Type
1	Susan	Sep/5	Oral
2	Cathy	Sep/5	Tymp
3	Joan	Sep/5	Tymp
4	Helen	Sep/6	Oral
5	Cathy	Sep/6	Oral
6	Susan	Sep/7	Oral
7	Joan	Sep/7	Oral

temperature around noon every day, to follow his evolution. The information that John needs appears in the *TempNoon* relation of Table 1, which contains the temperatures between 11:30 and 12:30 per day for each of John's patients. John has additional *quality* requirements for the temperature measurements of his patients: they need to be taken by a certified nurse with an oral thermometer. On Sep/5, unaware of the new requirements, Cathy takes Tom's temperature at 12:10 with a *tympanal* thermometer and records the result as the tuple number 2 in Table 1. Since the instrument used does not appear in the view that John has of the data, he interprets the 38.2^{o}C value as taken with an *oral* thermometer.

This is an example of a discrepancy between the semantics of the value as intended by the data producer (38.2^{o}C taken with a tympanal thermometer) and the semantics expected by the data consumer (38.2^{o}C taken with an oral thermometer). This tuple should not appear in a quality table, i.e., one that satisfies John's quality requirements, since such a table would contain only temperatures taken with an oral thermometer.

A similar problem appears in the third tuple in Table 1: It was taken by a new nurse, Helen, who is not yet certified and, thus, does not satisfy one of the doctor's requirements. This tuple should not appear in a quality table containing only temperatures taken by certified nurses.

Table 2 fixes the problems of Table 1 with respect to the doctor's specification: The problematic second and third tuples do not appear in it.

How can we say or believe that Table 2 does contain only quality data? Prima facie it does not look much different from Table 1. This positive assessment would be possible if we had a *contextual database* containing the additional information, e.g., Tables 3, 4 and 5.

The first relation contains the name of the nurses in Tom Waits' ward and the shifts they work in by day. These are the nurses taking the measurements; since it is a small ward there is only one nurse per shift with that task. The second relation records the name of the certified nurses in the ward and the year they got the certification. The last relation contains the type of thermometer each nurse is using by day (e.g., oral or tympanal); each nurse takes all temperature measurements of the day using the same type of thermometer. This contextual information allows us to assess the quality of the data in Tables 1 and 2. ■

In this paper we take seriously the intuition and experience that data quality is context dependent. Our formalization of context is given as a system of integrated data and metadata of which the data source under quality assessment is a particular and special component. More precisely, the context for quality assessment of data in a certain instance D of schema $\mathcal{S}$ is given by an instance I of a possibly different schema $\mathcal{C}$, which could be an extension of $\mathcal{S}$. In order to assess the quality of D, it has to be "put in context", which is achieved by *mapping* D (and $\mathcal{S}$) into the contextual schema and data. Actually, $\mathcal{C}$ can be more complex that a single schema or instance, namely a collection of database schemas and instances interrelated by data- and schema mappings.

In our framework, a quality database instance D could be seen as a "footprint" of a the contextual, extended database I. The possibly extra information in I is what gives context to- and explains the data in D. The contextual schema and data is not used to enforce quality of a given instance. Instead, it is used to: (a) Assess the quality of the data in the instance at hand; (b) Characterize the quality answers to queries; and (c) Possibly obtain those quality answers to a user query. All this is achieved by comparing the given instance D with instance I, virtual or material, that can be defined for the contextual schema on the basis of D, external sources that contribute with data to the contextual schema, and possibly additional data at the contextual level, as shown in Example 1.

Instance I above could be replaced by a much richer contextual description, e.g. a full-fledged ontology. Along this line, but still in a classic database scenario, we might define some additional *quality predicates* on $\mathcal{C}$ [19]. They could be used to assess the quality of the data in D (and also the quality of query answers from D as we will explore later).

The following contributions can be found in this paper: (a) A model of context for data quality assessment. (b) Its application to clean or quality query answering. (c) Its application to data quality assessment via some natural measures that emerge from the model. (d) Some algorithms for the previously mentioned tasks in a few particular, but common and natural cases. (e) The creation of a framework that can be naturally extended in subsequent work to include more general contextual ontologies and externally defined quality predicates.

The rest of the paper is organized as follows. In Section 2, we present a general framework for contextual data quality and illustrate it with a running example. In Section 3, we consider two special cases of the general framework where we assume we have a contextual instance I that we can use for quality assessment and present an algorithm for quality query answering under this assumption. In Section 4, we explore more complex cases, e.g., where such contextual instances do not exist. We discuss related work in Section 5; and conclude and point out to our ongoing and future work in Section 6.

2 A Framework for Contextual Data Quality

Consider a relational schema $\mathcal{S}$, with relational predicates $R, \ldots \in \mathcal{S}$. This schema determines a language $L(\mathcal{S})$ of first-order predicate logic. In this paper we consider only monotone queries and views, e.g. conjunctive queries and unions there of, which we will usually write in non-recursive Datalog with built-ins [1]. We also consider an instance D of $\mathcal{S}$, with extension $R(D)$ for R, etc. If database instances are conceived as finite sets of ground atoms, then, for each $R \in \mathcal{S}$, $R(D) \subseteq D$. Instances $D, R(D), \ldots$ are those under quality assessment wrt to a *contextual system*.

In its simplest form, a contextual system consists of a contextual relational schema $\mathcal{C}$ that may include a set $\mathcal{B}$ of built-in predicates. We may have or not an instance for $\mathcal{C}$. In a more complex scenario, the contextual system may consist of several contextual schemas $\mathcal{C}_1, \ldots, \mathcal{C}_n$ and also a set of external schemas $\mathcal{E}$ that can be used by the contextual system for the assessment of an instance D of $\mathcal{S}$.

In this general framework, the participating schemas are related by *schema mappings*, like those found, for instance, in virtual data integration systems (VDISs) [22,4] or data exchange [21], or even more complex logical relationships, like those common in peer data management systems [5,6]. (Cf. [13] for an analysis of the connections between these three areas.) Schema mappings take the form of correspondences between two formulas, like queries or view definitions, each of them containing predicates from a single or several schemas. In particular, the data source under assessment D will be mappings into the contextual schema.

A common form of association, or mapping, is of the form $\forall \bar{x}(S(\bar{x}) \rightarrow \varphi_{\mathcal{G}}(\bar{x}))$, where S is a relational predicate of a data source and $\varphi_{\mathcal{G}}(\bar{x})$ is a conjunctive query over a global relational schema $\mathcal{G}$. These association can be found in *local-as-view* (LAV) VDISs with open (or sound) sources. Another common form of association is of the form $\forall \bar{x}(\psi_{\mathcal{S}}(\bar{x}) \rightarrow G(\bar{x}))$, found in *global-as-view* (GAV) VDISs with open sources, where $\psi_{\mathcal{R}}(\bar{x})$ is a conjunctive query over the union $\mathcal{R}$ of the relational schemas at the sources, and G is a global relational predicate. In *global-and-local-as-view* (GLAV) VDISs with open sources, we find associations between views (or queries), of the form $\forall \bar{x}(\psi_{\mathcal{R}}(\bar{x}) \rightarrow \varphi_{\mathcal{G}}(\bar{x}))$.

Figure 1 illustrates this general scenario. The relations R_i in D are under quality assessment, which is done via the contextual schema $\mathcal{C}$, which has relational predicates $C_1, \ldots, C_m$. There is also a set $\mathcal{P}$ of *contextual quality predicates* (CQPs) $P_1, \ldots, P_k$, which are defined as views over $\mathcal{C}$ plus possibly external

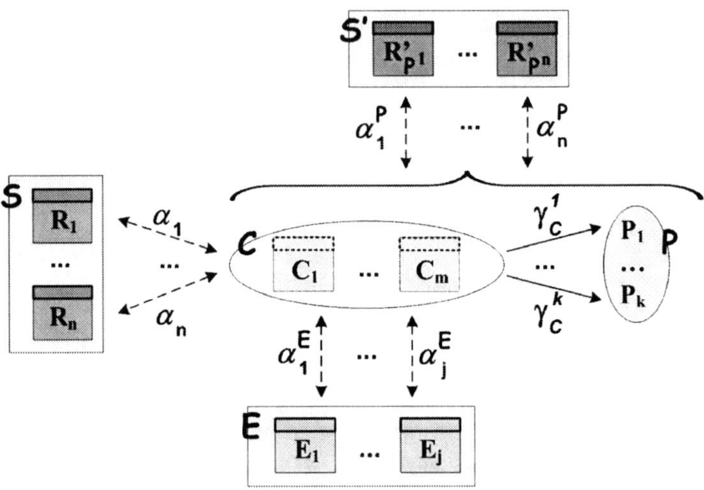

Fig. 1. General Framework for Contextual Data Quality

sources $E_1, \ldots, E_j$. In some cases, the combination of schemas $\mathcal{C}, \mathcal{P}, \mathcal{E}$ can be seen as a single, extended contextual schema. In other cases, it may be useful to tell them apart. The external predicates E_i could have "nicknames" E_i' in $\mathcal{C}$, with simple view definitions as mappings, of the form $\forall \bar{x}(E'(\bar{x}) \equiv E(\bar{x}))$ (or, in Datalog notation, $E'(\bar{x}) \leftarrow E(\bar{x})$).

We will usually have a copy $\mathcal{S}'$ of schema $\mathcal{S}$, with relational predicates $R_1', \ldots, R_n'$. The idea is that the R_i' stand for the quality versions of the R_i, and their extensions can be compared. Those ideal predicates are related with the (extended) contextual schema by the α mappings. If the mappings involve quality predicates in $\mathcal{P}$, we usually use a predicate $R_{\mathcal{P}i}'$, and mappings $\alpha^{\mathcal{P}}$ to emphasize the dependency on $\mathcal{P}$. In principle, each of the mappings in Figure 1 can be of any of the LAV, GAV, GLAV kind, plus additional assumptions about openness/closedness of the involved instances, or a usual view definition.[1]

For example, the γ's are view definitions of the quality predicates in terms of the elements in $\mathcal{C}$, plus possible the external sources in $\mathcal{E}$. All these elements, as in the case of virtual data integration and peer data management systems, determines a collection of admissible instances I for the contextual instance $\mathcal{C}$.

In following sections we consider and study some relevant special cases of this general framework. In each of them, we address: (a) The problem of assessing the quality of the instance D consisting of the relations $R_1(D), \ldots, R_n(D)$. This has to do with analyzing how they differ from ideal, quality instances of the R_i. (b) The problem of characterizing and obtaining quality answers to queries

[1] In virtual data integration it is possible to find semantics and algorithms for dealing with sources that coexist under different combinations of openness/closure assumptions [16,4].

that are expected to be answered by the instance D that is under assessment. As we will see, the two problems are related to each other. Actually, the former problem can be seen as a particular case of the latter.

We can present the main ideas already in the general framework: Given the different schemas involved, the mappings, and some materialized relations (e.g. the R_i, the E_k, some (parts) of the C_j) the relational predicates R_i' (or $R'_{\mathcal{P}i}$) will have (possibly virtual) admissible extensions, say $R_i'(I)$. The quality of $R_i(D)$ is determined by its "distance" to $R_i'(I)$, e.g. by the cardinality, $|R_i(D) \bigtriangleup R_i'(I)|$, of the symmetric difference. Different distance functions could be considered, specially if there are several admissible extensions for the R_i', as is often the case in VDISs, where several virtual *legal* instances may appear.

With respect to quality query answering, if a query $\mathcal{Q}$ is posed to D, but only quality answers are expected, the query could be rewritten in terms of the predicates R_i' and answered on the basis of their extensions.

Example 2. (example 1 continued) Consider query about patients and their temperatures around noon on Sep/5: $\mathcal{Q}(p, v) : \exists t \exists d(\mathit{TempNoon}(p, v, t, d) \wedge d =$ Sep/5). The *quality answers* to this query posed to Table 1 should be $\langle$*Tom Waits*, 38.5$\rangle$, namely the projection on the first two attributes of tuple 1, but not of tuple 2 because it does not comply with the quality requirements according to the contextual tables 3, 4, and 5. Notice that if the same query is posed to Table 2 instead, which contains only quality data with respect to the quality requirements, we get exactly the same answer. ■

If there are several admissible instances, forming a class $\mathcal{I}$, the schema $\mathcal{S}'$ can be instantiated in them, obtaining instances $R'(I)$, with $I \in \mathcal{I}$. In consequence, $\mathcal{S}'(I) := \{R'(I) \mid R \in \mathcal{S}\}$ forms an instance for schema $\mathcal{S}'$. The *quality answers* to $\mathcal{Q} \in L(\mathcal{S})$, can thus be defined as those that are *certain*:

$$QAns_D^{\mathcal{C}}(\mathcal{Q}) = \{\bar{t} \mid \mathcal{S}'(I) \models \mathcal{Q}'[\bar{t}], \text{ for all } I \in \mathcal{I}\} \tag{1}$$

where $\mathcal{Q}'$ is obtained from $\mathcal{Q}$ by replacing the R_i predicates by their copies, R_i'.

The notion of quality answer could be used to define the quality of instance D: For each of the relations $R \in \mathcal{S}$, we can pose the query $R(\bar{x})$ and obtain the quality answers $QAns(\mathcal{R})$. Each of the $QAns(\mathcal{R})$ becomes an instance for predicate R and can be compared with $R(D)$.

3 Instances as Views and Contextual Instances

As a broad and common case of the general framework, in addition to schema $\mathcal{S}$, the contextual schema $\mathcal{C}$, and an instance D of $\mathcal{S}$, we have the following:
(a) Each CQP $P \in \mathcal{P}$ defined as a conjunctive view, $P(\bar{x}) \leftarrow \gamma_{\mathcal{C}}(\bar{x})$, in terms of elements of $\mathcal{C}$ (and possibly built-in predicates). We denote with $\mathcal{C}^{\mathcal{P}}$ the schema $\mathcal{C}$ expanded with schema $\mathcal{P}$.
(b) For each database predicate $R \in \mathcal{S}$, a copy of it, R', which is defined as a conjunctive view of schema $\mathcal{C}^{\mathcal{P}}$:

$$R'_{\mathcal{P}}(\bar{x}) \longleftarrow \varphi_R^{\mathcal{C}}(\bar{x}), \ \varphi_R^{\mathcal{P}}(\bar{x}), \tag{2}$$

where $\varphi^{\mathcal{C}}_{R}(\bar{x}), \varphi^{\mathcal{P}}_{R}(\bar{x})$ are in their turn conjunctions of atomic formulas with predicates in $\mathcal{C}$, $\mathcal{P}$, respectively. A particular case is obtained when in (2) there are no CQPs in the view definition:

$$R'(\bar{x}) \longleftarrow \psi^{\mathcal{C}}_{R}(\bar{x}). \tag{3}$$

If we have an instance I for schema $\mathcal{C}$, then we will obtain a computed extensions $R'(I)$ and $R'_{\mathcal{P}}(I)$ by applying definitions (2) or (3). Now, if we also have an instance D of $\mathcal{S}$, the one under quality assessment, then $R(D)$ can be compared with $R'(I)$ and $R'_{\mathcal{P}}(I)$.

Intuitively, each CQP can be used to express an atomic quality requirement requested by a data consumer or met by a data producer. With the CQPs we can restrict the admissible values for certain attributes of tuples in I, so that only quality tuples find their way into D.

Although CQPs can be eliminated by unfolding their Datalog definitions, we make them explicit here, for several reasons: (a) To emphasize their role as predicates capturing quality requirements. (b) They allow us to compare data quality requirements in a more concrete way. For example, it is obvious that the quality requirement "temperature values need to be measured by an oral *or* tympanal thermometer" is less restrictive than "temperature values need to be measured by an oral thermometer". (c) Our approach allows for the consideration of CQPs that are not defined only in terms of $\mathcal{C}$ alone, but also in terms of other external sources, as indicated in Figure 1, that is, by view definitions of the form $P(\bar{x}) \leftarrow \gamma_{\mathcal{C}}(\bar{x}), \gamma_{\mathcal{E}}(\bar{x})$.

3.1 The Simple Case

A simple, restricted case of the general framework, and of the one in the previous section, in particular, occurs when the instance at hand D under assessment is exactly a materialized view of a contextual instance via a definition of the form (3). That is, for each $R \in \mathcal{S}$, we assume that $R(D) = R'(I)$. However, we may add additional quality requirements, thus obtaining an instance $R'_{\mathcal{P}}(I)$ via a view definition of the form (2). This would be an ideal instance of predicate R obtained from I using additional quality conditions.

In this case, $R(D) = R'(I)$, and $D(I) := \{R'(I) \mid R \in \mathcal{S}\} = D$. We also have the following instance for schema $\mathcal{S}$:

$$D_{\mathcal{P}}(I) = \{R'_{\mathcal{P}}(I) \mid R \in \mathcal{S} \text{ and } R'_{\mathcal{P}} \text{ is defined by (2)}\}. \tag{4}$$

As expected, there may be differences between D and $D_{\mathcal{P}}(I)$. The latter is intended to be the clean version of D. Actually, it holds $R'_{\mathcal{P}}(I) \subseteq R'(I) = R(D)$, for each $R \in \mathcal{S}$.

Example 3. (example 1 continued) Schema $\mathcal{S}$ contains the database predicate *TempNoon(Patient, Value, Time, Date)* with the instance in Table 1 under assessment. The contextual schema $\mathcal{C}$ contains the database predicates *S*(*Date, Shift, Nurse*), *T*(*Nurse, Date, Type*) and *C*(*Name, Year*) introduced before. We have instances for them: Tables 3, 4 and 5, respectively. In addition, $\mathcal{C}$ contains

Table 6.

M

	Patient	Value	Time	Date	Instr
1	T. Waits	37.8	11:00	Sep/5	Therm.
2	T. Waits	38.5	11:45	Sep/5	Therm.
3	T. Waits	38.2	12:10	Sep/5	Therm.
	...	...	...	...	...
4	T. Waits	110/70	11:00	Sep/6	BPM
5	T. Waits	38.1	11:50	Sep/6	Therm.

M (cont.)

	Patient	Value	Time	Date	Instr
6	T. Waits	38.0	12:15	Sep/6	Therm.
	...	...	...	...	...
7	T. Waits	37.6	10:50	Sep/7	Therm.
8	T. Waits	120/70	11:30	Sep/7	BPM
9	T. Waits	37.9	12:15	Sep/7	Therm.

predicate *M*(*Patient, Value, Time, Date, Instr*), which records the values of all measurements performed on patients by nurses (e.g., temperature, blood pressure, etc.), together with their time, date, instrument used (e.g., thermometer, blood pressure monitor), and the instance for it in Table 6.

Relation *TempNoon*(*Patient, Value, Time, Date*) can be seen as a materialized view over the instance in Table 6. It contains, for each patient and day, only temperature measurements close to noon.

According to (3), we can have the following view definition that captures the temperatures taken between 11:30 and 12:30:

$$TempNoon'(p, v, t, d) \leftarrow M(p, v, t, d, i), 11{:}30 \leq t \leq 12{:}30, i = \text{therm}. \qquad (5)$$

By materializing this view we obtain the instance shown in Table 1.

In order to express quality concerns, we now introduce some CQPs. In this way we will be in position to define the relation that contains only tuples satisfying the doctor's requirements, i.e., that the temperature has to be taken by a certified nurse using an oral thermometer. Accordingly, $\mathcal{P} = \{\ Oral(Instr),$ $Certified(Patient, Date, Time),\ Valid(Value)\}$.

In order to facilitate the definitions, we first introduce an auxiliary predicate, $Temp(Patient, Date, Time, Nurse, Instr, Type)$, that compiles information about the temperature measurements, the instruments used, and the name of the nurses for the morning and afternoon shifts – we do not care at this point for the evening shift because it does not overlap with the 11:30-12:30 interval of interest. *Temp* associates to each measurement in *M* the nurse and type of thermometer used depending on the time at which the temperature was taken.

$$\begin{aligned} Temp(p, d, t, n, i, tp) \leftarrow\ & M(p, v, t, d, i), S(d, s, n),\ T(n, d, tp), i = \text{therm}, \\ & 4{:}00 < t \leq 12{:}00, s = \text{morning}. \\ Temp(p, d, t, n, i, tp) \leftarrow\ & M(p, v, t, d, i), S(d, s, n),\ T(n, d, tp), i = \text{therm}, \\ & 12{:}00 < t \leq 20{:}00, s = \text{afternoon}. \end{aligned}$$

With the help of this auxiliary predicate, the first two CQPs are defined by:

$$Oral(i) \leftarrow Temp(p, d, t, n, i, tp),\ tp = \text{oral}. \qquad (6)$$

$$Certified(p, d, t) \leftarrow Temp(p, d, t, n, i, tp),\ C(n, y). \qquad (7)$$

The first quality predicate is satisfied only when the instrument used is an oral thermometer. (The only instruments that appear in *Temp*'s tuples are thermometers and the additional requirement is specified by $tp = \text{oral}$). The second predicate can be used to specify that a measurement (uniquely identified by the patient, the date and the time) is made by a certified nurse.

A third CQP takes care of potential typing errors by checking that the temperature is in a predefined valid range. It is defined by:

$$\mathit{Valid}(v) \leftarrow M(p, v, t, d, i), 36 \leq v \leq 42. \tag{8}$$

With these three CQPs, we can define, according to (2), a new relation:

$$\begin{aligned} \mathit{TempNoon}'_{\mathcal{P}}(p, v, t, d) \leftarrow M(p, v, t, d, i),\ & 11{:}30 \leq t \leq 12{:}30, \\ & \mathit{Valid}(v), \mathit{Oral}(i), \mathit{Certified}(p, d, t). \end{aligned} \tag{9}$$

The new extension, for predicate $\mathit{TempNoon}'_{\mathcal{P}}$, is intended to contain only measurements satisfying the doctor's requirements, which corresponds to the instance shown in Table 2. ■

3.2 Quality Query Answering

Queries are written in the language associated to schema $\mathcal{S}$ and posed to instance D. However, clean answers to queries over D should be, in essence, the answers to the same query posed to $D'(I)$ or $D'_{\mathcal{P}}(I)$ instead. In consequence, and as a particular case of (1), for a query $\mathcal{Q}(\bar{x}) \in L(\mathcal{S})$, the set of *quality answers to* $\mathcal{Q}$ *wrt* D becomes:

$$QAns^{\mathcal{C}}_{D}(\mathcal{Q}) := \mathcal{Q}(D_{\mathcal{P}}(I)). \tag{10}$$

For monotone queries, e.g. conjunctive queries, it holds $QAns^{\mathcal{C}}_{D}(\mathcal{Q}) \subseteq Q(D)$, where the latter denotes the set of answer to Q from D.

Since the $R(D)$s are obtained as materialized Datalog views of the contextual instance I, query answering can be done via view unfolding. That is, in order to get quality answers, we evaluate the original query on the clean relations $R'(I)$ via view unfolding:

Quality Unfold Algorithm: (QUA)

1. Replace each predicate R in $\mathcal{Q}$ by its corresponding R' (or $R'_{\mathcal{P}}$), obtaining query $\mathcal{Q}'$.
2. Replace $\mathcal{Q}'$ by a query $\mathcal{Q}^{\mathcal{C}}_{\mathcal{P}} \in L(\mathcal{C} \cup \mathcal{P})$ via view unfolding based on (2).
3. If desired, or possible, unfold the definitions of the CQPs, obtaining the "quality query" $\mathcal{Q}^{\mathcal{C}} \in L(\mathcal{C})$, which can be evaluated on I.

The last step of the algorithm opens the possibility of considering CQPs that are not defined on top of schema $\mathcal{C}$ only. This is the case, for example, when they appeal to external sources, and also when they represent other kinds of *quality predicates*, e.g. of the form introduced in [19].

The quality of D could be assessed by comparing each $R(D)$ with the corresponding $R'_{\mathcal{P}}(I)$. This is just a particular case of quality query answering: The set of clean answers to each of the atomic queries $\mathcal{Q}(\bar{x}) : R(\bar{x})$ can be compared with the corresponding $R(D)$s.

Example 4. Consider the query on schema $\mathcal{S}$ of our running example that asks for the temperature of the patients on Sep/5: $\mathcal{Q}(p, v) : \exists t \exists d(\mathit{TempNoon}(p, v, t, d) \wedge d = \text{Sep/5})$, which in Datalog notation becomes:

$$\mathcal{Q}(p, v) \leftarrow \mathit{TempNoon}(p, v, t, d),\ d = \text{Sep/5}. \tag{11}$$

To get quality answers, $\mathcal{Q}$ is rewritten in terms of schema $\mathcal{S}'$. Hence, $\mathcal{Q}$ is trivially rewritten as: $\mathcal{Q}'(p, v) \leftarrow \mathit{TempNoon}'_{\mathcal{P}}(p, v, t, d),\ d = \text{Sep/5}$. Now, $\mathit{TempNoon}'_{\mathcal{P}}$ is defined by (9). Thus, by view unfolding we get:

$$\begin{aligned} \mathcal{Q}^{\mathcal{C}}_{\mathcal{P}}(p, v) \leftarrow\ & M(p, v, t, d, i),\ 11{:}30 \leq t \leq 12{:}30,\ d = \text{Sep/5}, \\ & \mathit{Valid}(v), \mathit{Oral}(i), \mathit{Certified}(p, d, t). \end{aligned} \tag{12}$$

This query can be evaluated directly on I, which contains relation M, by unfolding the definitions (6)-(8) of the quality predicates or directly using their extensions if they have been materialized. ■

Notice that in (12) we could have quality predicates that are not defined only in terms of the contextual schema $\mathcal{C}$, but defined also in terms of other external sources. In consequence, the query cannot be evaluated on I alone, and this might trigger requests for additional data.

Example 5. (example 4 continued) Consider now that, instead of having an instance for $C(\mathit{Nurse}, \mathit{Year})$, we have its definition in terms of an external source $\#X(\mathit{Nurse})$ that contains information about certified nurses; $\#X(\mathit{Nurse})$ returns *true* if the input nurse appears in the source, and *false* otherwise. Since $C(\mathit{Nurse}, \mathit{Year})$ is part of the definition of the *Certified* CQP (rule (7)), the evaluation of the unfolded query in (12) will trigger a request for data from $\#X$ in order to evaluate the *Certified* predicate. ■

This independence of the quality predicates from the contextual data or schema is particularly interesting in the case we want to use them to filter tuples from a relation, say R, in D. This situation can be easily accommodated in our framework, as follows. For predicate $R \in \mathcal{S}$, we consider a copy, or *nickname*, $R' \in \mathcal{C}$. Each R' shares the arity, the attributes of R, and their domains. We also have a simple GAV definition for R': $R'(\bar{x}) \leftarrow R(\bar{x})$, considering R as an *exact source*, in the terminology of virtual data integration [22] (this is usual in view definitions over a single instance). This creates a copy $R'(D)$ of $R(D)$ as a part of the contextual instance, and the contextual instance becomes $I := \{R'(D) \mid R \in \mathcal{S}\}$.

Now, if we want to obtain quality answers to a query $\mathcal{Q}$ on instance D (with schema $\mathcal{S}$), taking into account the quality predicates, we replace each predicate $R \in \mathcal{S}$ in $\mathcal{Q}$ by the conjunction $R'(\bar{x}) \wedge \varphi^{\mathcal{P}}_{R}(\bar{x})$. The data to evaluate the additional, quality formula $\varphi^{\mathcal{P}}_{R}(\bar{x})$ would be obtained from the external sources. The resulting query would be evaluated on I and extensions for the quality predicates. If the latter is missing, the query evaluation process could trigger *ad hoc* requests for external data.

In this section we considered the convenient, but not necessarily frequent, case where the instance D under assessment is a collection of exact materialized views of a contextual instance I. Alternative and natural cases we have to consider may have only a partial contextual instance I^- together with its metadata for contextual reference. We examine this case in Section 4.

4 Missing Contextual Data

Against what may be suggested by the examples above, we cannot assume that we always have a contextual instance I for schema $\mathcal{C}$. There may be *some* data for $\mathcal{C}$, most likely an incomplete (possibly empty) instance I^-, also data from other external sources, and the data in the instance D under assessment mapped into $\mathcal{C}$. In this more general case, a situation similar to those investigated in virtual data integration systems naturally emerges. Here, the contextual schema acts as the mediated, global schema, and instance D as a materialized data source. In the following we will explore this connection.

Let us now assume that we do not have a contextual instance I for schema $\mathcal{C}$, i.e. $I^- = \emptyset$. We could see D as a data source for a virtual data integration system, $\mathfrak{C}$, with a global schema that extends the contextual schema $\mathcal{C}$ [22,4]. We may assume that all the data in D is related to $\mathfrak{C}$ via $\mathcal{C}$, but $\mathfrak{C}$ may have potentially more data than the one contributed by D and of the same kind as the one in D. In consequence, we assume D to be an *open source* for $\mathfrak{C}$. This assumption will be captured below through the set of intended or *legal* global instances for $\mathfrak{C}$.

Since not all the data in D may be up to the quality expectations according to $\mathcal{C}$, we need to give an account of the relationship between D and its expected quality version. For this purpose, as in the previous cases, we extend $\mathcal{C}$ with a copy $\mathcal{S}'$ of schema $\mathcal{S}$: $\mathcal{S}' = \{R' \mid R \in \mathcal{S}\}$. Now, $\mathcal{C}' := \mathcal{C} \cup \mathcal{S}'$, and it also becomes part of the global schema for $\mathfrak{C}$.

Definition 1. Assume each $R \in \mathcal{S}$ is defined as a Datalog view: $R(\bar{x}) \leftarrow \varphi_R^{\mathcal{C}}(\bar{x})$.
(a) A *legal instance* for system $\mathfrak{C}$ is an instance I' of the global schema, such that: (a1) For every $R \in \mathcal{S}$, $R(D) \subseteq R(I')$; (a2) $I' \models \forall\bar{x}(R'(\bar{x}) \equiv \varphi_R^{\mathcal{C}}(\bar{x}) \wedge \varphi_R^{\mathcal{P}}(\bar{x}))$.
(b) An instance I of $\mathcal{C}$ is *legal contextual instance* (LCI) if there is a legal instance I' for $\mathfrak{C}$, such that $I = I' \!\downarrow\! \mathcal{C}$ (the restriction of I' to schema $\mathcal{C}$). ■

The condition in (a1) essentially lifts D's data upwards to $\mathfrak{C}$. The legal instances have extensions that extend the data in D when the views defining the Rs are computed. The sentences in (a2) act as global integrity constraints, i.e. on schema $\mathcal{C}'$, and have the effect of cleaning the data (virtually) uploaded to $\mathfrak{C}$.

We can also consider a variation of this case, where, in addition to D, we have only a fragment I^- of the potential contextual instances I. That is, we have a *incomplete* contextual data. In this case, Definition 1 has to be modified by adding the condition on I: (a3) $I^- \subseteq I' \downarrow \mathcal{C}$, which requires that the legal instance I' is "compatible" with the partial instance I^- at hand. With $I^- = \emptyset$, we obtain the previous case.[2]

Now, the idea is to pose queries in terms of the R', to obtain quality answers.

Definition 2. A ground tuple $\bar{t}$ is a *quality answer* to query $\mathcal{Q}(\bar{x}) \in L(\mathcal{S})$ iff $\bar{t} \in \bigcap\{\mathcal{Q}'(I) \mid I \text{ is an LCI}\}$, where $\mathcal{Q}'$ is obtained from $\mathcal{Q}$ by replacing every $R \in \mathcal{S}$ in it by R'. ■

As before, we denote with $QAns^{\mathcal{C}}_{D}(\mathcal{Q})$ the set of quality answers to $\mathcal{Q}$ from D wrt $\mathcal{C}$.

Example 6. Let us revisit the query $\mathcal{Q}(p, v)$ in (12) in Example 4. Let $\mathcal{Q}'(p, v)$ denote the same query, now expressed in terms of schema $\mathcal{S}'$. The instance of *TempNoon(Patient, Value, Time, Date)* in Table 1 is D, the instance under quality assessment.

We now define a VDIS $\mathfrak{C}$ with D as an open source, and the relations in Tables 3, 4 and 5 as forming a partial global instance I^-. In this case, there is no instance (relation) for predicate *M(Patient, Value, Time, Date, Instr)* in $\mathcal{C}$.

According to Definition 2, a quality answer to $\mathcal{Q}(p, v)$ has to be obtained *from every* LCI for $\mathfrak{C}$. Now, every LCI will contain tuples from *TempNoon(Patient, Value, Time, Date)* satisfying the conditions imposed by (9). In fact, Table 2 corresponds to the smallest LCI for $\mathfrak{C}$: No subset of it is an LCI and any superset satisfying (9) is also an LCI. In consequence, the first tuple in Table 2 is the only one satisfying the additional query condition $d = \text{Sep/5}$. We obtain: $QAns^{\mathcal{C}}_{D}(\mathcal{Q}(p, v)) = \{\langle \text{Tom Waits}, 38.5\rangle\}$. ■

Since we have the original instance D defined as an open source, we can take advantage of any of the existing algorithms for the computation of the certain answers to global queries under the openness assumption [17]. Since we are assuming that queries and view definitions are conjunctive, we can use, e.g. the *inverse rules algorithm* [14] or extensions thereof [4,11]. We illustrate its application with an example.

Example 7. (example 6 continued) If we invert the definition of *TempNoon* in (5), we get:

$$M(p, v, t, d, i) \leftarrow \mathit{TempNoon}(p, v, t, d), 11{:}30 \leq t \leq 12{:}30, i = \text{therm}. \qquad (13)$$

We can evaluate $\mathcal{Q}^{\mathcal{C}}_{\mathcal{P}}(p, v)$ in (12) by unfolding the definition of predicate M according to (13), obtaining:

$$\begin{aligned}\mathcal{Q}^{\mathcal{C}}_{\mathcal{P}}(p, v) \leftarrow\ & \mathit{TempNoon}(p, v, t, d),\ 11{:}30 \leq t \leq 12{:}30,\ i = \text{therm},\ d = \text{Sep/5},\\ & \mathit{Valid}(v), \mathit{Oral}(i), \mathit{Certified}(p, d, t).\end{aligned}$$

The rewritten query can be now evaluated on the instances of *TempNoon*, S, C, and T (Tables 1, 3, 4 and 5, respectively). This produces the same result as in the previous example. ■

[2] The occurrence of partial and materialized global instance I^- can be accommodated in the scenario of VDISs by considering I^- as a separate exact "source" for $\mathfrak{C}$.

Finally, wrt data quality assessment, some alternatives naturally offer themselves. If we want to assess D, we can consider, for each LCI I, the instance $\mathcal{S}'(I) := \{R'(I) \mid R \in \mathcal{S}\}$. We have $\mathcal{S}'(I) \subseteq D$. A possible quality measure could be $QM_1(D) := (|D| - max\{|\mathcal{S}'(I)| : I \text{ is LCI}\})/|D|$, inspired by the G_3 measure in [20].

Another possible measure is based, as suggested above, on quality query answering: For each predicate $R \in \mathcal{S}$, compute the query $\mathcal{Q}_R : R(\bar{x})$. Then, compute $QM_2(D) := (|D \smallsetminus \bigcup_{R \in \mathcal{S}} QAns_D^{\mathcal{C}}(\mathcal{Q}_R)|)/|D|$. The analysis and comparison of these and other possible quality measures are left for future work.

5 Related Work

The study on data quality spans from the characterization of types of errors in data (e.g., [26]), to the modeling of processes in which these errors may be introduced (e.g., [2]), to the development of techniques for error detection and repairing (e.g., [7]). Most of these approaches, however, are based on the implicit assumption that data errors occur exclusively at the syntactic/symbolic level, i.e., as discrepancies between data values (e.g., Kelvin vs. Kelvn).

As argued in [19], data quality problems may also occur at the semantic level, i.e., as discrepancies between the meanings attached to these data values. More specifically, according to [19], a data quality problem may arise when there is a mismatch between the *intended* meaning (according to its producer) and interpreted meaning (according to its consumer) of a data value. A mismatch is often caused by ambiguous communication between the data producer and consumer; such ambiguity is inevitable if some sources of variability (e.g., the type of thermometer used and the conditions of a patient) are not explicitly captured in the data (or metadata). Of course, whether or not such ambiguity is considered a data quality problem depends on the purpose for which the data is used.

In [19] a framework was proposed for *defining* both syntactic- and semantic-level data quality in an uniformed way, based on the fundamental notion of signs (values) and senses (meanings). A number of "macro-level" quality predicates were also introduced, based on the comparison of symbols and their senses (exact match, partial match and mismatch). In this work, we take the next step to propose a specific mechanism for capturing and comparing semantic-level data quality requirements using context relations and quality predicates, and show how they are *used* in query answering.

Use of contexts in data management has been proposed before (see [9] for a survey). Of course, there are different ways to capture, represent and use contexts. For instance, contextual information has been used to support a semi-automatic process for view design (see [8] for an overview). A context in [8] consists of a number of context elements, which are essentially attribute-value pairs (e.g., role='agent', situation='on site', time='today'); certain constraints can also be specified on a context (e.g., when role is 'manager', situation cannot be 'on site').

A context specification allows one to select from a potentially large database schema a small portion (a view) that is deemed relevant in that context. Given a context specification, the design of a context-aware view may be carried out manually or semi-automatically by composing partial views corresponding to individual elements in that context [10]. In this paper, a context is specified in a similar manner as in [8], but with a different purpose. The main purpose in [8] is size reduction (i.e., separating useful data from noise in a given context); in our work however, the main purpose is quality-based selection (i.e., selecting a subset of data that best meets certain quality requirements).

On the use of quality assessments for query answering, one of the most relevant works is [24]. Naumann's proposal is based on a universal relation [23] constructed from the global relational schema for integrating autonomous data sources. Queries are a set of attributes from the universal relation with possible value conditions over the attributes. To map a query to source views, user queries are translated to queries against the global relational schema. Naumann defines several quality criteria to qualify the sources, such as believability, objectivity, reputation and verifiability, among others. These criteria are then used to define a quality model for query plans.

According to [24], the quality of a query plan is determined as follows. Each source receives information quality (IQ) scores for each criterion considered relevant, which are then combined in an IQ-vector where each component corresponds to a different criterion. Users can specify their preferences of the selected criteria by assigning weights to the components of the IQ-vector, hence obtaining a weighting vector. This weighting vector is used in turn by multi-attribute decision-making (MADM) methods for ranking the data sources participating in the universal relation. These methods range from the simple scaling and summing of the scores (SAW) to complex formulas based on concordance and discordance matrices. The quality model is independent of the MADM method chosen, as long as it supports user weighting and IQ-scores. Given IQ-vectors of sources, the goal is to obtain the IQ-vector of a plan containing the sources. Plans are described as trees of joins between the sources: leaves are sources whereas inner nodes are joins. IQ-scores are computed for each inner node bottom-up and the overall quality of the plan is given by the IQ-score of the root of the tree.

There has been some work on the formalization and use of contexts done by the knowledge representation community. There are general, high level ideas in that line of research that are are shared with our work, namely, the idea of integration and interoperability of models and theories. In [15], the emphasis is placed on the proper interaction of different logical environments. More recently, the notion of context, or better, multi-contexts, has been formalized through the use of *bridge rules* between denoted contexts, each of which can have a knowledge base or ontology on its own [12]. The bridge rules are expressed as propositional logic programming rules. It is not clear that they can express the rich mappings found in data management applications. Not necessarily explicitly referring to contexts, there is also recent work on the integration of ontologies and distributed description logics (cf. [18] and references therein) that shows ideas similar to those found in the literature on contexts in knowledge representation.

6 Discussion and Conclusions

We have proposed a general framework that allows for the assessment of a database instance in terms of quality properties. These properties are captured in terms of alternative instances that are obtained by interaction with additional contextual data or metadata. Our framework involves mappings between database schemas like those found in data exchange, virtual data integration and peer data management systems (PDMSs). Quality answers to a query also become relative to the alternative instances that emerge from the interaction between the instance under assessment and the contextual data or metadata.

These are first steps in the direction of capturing data quality and quality query answering as context dependent activities. We examined a few natural cases of the general framework. We also made some assumptions about the mappings, views and queries involved. The general framework and also cases of more intricate mappings (cf. [5,6] for more complex mappings in PDMs) remain to be investigated. More algorithms have to be proposed and investigated, both for quality assessment and for quality query answering.

Among the most prominent objects of ongoing research, we can mention: (a) The use of external quality predicates and data in the assessment of a given database instance. (b) The use and integration in our framework of more "intrinsic" and "absolute" quality predicates of the kind introduced in [19]. They can capture aspects as deep as data value syntax, correctness, sense, meaning, timeliness, etc. (c) A detailed and comparative analysis of the quality measures mentioned in this paper and others. (d) The implementation of the current framework using relational technology and its extension with contextual ontologies modeled within the Protégé knowledge-base platform [25].

Contexts have appeared in the data management literature, mostly in relation with obvious contextual aspects of data, like geographic and temporal dimensions. However, in our view, a general notion of context, its formalization, and use in data management have been missing so far. This is a most important problem that still has to be fully investigated. We have proposed some first ideas in this direction.

References

1. Abiteboul, S., Hull, R., Vianu, V.: Foundations of Databases. Addison-Wesley, Reading (1995)
2. Ballou, D., Wang, R., Pazer, H., Tayi, G.: Modeling Information Manufacturing Systems to Determine Information Product Quality. Management Science 44(4), 462–484 (1998)
3. Batini, C., Scannapieco, M.: Data Quality: Concepts, Methodologies and Techniques. Springer, Heidelberg (2006)
4. Bertossi, L., Bravo, L.: Consistent Query Answers in Virtual Data Integration Systems. In: Bertossi, L., Hunter, A., Schaub, T. (eds.) Inconsistency Tolerance. LNCS, vol. 3300, pp. 42–83. Springer, Heidelberg (2005)
5. Bertossi, L., Bravo, L.: Query Answering in Peer-to-Peer Data Exchange Systems. In: Lindner, W., Fischer, F., Türker, C., Tzitzikas, Y., Vakali, A.I. (eds.) EDBT 2004. LNCS, vol. 3268, pp. 476–485. Springer, Heidelberg (2004)

6. Bertossi, L., Bravo, L.: The Semantics of Consistency and Trust in Peer Data Exchange Systems. In: Dershowitz, N., Voronkov, A. (eds.) LPAR 2007. LNCS (LNAI), vol. 4790, pp. 107–122. Springer, Heidelberg (2007)
7. Bleiholder, J., Naumann, F.: Data Fusion. ACM Computing Surveys 41(1), 1–41 (2008)
8. Bolchini, C., Curino, C., Orsi, G., Quintarelli, E., Rossato, R., Schreiber, F., Tanca, L.: And What Can Context Do for Data? Communications of the ACM 52(11), 136–140 (2009)
9. Bolchini, C., Curino, C., Quintarelli, E., Schreiber, F., Tanca, L.: A Data-Oriented Survey of Context Models. SIGMOD Record 36(4), 19–26 (2007)
10. Bolchini, C., Quintarelli, E., Rossato, R.: Relational Data Tailoring Through View Composition. In: Parent, C., Schewe, K.-D., Storey, V.C., Thalheim, B. (eds.) ER 2007. LNCS, vol. 4801, pp. 149–164. Springer, Heidelberg (2007)
11. Bravo, L., Bertossi, L.: Logic Programs for Consistently Querying Data Integration Systems. In: Proc. International Joint Conference on Artificial Intelligence (IJCAI 2003), pp. 10–15. Morgan Kaufmann, San Francisco (2003)
12. Brewka, G., Eiter, T.: Equilibria in Heterogeneous Nonmonotonic Multi-Context Systems. In: Proc. AAAI 2007, pp. 385–390 (2007)
13. De Giacomo, G., Lembo, D., Lenzerini, M., Rosati, R.: On Reconciling Data Exchange, Data Integration, and Peer Data Management. In: Proc. PODS 2007, pp. 133–142 (2007)
14. Duschka, O., Genesereth, M., Levy, A.: Recursive Query Plans for Data Integration. Journal of Logic Programming 43(1), 49–73 (2000)
15. Giunchiglia, F., Serafini, L.: Multilanguage Hierarchical Logics. Artificial Intelligence 65, 29–70 (1994)
16. Grahne, G., Mendelzon, A.O.: Tableau Techniques for Querying Information Sources through Global Schemas. In: Beeri, C., Bruneman, P. (eds.) ICDT 1999. LNCS, vol. 1540, pp. 332–347. Springer, Heidelberg (1998)
17. Halevy, A.: Answering Queries Using Views: A Survey. VLDB Journal 10(4), 270–294 (2001)
18. Homola, M., Serafini, L.: Towards Formal Comparison of Ontology Linking, Mapping and Importing. In: Proc. DL 2010. CEUR-WS 573, pp. 291–302 (2010)
19. Jiang, L., Borgida, A., Mylopoulos, J.: Towards a Compositional Semantic Account of Data Quality Attributes. In: Li, Q., Spaccapietra, S., Yu, E., Olivé, A. (eds.) ER 2008. LNCS, vol. 5231, pp. 55–68. Springer, Heidelberg (2008)
20. Kivinen, J., Mannila, H.: Approximate Inference of Functional Dependencies from Relations. Theoretical Computer Science 149, 129–149 (1995)
21. Kolaitis, P.: Schema Mappings, Data Exchange, and Metadata Management. In: Proc. PODS 2005, pp. 61–75 (2005)
22. Lenzerini, M.: Data Integration: A Theoretical Perspective. In: Proc. PODS 2002, pp. 233–246 (2002)
23. Maier, D., Ullman, J., Vardi, M.: On the Foundations of the Universal Relation Model. ACM Transactions on Database Systems 9(2), 283–308 (1984)
24. Naumann, F.: Quality-Driven Query Answering for Integrated Information Systems. Springer, Heidelberg (2002)
25. Stanford Center for Biomedical Informatics Research. The Protégé knowledge-base framework (2010), `http://protege.stanford.edu/`
26. Wang, R., Strong, D.: Beyond Accuracy: What Data Quality Means to Data Consumers. J. Management and Information Systems 12(4), 5–33 (1996)

An Efficient Heuristic for Logical Optimization of ETL Workflows

Nitin Kumar and P. Sreenivasa Kumar

Indian Institute of Technology Madras,
Chennai, India 600036
{nitinkr,psk}@cse.iitm.ac.in
http://www.cse.iitm.ac.in

Abstract. An ETL process is used to extract data from various sources, transform it and load it into a Data Warehouse. In this paper, we analyse an ETL flow and observe that only some of the dependencies in an ETL flow are *essential* while others are basically represents the flow of data. For the linear flows, we exploit the underlying dependency graph and develop a greedy heuristic technique to determine a reordering that significantly improves the quality of the flow. Rather than adopting a state-space search approach, we use the cost functions and selectivities to determine the best option at each position in a right-to-left manner. To deal with complex flows, we identify activities that can be transferred between linear segments in it and position those activities appropriately. We then use the re-orderings of the linear segments to obtain a cost-optimal semantically equivalent flow for a given complex flow. Experimental evaluation has shown that by using the proposed techniques, ETL flows can be better optimized and with much less effort compared to existing methods.

Keywords: Data integration, Data Warehousing, ETL Optimization.

1 Introduction

A Data Warehouses(DW) [1] plays an important role in decision making for any organization. A DW is a data repository which is primarily used for reporting and analysis. ETL (Extract, Transform and Load) tools are used for consolidating the data from different sources to the DW. These tools are used to define an interconnected set of activities that is known as an ETL flow. An ETL flow can be represented at three levels: Conceptual, Logical and Physical. At the Conceptual level [2,3] details like source schema, target schema and the relationships between their attributes are defined.

The logical level defines the flow of data from the sources to the target. The flow consists of a set of activities which extract the data from the data sources, transform it and finally load it. Studies [4] have shown that designing the ETL flows requires a lot of effort. It can take upto 80% of the time and at least 30% of the cost of the DW. Any fault in the ETL design can lead to erroneous data

M. Castellanos, U. Dayal, and V. Markl (Eds.): BIRTE 2010, LNBIP 84, pp. 68–83, 2011.

in the DW and affects business decisions. Thus, ETL design is a very resource intensive, critical and time consuming process.

Most of the commercial tools currently available in market [5,6,7] allow the designer to work at the logical level. But unfortunately, these tools do not provide any kind of techniques to automatically optimize the flow. The designer is solely responsible for it.

Simitsis et al. [8] was one of the first works to recognize that there is a pressing need for optimization of ETL flows. They also point out that since some of the operations involved in the ETL flows are not relational algebra operators, optimization of ETL flows is different from traditional query optimization. However, one cannot deny that some of the ideas from the query optimization are applicable in the context of ETL process optimization. Simitsis et al. [8] introduced a theoretical framework for ETL flow optimization where they model the flow as a DAG and identify a set of operations that can be used to transform one flow into another under certain circumstances. These operators of course preserve the semantics of the ETL flow. Using this framework, Simitsis et. al propose a state-space based method for finding the minimum cost ETL flow that is equivalent to the given flow under a cost model. They also propose heuristics based variants of the method as they find that state-space search is not scalable.

In this paper, we adopt the above framework for ETL flow representation and meaning-preserving flow transformation operators while we abandon the state-space search approach. Starting with linear flows, we observe that only certain dependencies of the ETL flows are *essential* while others are there to basically represent flow of data. This insight leads us to come up with a dependency graph that captures the essential dependencies of a linear flow. We then use the cost functions and selectivities of the activities to come up with a greedy heuristic that reorders a linear flow and achieves significant improvement in its quality.

The proposed techniques can be incorporated in a ETL design tool to shift the burden of the logical optimization of the flow from the designer to the tool. The main contributions of the work are:

1. We introduced an efficient heuristic for optimization of linear flows. The algorithm finds the dependencies among the activities and reorganizes them to an optimized flow.
2. We extended the heuristic for the complex flows by finding the linear components in it. Transferable activities are identified in the flow and the most suitable positions for them are computed.
3. Implementation of the methods has shown that the proposed method is highly scalable compared to the earlier approaches.

The paper is structured as follows. Section 2 describes the need for ETL optimization and the preliminaries of the area, while Section 3 gives the review of the existing approaches. Section 4 and Section 5 describe the proposed approach for the linear and complex flows respectively. The correctness of the algorithm is established in Section 6. In Section 7, we present our evaluation set-up and the results. Finally, Section 8 concludes with our findings.

2 Preliminaries

At the logical level an ETL flow is usually represented as a DAG (Directed Acyclic Graph) [9,10]. The activities (or operators) are represented as nodes and the data flow among them as directed edges of the graph. Each activity processes the data and forwards it to the next activity(s). Every activity has an associated selectivity and a cost. Selectivity is defined as an estimate of percentage of the data that would be allowed to pass through it. It is the ratio of output to input data volume processed. For an activity, selectivity can be computed by processing some sample data. The cost of each activity depends on the volume of the data processed by it. It is expressed as the function of input size. As the volume of data differs at different places in the flow, it results in different costs for the same activity at different positions. Due to variation in the input size the cost of the activity varies. The cost of the flow can be altered by rearranging the activities. While rearranging the activities the semantics of the flow must be preserved. The problem of logical optimization can be viewed as finding a semantically equivalent flow having minimum cost.

Consider the sample flow in Figure 1. It has two sources (S1, S2) and two target databases (T1, T2). The Sources S1, S2 are the databases from different regions having schema (AccNo, Name, Gender, ContactNo, Opening Date, Currency, Bal). The activities defined transform the source data to the required target specifications. The activities (1, 5) perform Not-Null check on the attribute Opening Date, activities (3, 6) also perform the Not-Null check but on attribute Account No (AccNo). Since the source data belongs to different regions, the activity 2 converts the currency of the first region to another. Activities (4, 7) format balance and PhoneNo respectively. Activity 8 combines the different datasets into one, activity 9 generates the surrogate key for the AccNo, activity 10 selects only the female customers, activity 11 splits the dataset as per the opening date, activities (12, 13) encrypt the name of the customers.

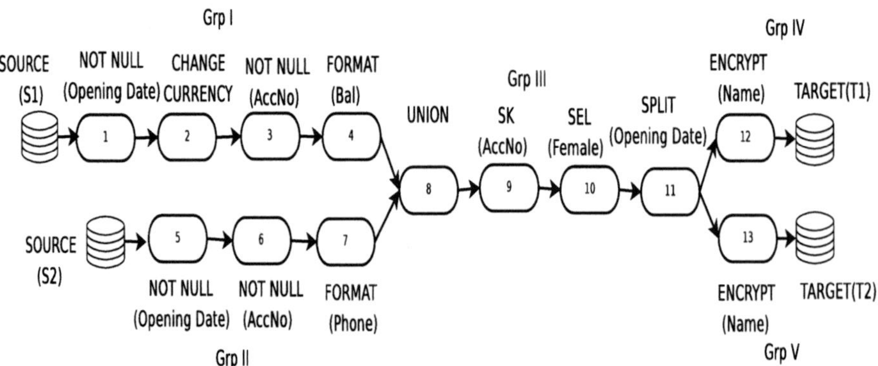

Fig. 1. An ETL workflow example

The flow shown in the Figure 1 can be optimized by moving the activity 10 which selects the data on the basis of Gender to both the sources. This activity is highly selective. Due to this repositioning the input data volume of other activities will be reduced resulting in the change of their cost and the overall cost of the flow.

An Activity (or an Operator) is the basic unit of an ETL flow. On the basis of input and output, activities can be classified into unary activities and binary activities. Activities having only one input and one output. e.g. sort, currency conversion, date formatting are unary activities and on the other hand activities having more than one input or output. e.g. join, difference are binary.

Local Group (or Linear Group) : A local group is a subset of the graph, the elements of which form a linear path of unary activities [8]. In the Figure 1 activities (1, 2, 3, 4) form a linear group.

Signature : A Signature is a concise way of representing an ETL flow introduced in [11]. Here activities are represented by numbers and the structure is captured using double slashes // and parenthesis (). The activities between immediate opening and closing parenthesis form a linear group while the parallel groups are represented by pipes. For example signature for the Figure 1 is (((S1.1.2.3.4)//(S2.5.6.7))8.9.10.11((12.T1)//(13.T2))). It gives an efficient way to distinguish one flow from other.

The following operations were introduced in [8] for transforming a flow into an equivalent flow.

Swap : The sequence of execution of the activities can be altered by swapping the activities in a given flow. This transition is applicable to the unary activities only.

Factorize and Distribute : Factorize means performing a transformation once if it occurs in two parallel flows. This operation is applicable for one binary activity (e.g. join, union) and two unary activities. The unary activities on different inputs of the binary activity are replaced by one single activity after the binary activity. Distribute is the inverse of Factorize.

Merge and Un-Merge : Merging two activities into one can be viewed as creating a black box activity that performs the combined transformation. These kind of transformations are used to implement user constraints where the user wants two activities to execute sequentially. Un-Merge[1] is inverse of Merge.

Cost Model

The cost model adopted would enable us to compare different ETL flows. The cost of an activity depends on the operation performed (such as de-duplication, sorting etc.) and also the I/O operations. In this paper, we assume that the cost of an activity can be modelled as function of the volume of data processed by it. These functions can be appropriately chosen before the proposed heuristic

[1] Referred as Split in [8].

based optimization is used. We have chosen well-known upper bounds based on the computational complexity of the operation involved in an activity. For example for the activity involving the sorting of n items, the associated cost function $\phi(n)$ would be $O(nlogn)$. The constant implied by the big O notation can be determined empirically. Once the cost function for an activity is chosen, the actual cost of an activity node can be computed for any specific volume of the data processed. The cost of an ETL flow is the sum of cost of all the activities in it. These values are appropriately used to compare ETL flows. These details are explained fully in Section 4.1.

3 Related Work

An earlier attempt [8] for logical optimization of an ETL work flow models the problem as a State Space Search problem. It introduces various transitions like swap, factorize, distribute, merge, split etc. to transform an ETL flow to an another semantically equivalent flow. Three variants of the algorithms- Exhaustive, Heuristic and Greedy are proposed. The Exhaustive approach applies all the possible transitions to an existing state to search the entire space for the minimum cost flow. The Heuristic approach organizes the transitions to speed up the process. It defines an order among the transitions. The Greedy algorithm further reduces the search space by allowing only those transitions which result in the cost reduction of the flow. These heuristics work efficiently for small flows but with the increase in the number of activities i.e. the size of the flow, the deviation from the optimal flow increases. In real world scenarios where the flows are very large, getting the optimal or near optimal solution is desired.

4 Dependency Based ETL Optimization

In this Section, we present the dependency based ETL optimization algorithm. Initially we apply the algorithm to linear flows and then extend it to complex or non-linear flows by detecting linear sections in it.

4.1 Optimizing Linear Flows

The linear structure is the most fundamental flow in the ETL process. In a linear structure every activity has only one input and one output. Simitis et al. [8] demonstrated that a significant improvement in cost can be achieved by optimizing the linear groups in a complex flow. Every complex flow can be divided into a number of linear flows. These flows can be optimized and combined into semantically equivalent optimized flow.

For a given linear ETL flow L, the edges in the transitive closure, say $T_c(L)$, should represent the set of all dependencies among the activities. When we carefully examine the edges in $T_c(L)$ graph, we find that there are two kinds of edges: *flow* edges and *dependency* edges. Flow edges are those that indicate the flow of

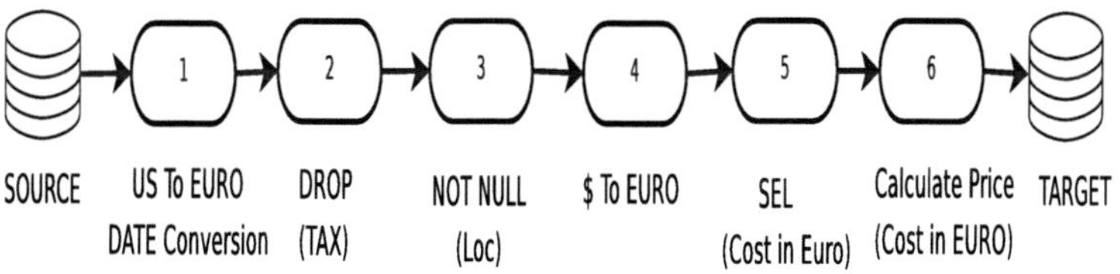

Fig. 2. A linear ETL flow example

data from one node to another node but not necessarily an operational dependency between nodes. For example the edge between node 2 and 3 in Figure 2 is a flow edge. It is easy to see that the two activities can be carried out in either order: (2, 3) or (3, 2). However one of the orders has to be chosen while designing the ETL flow in a design tool. On the other hand, the edge (4, 5) is not only a flow edge but also a dependency edge. In the Figure 2, Activity 5 performs selection on cost in Euros, while activity 4 performs conversion from Dollar to Euro. Activity 5 cannot be executed ahead of activity 4 because it is dependent on activity 4. Thus it is clear that not all edges of $T_c(L)$ are dependencies. Some of them are induced by flow edges that are not dependency edges. In our approach for logical optimization of ETL flows, we use "swappability" test to identify dependency edges and define the dependency graph G_L corresponding to the linear flow L. We find that the given flow L is one of the linearisation of G_L and there may be other linearisation that are better than L in terms of cost. We propose heuristics to compute a different linear ETL flow so that all the dependencies are respected but the ETL flow is cost optimized.

Our Algorithm works in two phases: 1. Identify the dependencies between activities, 2. Using the dependencies identified and the cost model to generate an equivalent linear flow. The preprocessing step is to merge certain activities which is also used in [8]. Once the optimization is over the merged activities are un-merged to their original status.

Dependency Graph Computation

Each activity has an input(s) and output(s) schema. In additions to these schemata, [8] characterizes an activity with certain additional schemata, they are functional, generated and projected-out schemata. Functionality schema has the parameters of the operation performed by the activity. Generated schema is the list of attributes generated by activity while the projected-out schema is the list of input attributes discarded by the activity. For example, an activity with input schema [EmpNo, Name, Salary] and calculating Bonus from Salary has a functionality schema of [Salary]. If the activity produces the output as [EmpNo, Name, Bonus]. The discarded schema will be [Salary] and the generated schema will be [Bonus].

For a given flow $(a_1, a_2, a_3, ..., a_n)$, two activities (a_i, a_m) are *swappable* if the they have non intersecting functionality schema and their input schema

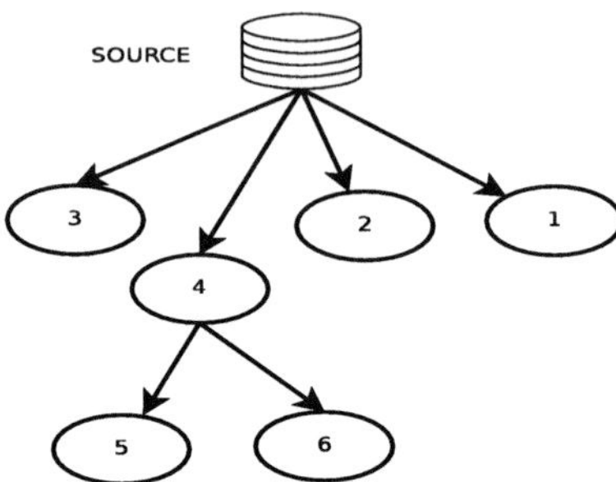

Fig. 3. Dependency graph of the ETL flow shown in Figure 2

requirements are satisfied after the swap. Dependencies of an activity can be found by testing whether it can be swapped with any of its succeeding activities. In the Figure 2, the activities 2 (Drop) and 3 (Not Null) are swappable because they have non-intersecting functionality schemas (Tax and Loc respectively) and the required input schema for them is satisfied after the swap. A more detailed definition of swap and it's proof of correctness is given in [8].

We can start from the first activity and compare it to the activities succeeding it. If they are swappable then they are not dependent otherwise they are dependent. The dependants of an activity are maintained in a list. This process is repeated to find all the dependants of the first activity. Similarly for all other activities their dependants can be found out. In the Figure 2, activity (4, 5) and (4, 6) are not swappable, So 5 and 6 are dependent on 4. The end result of this process can be represented in the form of a DAG. This DAG is called as *dependency graph.* Figure 3 represents all the dependencies of the flow given in Figure 2.

Flow Reconstruction

In order to optimize a linear flow we must ensure that costly activities process less amount of data, at the same time highly selective activities should be pushed towards the source. While rearranging the activities in the flow the dependencies must be taken care of so that the resultant flows are semantic equivalent to the original flow.

A new linear semantically equivalent flow can be constructed from the dependency graph either in the forward direction or backward direction. If we start from the forward direction, to evaluate a candidate activity we know the succeeding activities but we don't have any information about the order of those activities. The order is necessary because different arrangements of succeeding activities will result in different costs. This makes evaluation of the candidate difficult. However, if we proceed from the backward direction i.e. reconstruct the flow in right-to-left manner, the activity near to the target will be the first to get selected. Now the other activities can be evaluated by calculating their effect

Algorithm 1. Flow Reconstruction

Input : :Dependent list of all the Activities
Output: :Linear ETL flow

$SelectedActivityList \leftarrow null$
$currentPos \leftarrow m$
$f_i(n) \leftarrow 0$
while $CurrentPos \mathrel{!=} 0$ **do**
    foreach $Activity\ a \in Sig$ **do**
        if $(dependent[a] \epsilon SelectedActivityList)$ **then**
            Add a to the $candidateSet$
    foreach $c \in CandidateSet$ **do**
        $M_c = \phi_c(n) + f_i(sel_c \times n)$
    CurrentSelectedAct c' = Activity having $\max(M_c)$;
    Append c' to $SelectedActivityList$;
    $f_{i+1}(n) = \phi_{c'}(n) + f_i(sel_{c'} \times n)$
    $CurrentPos = CurrentPos$ - 1;
    $f_i(n) = f_{i+1}(n)$

on the current state of the flow. Suppose in the above example activity 6 gets selected. Now the other candidate activities can be evaluated by assuming that the activity 6 is already present in the flow. This process is repeated till all the activities are processed.

At each iteration the activities on which no other unselected activity is dependent are the candidates for the next position in the flow. The first iteration starts with all leaf nodes of the dependency graph as candidate set. In this case only the cost of the activity will be considered, ties are broken by giving priority to less selective activity. Recall that the activities that allow high volume of data to pass through them have lower selectivity. For the second iteration, the candidates are evaluated by taking into consideration its effect on current selected activities (in this case it will be the activity selected in the first iteration).

The candidate activities are evaluated by using the measure

$$M_c(n) = \phi_c(n) + f_i(sel_c \times n) \tag{1}$$

where $f_i(n)$ is the cost function of the flow partially constructed having i activities. sel_c is the selectivity of the candidate. ϕ_c is the cost function of the candidate. Suppose there are m activities and i activities of the linear flow are already selected and placed in positions $m, m-1, ..., m-(i-1)$. We now evaluate the candidates for the position $m-i$ as shown in the Figure 4. The candidates are compared by evaluating their corresponding measure expressions asymptotically. That is, the measure $M_c(n)$ would be calculated by taking n to be a large value, say one million, for different candidates c. (Note that The value for n can be chosen to be approximately same as the volume of the data processed by the ETL flow). The candidate activity having maximum measure gets selected for

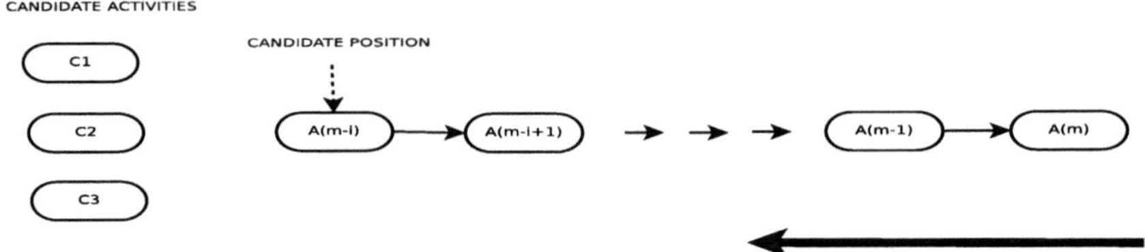

Fig. 4. Reconstruction of a linear flow in right-to-left order

the position under consideration. The measure is basically the cost of the currently constructed flow having the activities selected so far and the candidate being evaluated.

Now, the measure function for the next iteration uses the following f_{i+1} function. Here, c' is the selected activity in the iteration i.

$$f_{i+1} = (\phi_{c'}(n) + f_i(sel_{c'} \times n)) \tag{2}$$

The measure is updated after each iteration to reflect the changes due to the newly selected activity. Note that the function f_{i+1} after i iterations can also be written as:

$$f_{i+1} = \phi_{m-i}(n) + \phi_{m-i-1}\left(sel_{m-i} \times n\right) + \phi_{m-i-2}\left(\left(\prod_{j=m-i}^{m-i-1} sel_j\right) \times n\right) + ... + \phi_m\left(\left(\prod_{j=m-i}^{m-1} sel_j\right) \times n\right) \tag{3}$$

It can be recalled that the selectivity of the candidate affects the costs of the succeeding activities. The measure M takes into account the selectivity and the cost of the candidate activity. The activity having lower selectivity and high cost will have higher measure.

Algorithm 1 describes this process of flow reconstruction. The activities having the higher selectivity and lower cost do not get selected early and due to the right to left approach these activities are pushed towards the source. This reduces the amount of data processed by succeeding activities and results in reduction of the cost of the flow.

5 Optimizing Complex Flows

There are some activities for which

$$\phi(n) > \phi(n_1) + \phi(n_2); \text{where } \phi(n) \text{ is activity cost function and } n_1, n_2 < n \tag{4}$$

i.e. it is better to perform them on smaller inputs rather than on large inputs. On the other hand, for some activities it is better to perform them on large inputs. To optimize an ETL flow such kind of activities must be identified and positioned to have minimum cost.

5.1 Finding Transferable Activities

Activities that can be pushed from one linear group to another are called *transferable* activities. They can be swapped with the binary activity (e.g. join, split) of their linear groups. Binary activities either have two inputs (join) or two outputs (split), they connect linear groups. In the case of linear groups that converge[2] (e.g. input of join) the activities that have same semantics (i.e. homologous activities) can be transferred to the output group. Similarly activities can be transferred form the output group to the input groups. These kind of activities can be determined using Factorize and Distribute operations described in Section 2. Transferable activities for the diverging linear groups can also be determined in a similar manner. Since an ETL flow is represented as a directed graph, the order of execution among the linear groups is determined by the order implied by the DAG. The transferable activities are of two types: Forward transferable and Backward transferable. Forward transferable activities can be transferred to the output linear group(s) in the direction of the flow while the Backward transferable activities can be transferred to the input linear group(s). Our approach finds the transferable activities in two phases: 1. Forward Pass and 2. Backward Pass.

Forward Pass

In this pass the activities of a group that can be transferred to the next linear groups are determined. These activities are added at the start of the next group(s). Suppose in the Figure 1, for the linear groups I, II activities (1, 3) and (5, 6) are transferable respectively. The activities (1, 5) and (3, 6) are homologous. The next linear group (Grp III) will now become as (1_5, 3_6, 9, 10) where (1_5 and 3_6) are the newly added activities having same semantics as 1 and 3 respectively. The activities present initially in this group (i.e. Grp III) may be dependent on the these transferable activities. In order to preserve these dependencies, the new activities (1_5, 3_6 in this case) are added at the start of the group. Now the transferable activities for this new enhanced group are determined. In this approach, we will be able to determine if an activity can get transferred transitively that is, it can be transferred from linear group Grp_i to Grp_j and then to Grp_k. For the last linear groups i.e. having no next groups, there are no activities that be forwarded. At the end of this phase all the forward-transferable-activities of each groups are determined. Further, for each transferable activity we determine how far it can be transferred in the forward direction.

Backward Pass

In this phase, the activities of a group that can be transferred to the previous group are determined. But, now the activities are added at the end of the group to preserve the dependencies.

[2] Converging linear groups [8].

5.2 Reconstructing the Original Flow

The process of reconstructing the original flow is described in Algorithm 2. To optimize each linear group all possible activities that can be present are considered. Each linear group is enhanced with the activities that can be forward-transferred from the previous group and the activities that can be backward-transferred from the next group. For example the Grp III of the ETL flow shown in Figure 1 becomes {1_5, 3_6, 9, 10, 12_13 }. Now, all of these enhanced linear groups are optimised. For the transferable activities there are many possible positions. So, the enhanced linear group contains many occurrences of the same activity. For instance, the activities 3, 6 can be present in {GrpI, GrpII}, {GrpIII}, {GrpIV, GrpV}. These activities are sorted in the order of their selectivity. For each transferable activity, the costs of the signatures for its different valid positions are calculated. The position having the maximum effect i.e. the signature having the minimum cost is retained, all of the remaining instances are deleted from the enhanced signature. This process is repeated till the most profitable position for each one of the transferable-activities is calculated. At the end of this process a semantically equivalent optimized flow is obtained.

5.3 Handling Inter-dependent Transferable Activities

Transferable activities may have dependencies between them. So while calculating the optimal position for them, it may happen that their dependencies may be lost. In the Figure 1, the activities 3_6 and 9 are transferable for the enhanced linear Grp III. Both these activities have the same functional schema. Hence the activity 9 is dependent on the activity 3_6. Let us assume that the optimal position for the 3_6 may turn out to be in the linear groups after the split i.e. GrpIV, GrpV and for the activity 9 as in its current position. In that case the earlier dependency constraint will be violated.

To prevent such cases the dependent-transferable activities are handled in a different manner. For all such groups, instead of possible positions of individual activities, valid combinations for these activities are computed. {[GrpI, GrpII], [GrpIII]}, {[GrpIII], [GrpIII]}, and {[GrpIV, GrpV], [GrpIV, GrpV]} are valid combinations for the activities {3, 6, 9} respectively. While {[GrpIV, GrpV], [GrpIII]} violates the dependency and is an invalid combination. Then the valid combinations are tested for finding the optimal position for these activities.

Algorithm The Algorithm-2 describes the process of optimizing the complex flows. Line 4-7 describes the forward pass. The forward transferable activities are added to the start of each linear group. The backward pass is presented in the lines 8-10. In this case the backward transferable activities are appended at last of each linear group. The enhanced linear groups are optimised in line 12-14. Lines 14-15 finds the dependency among the transferable activities. The positions for the dependent groups are determined in the lines 17-19 while for other transferable activities, lines 20-21 computes the most profitable position.

Algorithm 2. Handling Complex Flow

```
Input  : Signature of an flow Sig[]
Output: Optimized ETL flow
Apply all Merges according to constraints
Determine Linear Groups[ ]
Topological Sort to determine order among the groups
foreach Linear_Grp[i] in topological Order do
    enchancedLinear = Add(Fwd_Trans_Act(prev_grp{s}), Linear_Grp[i]))
    Calculate Fwd_Trans_Act[enchancedLinear]
    Trans_Act = Trans_Act +Fwd_Trans_Act
foreach Linear_Grp[i] in reverse topological Order do
    enchancedLinear = Append(Linear_Grp[i],
    Bwd_Trans_Act(prev_grp{s})))
    Calculate Bwd_Trans_Act[enchancedLinear]
    Trans_Act = Trans_Act +Bwd_Trans_Act
foreach Linear_Grp[i] do
    enchancedLinearGrp =
    Add(Fwd_Trans_Act,Bwd_Trans_Act(prev_grp{s}),Linear_Grp[i]));
    OptimizedEnchancedGrp = Optimize(enchancedLinearGrp)
foreach Trans_Act do
    Find dependentGrps
foreach g in dependentGrps do
    Compute valid variations of g
    Calculate Optimal_Pos
foreach t in Trans_Act and not in dependentGrps do
    Calculate Optimal_Pos(t)
Apply all the Un-Merge
```

6 Proof of Correctness

In this section we will establish the proof of correctness for the proposed dependency based ETL optimization method. Two ETL flows are semantically equivalent if the same target data set can be obtained for the same input. The order of the activities may be different in the two flows, which may lead to different data in the intermediate stages, but the end result will be same.

Linear Flows

As we noted earlier in the Section 4.1, the given linear flow is one of the linearisation of the the underlying dependency graph of the activities in the flow. Step 1 of dealing with a linear flow constructs the dependency graph. It is clear that this is computed correctly as all possible pairs of the activities are considered while constructing the dependency graph. What remains to be shown is that the new linearisation computed in Step 2 of the algorithm is semantically equivalent to the given flow. Note that the algorithm presented constructs a linear flow from the dependency graph by first considering the leaf nodes. At each stage it chooses one of the nodes none of whose dependants are placed later to it. Thus the algorithms computes the topological sort of the underlying dependency graph. Hence it is clear that the linearisation obtained is semantically equivalent to the given flow.

Complex or Non Linear Flow

For a complex flow, the activities are transferred from one linear group to another. Transferable activities are identified using factorize and distribute operations. After transferring the activities each of the linear groups is optimised. It is shown in [8] that these operations preserve the semantic equivalence between the flows. In order to optimize the flow all the possible occurrences of the transferable activities are considered and the proposed algorithm retains only one valid occurrence for such activities thus ensuring the resultant flow has the same semantics as the original one.

7 Experimental Results

System set-up: The experiments were conducted on Linux (Ubuntu 7.10) PC based on Intel Core 2 Duo (2.0GHz CPU) with 1GB of RAM. We implemented the algorithms in Java and tested them for different measures quality of improvement, time taken. The Quality of Improvement (QoI) is can be expressed as:

$$QoI = \left(\frac{InitialCost - FinalCost}{InitialCost}\right) \times 100 \tag{5}$$

We have used 40 different ETL flows as test cases. We have tested the algorithms for different size and structures as described in [12]. The operators considered are filter, type conversion, lookup, union, join, difference, aggregation etc. We have used a simple cost Model described in [13]. The cost of an operation is determined by the core functionality of the operation. The Quality of Improvement and time taken was measured for all the State space based (Heuristic, Exhaustive and Greedy) algorithms and the proposed algorithm. The results are shown in Table 1.

Exhaustive Space Search (ES) starts with the given flow as the initial state and it applies all possible transition (as described in the Section 2) to generate new states. For each such state, all the possible transitions are applied again to

Table 1. Results

Sig	Exhaustive		Heuristic		Greedy		Proposed	
No. of Act(avg)	QoI	time(sec)	QoI	time(sec)	QoI	time(sec)	QoI	time(sec)
20	70	67540	68	150	65	6	71	2
40	51*	86400*	62	640	57	76	69	5
60	42*	86400*	55	1480	44	524	67	7

*the algorithm did not terminate, the values are when it is stopped

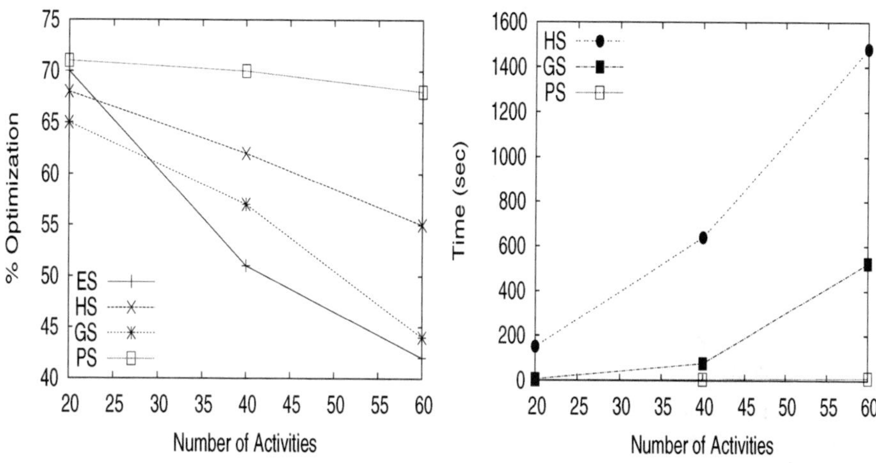

Fig. 5. Quality of improvement **Fig. 6.** Time taken

HS-Heuristic Search, PS-Proposed Algorithm, GS-Greedy Search, ES-Exhaustive Search

generate new sets of state. This process continues till all the possible states are searched. The search space is finite, but it takes a long time to terminate. Due to such a large space, as reported in the Table 1 as well as in [8] even after 36 hrs the algorithm does not terminate. This makes the algorithm inefficient and unsuitable for medium to large size flows.

In the state space based heuristic algorithm (HS), all the transferable activities (Homologous and Distributable) are computed from the initial signature of the flow. When these activities are processed they get shifted to the adjacent local group only. While in the proposed algorithm transferable activities are calculated from enhanced linear groups so the transferability of the activities is not restricted to the adjacent groups. For example in Figure 1, the activities (3, 6) can be transferred to the groups after the split while these kind of transfers are not possible in the HS. With the increase in the size of the flow, such kind transferability restriction affects the quality of the solution, which is also reflected in the result table.

The State Space based algorithms described in [14,8] consider only the converging linear groups (i.e groups connected by join operator) to transfer the activities. While the Proposed algorithm (PS) considers the positioning of activities across diverging groups (groups separated by split operator) as well. This allows us to explore more space than the existing algorithms to produce better results which are shown in the Figure 5.

The HS-Greedy algorithm reduces the search space by allowing only those swaps that result in cost reduction from the current state. The algorithm is fast as compared to the other state-space based algorithms as less number of states are visited. But due to the greedy nature of the algorithm it results in local optima. As expected and shown in Figure 6 there is huge difference between the time taken by the algorithms. The state space based algorithms search through the space for the optimal solution while the proposed algorithm reorganizes the activities according to the measure defined and directly computes it.

8 Conclusions and Future Work

In this paper, we study the problem of logical optimization of ETL workflows and present an efficient heuristic for optimizing them. A key observation is that not all dependencies implied by a given flow are essential dependencies. Following this, we capture the essential dependencies in a dependency graph. This gives us a way of computing a semantically equivalent linear flow in a much more efficiently manner compared to the state space approaches. We find that the approach can be extended to complex flows. The resulting solution has given considerable performance gain and can be used for ETL flows of large size. We devise a new measure function that uses the cost and selectivities of activities to evaluate partially constructed linear flows. We make use of it to heuristically compute a semantically equivalent flows. The proposed algorithm can be potentially incorporated in ETL design tools.

Future work includes the use of a complex cost model for the activities in view of their physical implementation.

References

1. Inmon, W.: Building the Data Warehouse, 3rd edn. Wiley & Sons, New York (2002)
2. Vassiliadis, P., Simitsis, A., Skiadopoulos, S.: Conceptual Modeling for ETL Processes. In: Proceedings of the 5th ACM International Workshop on Data Warehousing and OLAP (DOLAP 2002), pp. 14–21. ACM, New York (2002)
3. Trujillo, J., Luján-Mora, S.: A UML Based Approach for Modeling ETL Processes in Data Warehouses. In: Song, I.-Y., Liddle, S.W., Ling, T.-W., Scheuermann, P. (eds.) ER 2003. LNCS, vol. 2813, pp. 307–320. Springer, Heidelberg (2003)
4. Eckerson, W., White, C.: `http://www.dw-institute.com/etlreport` (2003)
5. IBM: IBM data warehouse manager, `www3.ibm.com/software/data/db2/datawarehouse`
6. Oracle: Oracle warehouse builder 11g, `http://www.oracle.com/technology/products/warehouse/`
7. Informatica: PowerCenter, `http://www.informatica.com/products/data+integration/powercenter/default.htm`
8. Simitsis, A., Vassiliadis, P., Sellis, T.: State-Space Optimization of ETL Workflows. IEEE Trans. on Knowl. and Data Eng. 17(10), 1404–1419 (2005)
9. Vassiliadis, P., Simitsis, A., Spiros, S.: Modeling ETL Activities as Graphs. In: 4th International Workshop on the Design and Management of Data Warehouses (DMDW 2002), pp. 52–61. IEEE Computer Society, Toronto (2002)
10. Vassiliadis, P., Simitsis, A., Baikousi, E.: A taxonomy of etl activities. In: DOLAP 2009: Proceeding of the ACM Twelfth International Workshop on Data Warehousing and OLAP, pp. 25–32. ACM, New York (2009)

11. Tziovara, V., Vassiliadis, P., Simitsis, A.: Deciding the Physical Implementation of ETL Workflows. In: Proceedings of the ACM Tenth International Workshop on Data Warehousing and OLAP (DOLAP 2007), pp. 49–56. ACM, New York (2007)
12. Vassiliadis, P., Karagiannis, A., Tziovara, V., Simitsis, A.: Towards a Benchmark for ETL Workflows. In: Proceedings of the 5th International Workshop on Quality in Databases (QDB 2007), in Conjunction with the 33rd International Conference on Very Large Data Bases (VLDB 2007), pp. 117–137 (2007)
13. Elmasri, R., Navathe, S.: Fundamentals of Database Systems. Addison-Wesley Pubs., Reading (2000)
14. Simitsis, A., Vassiliadis, P., Sellis, T.: Optimizing ETL Processes in Data Warehouses. In: Proceedings of the 21st International Conference on Data Engineering (ICDE 2005), pp. 564–575. IEEE Computer Society, Washington, DC (2005)

Augmenting Tables by Self-supervised Web Search

Alexander Löser, Christoph Nagel, and Stephan Pieper

DIMA Group, Technische Universität Berlin, Einsteinufer 17
10587 Berlin, Germany
firstname.lastname@tu-berlin.de

Abstract. Often users are faced with the problem of searching the Web for missing values of a spread sheet. It is a fact that today only a few US-based search engines have the capacity to aggregate the wealth of information hidden in Web pages that could be used to return these missing values. Therefore exploiting this information with structured queries, such as join queries, is an often requested, but still unsolved requirement of many Web users.

A major challenge in this scenario is identifying keyword queries for retrieving relevant pages from a Web search engine. We solve this challenge by automatically generating keywords. Our approach is based on the observation that Web page authors have already evolved common words and grammatical structures for describing important relationship types. Each keyword query should return only pages that likely contain a missing relation. Therefore our keyword generator continually monitors grammatical structures or lexical phrases from processed Web pages during query execution. Thereby, the keyword generator infers significant and non-ambiguous keywords for retrieving pages which likely match the mechanics of a particular relation extractor.

We report an experimental study over multiple relation extractors. Our study demonstrates that our generated keywords efficiently return complete result tuples. In contrast to other approaches we only process very few Web pages.

Keywords: information extraction, document collections, query optimization.

1 Introduction

Next-Generation Business Intelligence Applications require methods to mine the Web for actionable business insights. For example, consider the following query :

"Given a list of companies defined in table MyCompanies, augment information from news pages on the Web about acquisitions, company headquarter, size of employees, product customers and analyst recommendations.

It is a fact that today only a few US-based search engines have both the capacity and the know-how to index and to aggregate the Web for answering such queries. Because of this monopoly, previous systems for executing such queries [2,3,4] assumed a full access granted to all indexed pages for answering the query from above. For instance, a possible scenario for these systems is a query that is directly executed on the entire index by an employee of the Yahoo search engine.

M. Castellanos, U. Dayal, and V. Markl (Eds.): BIRTE 2010, LNBIP 84, pp. 84–99, 2011.

However, the majority of Web users do not have full access to these pages. Moreover, due to the nature of business models of Web search engines it is unlikely that a full access to the entire index is ever provided for each Web searcher. Because of the plethora of possible relation extractors, it is very unlikely that a Web search engine will ever provide extracted tuples for all of these extractors and for each Web site.

Contributions: Ideally, Web searchers could query the Web like a relational database. For realizing this interesting and novel application scenario the paper focuses on the specific problem of complementing a given list of values with information (values) from the Web. Our approach automatically identifies discriminating keywords to return a small set of relevant web pages using an existing search engine, like Yahoo Boss, from which tuples for a structured query are extracted. Other aspects of the overall process of augmenting given tuples with missing values from the Web have been presented in a previous publication [9].

Self-supervised Web search for obtaining missing values in a table: Extracting tuples from pages is costly and time consuming. For instance, state-of-the-art extraction services (such as OpenCalais.com) require multiple seconds to download a page and to extract relations. Ideally, generated keywords strategy return only pages that likely contain a missing relation. Thereby, keywords should help to retrieve only pages that also match the mechanics of the extractor, otherwise relevant pages are retrieved but relations are not recognized by the extractor. Keywords should be generated without analyzing a large set of sample pages from the search engine. Finally, keywords should adapt constantly to new pages published on the Web.

To solve this problem we designed a self-supervised keyword generation method. Our method returns highly selective keywords: It omits *ambiguous* keywords (keywords that appear with multiple relationships) and only returns most *significant* keywords (keywords that frequently correlate with a particular relationship).Our method is efficient since keywords are observed and extracted only from pages that are already retrieved during query execution. Contrary to the method proposed in [6], our method does not require processing additional pages before executing a structured query. Finally, generated keywords are constantly updated with words and grammatical structures of Web pages that are discovered during query processing.

Prototypical implementation and experimental study: We implemented our algorithms for the in-memory database *HSQLDB* [13]. In a preliminary study we test our algorithms findings on structured queries invoking multiple relationship extractors. We compared and identified keyword generation strategies that can effectively reduce the amount of processed documents.

The rest of the paper is organized as follows: Section 2 introduces our novel application scenario and reviews our existing work. In Section 3 we introduce our novel algorithm to generate discriminative keywords. In Section 4 we evaluate the performance of our algorithms. Section 5 compares our contributions to related work. Finally, in Section 6 we give a summary and discuss future work.

2 Augmenting Tables with Information from Web Search Results

In this Section we give a brief overview on our query processor for executing queries of the type 'augment specific-k items' on Web search results.

2.1 Answering Structured Queries from Web Search Results

The long term vision of our work is to answer structured queries from natural language text on Web pages [9, 19, 21]. In this paper we focused on queries of the type AUGMENT specific-k items. In this query type a list of known entities is complemented with relations that are extracted from Web pages. Consider again the query from the introduction:

***Example: Augment specific-k items**: "Given a list of companies defined in table MyCompanies, augment information from pages of cnn.com about acquisitions, company headquarter, size of employees, product customers and analyst recommendations.* ■

This query takes as input a table with one or multiple companies. For each company pages are retrieved from the search engines CNN.com that likely contain information about acquisitions, size of employees, product customers or analyst recommendations. In addition, we identified two additional, similar query types:

***Example: Discover any-k items**: Projects (or) funders) of climate adaptation projects in Africa from the Web.* ■

The goal of this query is to find names of projects and/or the names of funders associated with such projects or funders who work on climate adaptation in Africa more generally (even the name of the funder without the name of the project). However, this query does neither specify a search engine nor a Web page nor a list of already known entities, such as companies or project names. Queries for discovering any-k relations enable users exploring and discovering previously *unknown* relations without manually searching, browsing and reading thousands of Web pages. Users can browse and refine these tables further, e.g., by verifying the authenticity of surprising relations with additional search queries.

***Example: Verify structured data with information from Web pages**: The PPI database of the 'World Bank' includes lists of projects. Engineer a search that finds all privately financed water and sewerage projects in Colombia since 1984 (the PPI database lists names of 51 distinct projects).* ■

The goal of this query is to complement existing structured data with relations from the Web and to identify 'linage' information (such as Web pages or Blog authors) for retrieved relations.

Neither Web search engines nor business intelligence tools can answer this query today which requires an intersection of their business (and user access) models, content data bases and technical capabilities. For answering these queries our work address the following key-challenges.

Timely answer: Extracting relations from pages is costly and time consuming. For instance, state-of-the-art relation extractors (such as OpenCalais.com) require multiple seconds for downloading a page and for extracting relations. One possible approach is utilizing parallelization techniques for executing multiple queries in parallel [20]. The approach presented in this paper avoids forwarding irrelevant pages to relation extractors by generating highly discriminative keyword queries.

```
-- Assign search results and extractors to temporary tables
DEF Acquisition(Acquirer, Acquired, Status, DateString)
    AS OpenCalais.Acquisition FROM yahoo.com USING FIRST 10

-- Define result attributes and join predicate
SELECT  Acquisition.Acquirer, Acquisition.Acquired, Acquisition.Status,
Acquisition.DateString
FROM    MyCompany, Acquisition
LEFT OUTER JOIN Acquisition
    ON  MyCompany.company = Acquisition.Acquirer
```

MyCompany.Company	Acquisition.Acquirer	Acquisition.Acquired	Acquisition.Status	Acquisition.Datestring
United Natural Foods	United Natural Foods	Canadian Food Distribution	announced	Monday, August 5 2002
United Natural Foods	United Natural Foods	Food Distribution Ass	known	Jun 14, 2010
United Natural Foods	United Natural Foods	Boulder Fruit Express	known	November 2001
United Natural Foods	United Natural Foods	Blooming Prairie	announced	Wednesday, August 7 2002
United Natural Foods	United Natural Foods	SunOpta Distribution Group	known	May 19, 2010
Discovery Communications	Discovery Communications	HowStuffWorks.com	announced	Sunday, December 30, 2007
Oracle	Oracle	MySQL	planned	February 18th, 2006
Oracle	Oracle	Sun Microsystems	announced	April 20, 2009
Oracle	Oracle	Tacit Software	announced	November 4, 2008

Fig. 1. Example query and result excerpt

Data quality: Because of the nature of content on the Web, incomplete result tuples may frequently occur. One important quality criteria is result tuple completeness. For instance, queries invoking joins across multiple relations require complete values for join attributes. Moreover operators for cleansing, fusing, merging, verifying [10], aggregating and ranking [2] require complete tuples to create authentic results. Unfortunately, relation extractors frequently return incomplete tuples. The rationale for this incompleteness is to indicate human evaluators the existence of a relation on a Web page, even though precise values for each attribute of the relation are not extracted. Worse, extractors may frequently fail because of missing textual data in the Web page.

2.2 Expressing Queries of the Type '*augment specific-k items*'

Relation extractors and search engines as table generators: Our query language uses relation extractors as table generators which are integrated with data manipulation operations. With this functionality a user can select a powerful combination of qualitative search engines and of high-precision extractors that likely return relevant result tuples answering the structured query. Based on our language, representations of tuples in natural language from Web pages are mapped to the explicit integrated schema defined in the user query. The table generation is done by a *DEF*-clause (which is similar to the *WITH* clause in SQL). A *DEF*-clause defines the extractor, the search engine, the top-pages and optional keywords used to create tuples for a temporary table. In the temporary table we store attribute values of the tuple, pages from which attribute values are extracted and the completeness of each tuple.

***Left outer join**:* Our query language allows Select-Project-left outer join query structures. The outer table for the join should already contain relations. For executing a left outer joining on these relations users can define a join predicate. For instance, the join predicate can be an object identifier that is shared by objects in the outer table and relations that are returned from the relation extractor. Otherwise a fuzzy join can be executed on the textual representation of the object.

***Example:** Figure 1 illustrates the representation of the example from the introduction query in our language. The query augments a set of companies in table MyCompanies with tuples of the relationship type Acquisition(Acquirer, Acquired, Date, Status). The query defines the table generator 'Acquisition' which retrieves top-10 pages from the search engine "yahoo.com" and forwards pages to the extractor OpenCalais.Acquisition. Tuples from the 'left' table MyCompanies are joined with relations returned from the extractor on the text of the company attribute.* ■

2.3 Processing Queries of the Type '*augment specific-k items*'

In our previous work [9] we proposed a query processor for executing join operations on search results from Web search engines. This technique is applied for answering queries of the type 'augment specific-k items'. We briefly repeat the two main steps:

1. ***Iterate over outer table:*** Similar to a nested-loop join our query processor scans the outer table (which contains the specific-k items) row by row. For each row in the outer table we generate a keyword query for obtaining a missing relation.
2. ***Query index of search engine, retrieve pages, extract and combine relations:*** The keyword query scans the index of billions of pages of a Web search engine. This operation is executed in a timely fashion by leveraging the powerful infrastructure of existing search engines. A keyword query returns pages which are forwarded to a relation extractor. Relations extracted on the page are combined with rows of the outer table according to the structured query.

Query termination: The adaptive process of generating keyword queries, extracting relations, combing relations into result tuples is terminated when all rows in the outer table are processed. During query processing the keyword generating component learns how likely a keyword query returns a relevant page.

3 Continuous Keyword Query Generation

In this Section we introduce our strategy to identify, generalize and extract meaningful keyword phrases from Web pages.

3.1 Overview and Requirements

The average Web user is often not aware of relevant keywords for returning pages from an extractor can return tuples for a particular relationship. Even if such keywords are known, determining keywords that best fit the mechanics of a relation extractor is difficult.

Our keyword generation strategy is based on the key observation that human language has already evolved words and grammatical structures for relationships. Our approach monitors the ability of the 'mechanics' of an extractor to capture these words and grammatical structures for a particular relationship. Figure 2 gives an overview on this process: First, we observe if sentences share instances of the same relationship also share similarities in textual content. Next, we keep phrases from these sentences that indicate the existence of an instance of a specific relationship (i.e., an *acquisition*) by using an efficient *lexico–syntactic* classifier. Then, we determine for each phrase their clarity with respect to other relationships and their significance for a particular relationship. From phrases that achieved both, a high clarity and a high significance, we generate a keyword query for a specific search engine and relationship type.

Our method is designed towards an online classification setting: It is completely unsupervised, requires no parameter tuning and requires little computation overhead. As an important highlight the set of keywords is no longer static (i.e. defined by a human or learned from a static corpus [6]) but is constantly updated by new phrases which are observed during query exaction.

3.2 Step 1: Extract Candidate Phrases

A page may contain many irrelevant words for extracting a particular relationship. Therefore, we consider only words from sentences in which an extractor identified a relation and attribute values. We generalize attribute values to the name of the attribute type returned by the relationship extractor. Next, we obtain lexical information (phrases of words) appearing before, between and after these attribute values and we generate syntactic information (part-of-speech tags) for each sentence.

Example: *Figure 3a-c shows sentences which contain a relation of the type Acquisition (Acquisition.Acuqirer, Acquisition.Acquired). In each sentence, attributes and attribute values of the extract relation are labeled (Figure 3a). Next, attribute values in each sentence are generalized to their corresponding attribute type (Figure 3b). For instance, the values 'Tata Motors' and 'Brunswick Corp' are generalized to the attribute type 'Acquisition.Acquirer'. Finally, words before, between and after attribute values are labeled with part-of-speech information (Figure 3c).* ■

3.3 Step 2: Classify and Filter Phrases

Labeled sentences may still contain words that are not relevant for extracting relations of a particular type. For instance, in the sentence: "*<Acquisition.Aquierer> has sold <Acquisition.Acquired> for $2.3 billion.*" the adverbial information "for $2.3 billion" is not relevant for the type *Acquisition(Acquisition.Acuqirer, Acquisition.Acquired).* One option to identify the structure of complex and compound sentences is a time consuming deep linguistically analysis of each sentence. Fortunately, recent research [8] has shown that 95% of binary relationships are expressed in English sentences by a set of few *relationship independent* lexico-syntactic patterns that can be detected with a shallow analysis (part-of speech tagging). For instance, the pattern *<A><verb-phrase><A>* enforces an instance of an attribute type that is followed by a group of verbs that are followed by another instance of an attribute type. We keep only phrases that follow at least one of these patterns. Next, we label remaining phrase with the relationship type that is returned from the relation extractor.

a) Obtain extracted sentences, entities and relations from pages.

Acquisition	**<Acquisition.Acquirer:'Tata Motors'>** had acquired **<Acquisition.Acquired:'JLR'>** for $2.3 billion.
Acquisition	**<Acquisition.Acquirer:'Brunswick Corp'>** on Monday said it has sold **<Acquisition.Acquired: 'Sealine'>.**

b) Generalize relation-dependent patterns in sentences.

Acquisition	**<Acquisition.Acquirer>** had acquired **<Acquisition.Acquired>** for $2.3 billion
Acquisition	**<Acquisition.Acquirer>** on Monday said it has sold **<Acquisition.Acquired>** .

c) Classify words with relation-independent lexico-syntactic patterns.

Acquisition	**<Acquisition.Acquirer>** [VBD/had] [VBN/acquired] **<Acquisition.Acquired>** [IN/for] [$/$] [CD/2.3] [CD/billion].
Acquisition	**<Acquisition.Acquirer>** [IN/on] [NNP/Monday] [VBD/said] [PRP/it] [VBZ/has] [VBN/sold] **<Acquisition.Acquired>.**

d) Extract relation-dependent words and phrases.
(here <Acquisition.Acquirer> <Verb Group><Acquisition.Acquired>)

Acquisition	**<Acquisition.Acquirer>** had acquired **<Acquisition.Acquired>**
Acquisition	**<Acquisition.Acquirer>** has sold **<Acquisition.Acquired>**

e) Rank discriminative phrases for relation

Relation	**Existing Value Attribute Type**	**Generated Keywords**	**Missing Value Attribute Type**	DCM
Acquisition	Acquisition.Acquirer	had acquired	Acquisition.Acquired	0,4
Acquisition	Acquisition.Acquirer	has sold	Acquisition.Acquired	0,27

f) Generate keyword query with discriminative phrases
Parameters: *se=Yahoo.com; Relation="Acquisition"; Existing Attribute Type = Acquisition.Acquirer; Existing Attribute Type Value = "SAP AG"*

+"SAP AG" +("had acquired" OR "has sold")

Fig. 2. Generating discriminative keyword queries

Example: *Figure 3 shows our set of relationship independent lexico-syntactic patterns, five example relationship types and six candidate phrases. For instance, for relationship Producer(Product, Company) two phrases in diathesis voices are extracted. Figure 2d shows two phrases '<Acquisition.Acquirer> had acquired <Acquisition.Acquired>' and '<Acquisition.Acquirer> has sold <Acquisition.Acquired>' for relationship type Acqusition(Acquirer, Acquired).* ■

3.4 Step 3: Identify Discriminative Phrases

A crucial task of the keyword generation algorithm is to determine (1) if the phrase is ambiguous for multiple relationships and (2) if the phrase is significant for a particular relationship. For instance, the phrase *"announces"* is ambiguous, since it frequently appears together with relations of multiple relationships, such as *Acquisition*, *CareerChange* or *CompanyExpansion*. In addition, for the relationship *Acquisition* multiple phrases appear, such as *announces (97), acquires(78), compete(28) ... completes(18) ...rebuffed(1).*

Identifying highly significant and unambiguous phrases for a relationship is similar to the problem of identifying discriminative features for document classification [14]. Originally, the discriminative category matching approach (DCM) measures the (1) relative importance of a feature for describing a document and (2) for describing and the relative importance of a feature to describe a category of documents. We transfer these ideas to our scenario and measure the significance and clarity of a phrase for returning only pages which likely contain relations of a specific type.

Relative significance of a phrase for a relationship: We consider a phrase as significant, if it appears frequently among all phrases for a particular relationship. The significance is relative to the set of observed pages. The relative $Significance_{i,R}$ of a phrase i for a relationship R is given by the following equation:

$$Significance_{i,R} = \frac{\log_2(f_{i,R} + 1)}{\log_2(P_R + 1)}$$

The term $f_{i,R}$ denotes the number of sentences where phrase i was observed for relationship R. P_R denotes the number of *all* sentence where a phrase for *any* relationship R is detected. Since a phrase which appears n times cannot imply that the phrase is n times more important we use a logarithmic scale rather than a linear scale.

Lexico Syntactic Pattern	->	Example Relationship	->	Observed Canidate Phrase
<A> verb-phrase <A>		Acqusition(Acquirer, Acquired)		<Acqusition. Acquirer> had acquired <Acqusition. Acquired>
<A> verb-phrase <A>		HQ(Company, HeadQuarter)		<HQ. Company> headquarter in <HQ.Location>
<A> verb-phrase + prep <A>		Producer(Product, Company)		<Producer.Product> manufactured by <Producer. Company>
<A> to + infinitive <A>		Producer(Product, Company)		<Producer. Company> to produce <Producer.Product>
<A> verbphrase <A> noun-phrase		Award(Person, Company)		<Award.Person> was awarded <Award.Company> grant
<A> and | , <A> verb-phrase		Marraige(Person1, Person2)		<Marriage.Person1> and <Marriage.Person2> are expected to marry

Fig. 3. Lexico-syntactic pattern for the English Language

Relative clarity of an extracted phrase across relationships: Consider an extractor which recognizes multiple relationships. We consider a phrase as *ambiguous* if the *same* phrase is frequently observed for *multiple* relationship types $R_1 \ldots R_n$. A phrase achieves a high *clarity*, if we frequently observe the phrase only for a *single* relationship. The following equation captures this intuition. The $Clarity_i$ is relative to observed relationships and Web pages. We denote $Clarity_i$ of a phrase i as:

$$Clarity_i = \begin{cases} \log \dfrac{n * \max\limits_{j \in \{1..n\}} \left\{ Significance_{i,R_j} \right\}}{\sum_{j=1}^{n} Significance_{i,R_j}} * \dfrac{1}{\log n}, & n > 1 \\ 1, & n = 1 \end{cases}$$

In the equation above, $Signficance_{i,Rj}$ describes the significance of a phrase i for a specific relationship R_j. The variable n counts the number of relationships $R_1 \ldots R_n$ for which the significance of phrase i is observed. $Clarity_i$ has some interesting and intuitive characteristics: $Clarity_i$ of phrase i drops, if individual significance values of phrase i for multiple relationships are growing. Contrary, the $Clarity_i$ of phrase i is high, if we observe a high significance for a single relationship and low significance for other relationships. If we observe a phrase only once and only for a single relationship we set $Clarity_i=1$. We normalize $0 \le Clarity_i \le 1$ with the term $1/log(n)$.

Discriminative phrases for a relationship. A phrase has a high discriminative power, if we observe for both values, $Significance_{i,R}$ and $Clarity_{i,}$, *equally high values*. The following equation captures this intuition. We identify the most discriminative phrases i for a relationship R as with the metric $Discriminative_{i,R}$ as follows:

$$Discriminative_{i,R} = \frac{Significance_{i,R}^2 * Clarity_i^2}{\sqrt{Significance_{i,R}^2 + Clarity_i^2}} * \sqrt{2}$$

The term $\sqrt{2}$ serves as normalization factor with $0 \le DP_{i,R} \le 1$.

Example: *We observe two phrases with* $f_{has\ sold,\ Acquisition}=15$ *and* $f_{had\ acquired,\ Acquisition}=43$. *We compute* $Significance_{had\ aquired,Acquisition}$ *as:*

$$Significance_{had\ aquired,\ Acquisition} = \frac{log_2(43+1)}{log_2(15+43+1)} \sim 0.93$$

Analogue, we compute$Significance_{had\ aquired,\ CompanyInvestment} \sim 0.17$. *Then we compute* $Clarity_{had\ acquired}$ *as:*

$$Clarity_{had\ acquired} = log\frac{2*0.93}{0.17+0.93} * \frac{1}{log(2)} \sim 0.78$$

Finally, we compute $Discriminative_{had\ acquired,Acqusition}$ *as:*

$$Discriminative_{had\ aquired,\ Aquisition} = \frac{0.93^2 * 0.78^2}{\sqrt{0.93^2+0.78^2}} * \sqrt{2} \sim 0.61$$

In a similar way we compute $Discriminative_{had\ acquired,\ CompanyInvestment} \sim 0.03$. *We conclude that the phrase 'had acquired' is more discriminative for the relationship 'Acquisition' than for the relationship 'CompanyInvestment'.* ■

3.5 Step 4: Generate Search Engine-Specific Keyword Queries

We create the keyword query by concatenating the set of discriminative phrases for a particular relationship into a string. The string is complemented with the attribute value of the join predicate. Each search engine has a slightly different syntax to express conjunctions, disjunctions and phrases. Therefore, the generation of this string depends on the search engine e that was specified in query Q. The number of phrases considered by the search engine *e* is an unknown parameter to the user. We observed that most search engines tolerate at least five phrases. Future research is required to observe this parameter in a more automatic fashion.

***Example**: Figure 3f shows an example keyword query that is generated for the search engine boss.yahoo.com. It contains the two most discriminative keywords for the relationship Acquisition. Following the syntax of boss.yahoo.com the symbol '+' denotes a conjunction and the symbol "OR" a disjunction.* ■

Continuously update values for Significance$_{i,R}$, Clarity$_i$ and Discriminative$_{i,R}$. Our method is designed towards an online classification setting: It is completely unsupervised, requires no parameter tuning and requires little computation overhead. During query processing, we constantly update observations about common keyword phrases and values for *significance*, *clarity* and *discriminative*. Thereby, our set of keywords is no longer static (i.e. defined by a human or learned from a static corpus [9] at query definition time) and reflects additional phrases that are observed Web pages discovered during query execution. Note, that the DCM has been shown to provide similar high classification accuracy as a comparable classifier based on a Support Vector Machine (SVM) in many other classification scenarios.

4 Experimental Study

We designed a prototype for evaluating our keyword generation strategies based on the in-memory database HSQLDB [13]. In this Section we report on our results.

4.1 Evaluation Setup and Metrics

Queries and data set: Currently no benchmark for extracting and joining tuples across Web search results exists. In this study we tested our system on 5 queries which are shown in abbreviated form in Figure 4. As 'left table' we took a list of 200 randomly chosen companies from the Fortune list [16]. Our benchmark queries utilize 5 relationships with 10 different attribute types. The corresponding join predicate is underlined in each benchmark query. All queries utilize the extraction service OpenCalais.com [11] and the search service *Yahoo Boss* [10].

Competitor strategies: The most interesting comparative experiments are concerned with different keyword generation strategies for the same query. We tested the following strategies:

V (Attribute value): Keywords are generated from the text of the attribute value. With this strategy we consider a naïve user that takes as input for a search the name of a given attribute value (here a company). This strategy serves as our baseline.

V+RT (Attribute value + RT-Name): Authors in [12] proposed generating keywords from the attribute value and the name of the relationship. Names for relationship types are represented in OpenCalais.com by concatenating multiple words into a single string, for instance '*AnalystRecommendation*'. This string unlikely appears on a Web page. Therefore we manually tokenized names of relationship types into meaningful word sequences, such as '*analyst recommendation*'.

V+GK (Attribute value + generated and dynamically updated keywords): We generated keywords with our novel method from Section 4. In this strategy keywords are updated during query execution.

V+EK (Attribute value + keywords defined by experts): We utilized user generated Keywords. Only humans are familiar with the sheer endless expressiveness of common words and structures for expressing relationships of a particular domain. Therefore we consider as most competitive 'opponent' for our keyword generation strategy a human. Our human opponent is aware with technical limitations of state-of-the-art relationship extraction techniques. Contrary, the typical user of a search engine rarely combines such profound knowledge in practice. To simulate our human opponent, we studied the 'mechanics' of information extraction systems Textrunner [8] and DIAL [15] that are used by the service OpenCalais.org. In addition we observed words and structures for expressing relationships from common news sites (that are frequently returned from our queries). Based on this knowledge, we asked experienced engineers of our system to manually craft and tune the best possible keywords. Figure 7 presents those user-defined keywords.

```
ac: Acquisition(Acquirer, Acquired, Date, Status);
    'acquisition'
ar : AnalystRecommendation(Company_Rated, Company_Source, Financial_Trend);
    ' analyst recommendation'
ce : CompanyEmployeeNumber(Company, Employeesnumber);
    'company employees number'
cl : CompanyLocation(Company, City, LocationType)
    'company location'
cp : CompanyProduct(Company, Product, Producttype);
    ' company product'
```

Fig. 4. Relation extractors and join predicates for benchmark queries

Test environment: We implemented these strategies for the java-based in-memory database HSQLDB [13]. Experiments are conducted on a T61 laptop, with 4 GB of RAM, a core duo CPU with 2.2 GHz, Windows 7 professional and Java 1.6_017.b04. Each benchmark query was executed six times and the average value was computed across experiments.

Measurements: In each experiment we compared the different strategies. For instance, we are interested in the average costs to complete a single tuple for a query *(P/RT)*. Keeping this amount low significantly reduces monetary and processing costs[1]. In addition, we measure how many tuples from the left table are completed *(RT)* with a given amount of costs (in this experiment set to 2000 pages). A query may return irrelevant pages. For instance, a query may return pages from which tuples are extracted that could not be joined. Therefore we measured the proportion of the

[1] For instance, Yahoo Boss [10] charges currently $0.30 dollar per 1.000 requests for the top-10 search results and OpenCalais [11] charges $2000 per 3.000.000 pages that are extracted with their service.

overall size of extracted tuples *(Buf)* vs. extracted tuples that are part of the query result *(%RT/Buf)*. We also measured the proportion of relevant pages among the top-10 pages that contained a relevant tuple with *the mean average precision (MAP)* [17].

$$\mathrm{MAP}(Q) = \frac{1}{|Q|}\sum_{j=1}^{|Q|}\frac{1}{|m_j|}\sum_{r=1}^{N}\big(P(r) \times rel(r)\big)$$

MAP is a common metric to average the effectiveness of rankings from multiple keyword queries for each benchmark query Q. Among evaluation measures, MAP has been shown to have especially good discrimination and stability. In the formula above m_j denotes the number of relevant pages which are returned for a keyword query. Finally, we compared the speedup of each strategy in terms of pages per result tuple to our base line.

The list below shows our measurements and the abbreviations used in our diagrams:

Q-ID	: ID of Benchmark Query
#A	: Distinct attributes in result tuples for query
RT	: Returned complete result tuples for 2000 pages
Buf	: Complete and incomplete tuples in buffer
Usage (%)	: Proportion of complete tuples among all tuples in the buffer
P/RT	: Processed pages per single complete result tuple
Speedup	: (P/RT Baseline) / (P/RT Other strategy)
Terminated	: Either 2500 pages or 200 rows have been processed
MAP(10)	: Mean average precision (only among top-10 pages)

4.2 Experimental Results

Strategy 'V+GK' is a clear winner. We first compare quantitative measurements for different keyword generation strategies. Figure 5 presents our results: Strategy 'V+GK' consumes the fewest number of pages to obtain a single result tuple (P/RT). We observed a moderate speed up of strategy 'V+GK' in contrast to our baseline strategy 'V' by factor 2.5-5x. Strategy 'V+GK' is also efficient: It returned the largest result tuples size (RT) for our maximum of 2500 processed pages. For instance, for query *ac* we observed that 292 distinct relations for relationship type analyst recommendation are joined with companies from the left table. Moreover, we observe the most efficient buffer usage for strategy 'V+GK'. For instance, for query *cp* and *ce* more than half the tuples returned by this strategy contain values for all attributes. Except for query *cl,* we observed the highest mean average precision value, *MAP(10),* for strategy 'V+GK'. The comparable high value for *MAP(10)* indicates that our strategy likely returns Web pages among the top-10 search results.

Comparing generated keywords against expert keywords: Generated keywords capture tenses and reflections of verbs which are rather unusual for human-generated keyword queries. For instance, in Figure 5 shows generated keywords of the form 'to+infinitive' for relationship *Product* and keywords of the form 'noun+prepositions' for relationship *Employees.* We conclude that generated keywords are general applicable for various combinations extractors and search engines. Finally, and most importantly, generating keywords requires no involvement of the querying user requires no prior training and is therefore highly suitable for our online query setting.

Further observations: For the 'cl' query V+GK significantly outperforms V+EK despite a largely overlapping set of keywords. A closer investigation reveals that compound keywords of V+GK retrieve likely pages that contain multiple relations of the type 'company location'. Also, we observed the fraction of top-10 pages which likely contains these relations is significantly larger for V+GK. In outer future work we will systematically compound and other keyword types for retrieving multiple relations per page. Moreover, we will investigate a classifier that only forwards promising pages from top 10 pages to a relation extractor.

5 Related Work

We briefly present the state-of-the-art for generating keyword queries in 'text databases', which despite the difference between Web search results and text databases is closest to our work. In addition, we briefly review related work in the area of text analytics.

Automatic keyword query generation. A query processor requires discriminative keywords that likely return relevant pages from a Web search engine. Previous methods [6] obtained such keywords from a trained SVM-classifier. To train the classifier a large sample of training documents is collected prior executing a structured query from a 'text database' (with full access to all index pages). Next, tuples for each document in the sample are extracted. When a tuple is discovered in a document, words from the document are marked as positive examples for training a classifier. Finally, words are cross validated with documents from the training sample. The highest scoring words are used as keywords to obtain successive documents from the 'text database'. This approach has three major drawbacks for our setting: Training an SVM-based classifier is expensive, since costs are quadratic to the number of training examples. Next, training the classifier requires full access to documents which is an unrealistic assumption in our scenario. Finally, the set of training and test pages is not fixed in our scenario, but may vary from user query to user query. Contrary, in our approach initial keywords are used to randomly download pages. Keywords are constantly updated when new pages are returned by the search engine. Therefore, generated keywords also match the language of new Web sites that are discovered during query execution. Another idea is presented in [12] where candidate keywords are extracted from semantically meaningful attribute type names or predicate values from a structured query. We do not expect meaningful attribute type names in a structured query. Rather we trust that Web page authors have already evolved common words and grammatical structures for describing important relationships in human language.

Information extraction and text analytics. The CIMPLE project [5] describes an information extraction plan with an abstract, predicate-based rule language. More recently, open information extraction techniques generalize relationships with relationship-independent lexico-syntactic patterns [8]. We rely on the system Open Calais [11, 15] that uses both approaches.

Q-ID	RT	EK (Top 5)	GK (Top 5)
ac	"acquistion"	"acquire", "merger", "sale", "proposed", "said"	"acquires", "buys", "acquisition of", "sold", "takeover of"
ar	"analyst recommendation"	"downgrades", "upgrades," "rates", "recommends", "buy"	"upgraded", "buy from", "rating on", "rates", "upped"
ce	"company employee size"	"employees", "employees in", "employs", "employee size", "hires"	"employs", "employs over", "employs about", "employs around", "employing"
cl	"company location"	"located", "headquarter", "based", "founded", "resides"	"based in", "located in", "headquarters in", "corporation of", "incorporated"
cp	"company product"	"launched", "installed", "introduces", "puts to market", "provides"	"introduces", "launches", "launched", "introduced", "presents"

Strategy	Q-ID	#A	RT	Buf	Usage (%)	P/RT	Speedup	Terminated	MAP(10)
V	ac	4	89	396	22	28	1,00	max documents reached	0,07
V+RT	ac	4	211	802	26	12	2,38	max documents reached	0,21
V+GK	ac	4	**292**	1037	**28**	**9**	**3,28**	max documents reached	**0,29**
V+EK	ac	4	106	529	20	24	1,19	max documents reached	0,17
V	ar	4	0	200	0	--	--	max documents reached	0,00
V+RT	ar	4	17	**202**	8	139	--	max rows processed	0,01
V+GK	ar	4	**46**	218	**21**	**54**	--	max documents reached	**0,05**
V+EK	ar	4	32	209	15	78	--	max documents reached	0,01
V	ce	2	27	**208**	13	90	1,00	max rows processed	0,03
V+RT	ce	2	63	225	28	40	2,26	max documents reached	0,05
V+GK	ce	2	**141**	277	**51**	**18**	**5,07**	max documents reached	**0,17**
V+EK	ce	2	76	233	33	32	2,85	max rows processed	0,07
V	cl	3	37	**217**	17	68	1,00	max documents reached	0,05
V+RT	cl	3	71	252	28	35	1,92	max documents reached	0,06
V+GK	cl	3	**92**	251	**37**	**27**	**2,48**	max documents reached	0,10
V+EK	cl	3	85	253	34	29	2,30	max documents reached	**0,20**
V	cp	3	45	**217**	21	54	1,00	max rows processed	0,04
V+RT	cp	3	64	227	28	38	1,44	max rows processed	0,06
V+GK	cp	3	**146**	280	**52**	**17**	**3,14**	max documents reached	**0,11**
V+EK	cp	3	118	259	46	20	2,72	max rows processed	0,08

Fig. 5. Keyword phrases and experimental results

6 Summary

It is a fact that today only a few US-based search engines have the capacity to aggregate the wealth of information hidden in Web pages. Exploiting this information with structured queries is an often requested, but still unsolved requirement of many Web users. A major challenge is to define discriminative keywords to return a small set of relevant pages from which a relation extractor returns tuples for a structured query. Manually formulating and updating such keyword queries for every Web site is difficult and time consuming. In this paper we discussed and solved this challenge by generating keywords with a self supervised algorithm. We report from our preliminary study that our keyword generation strategy effectively returns result tuples while processing very few pages.

In our future work we incorporate cleansing [7,18] and tuple ranking techniques [1] into query processing to ensure informative and concise result tuples. We will extend our algorithms to complete missing information about existing objects in Freebase.com, DBPedia.com or other public databases for linked data. Moreover, we will significantly extend our preliminary study with additional experiments on relation extractors, for instance in the domains 'people', 'media' and 'nature'.

References

1. Kasneci, G., Ramanath, M., Suchanek, F.M., Weikum, G.: The YAGO-NAGA approach to knowledge discovery. SIGMOD Row 37(4), 41–47 (2008)
2. Jain, A., Doan, A., Gravano, L.: Optimizing SQL Queries over Text Databases. In: ICDE, pp. 636–645. IEEE Computer Society, Washington, DC (2008)
3. Jain, A., Srivastava, D.: Exploring a Few Good Tuples from Text Databases. In: ICDE, pp. 616–627. IEEE Computer Society, Washington, DC (2009)
4. Jain, A., Ipeirotis, P.G., Doan, A., Gravano, L.: Join Optimization of Information Extraction Output: Quality Matters! In: ICDE. IEEE Computer Society, Washington, DC (2009)
5. Shen, W., DeRose, P., McCann, R., Doan, A., Ramakrishnan, R.: Toward best-effort information extraction. In: SIGMOD 2008, pp. 1031–1042. ACM, New York (2008)
6. Agichtein, E., Gravano, L.: QXtract: a building block for efficient information extraction from Web page collections. In: SIGMOD 2003, p. 663. ACM, New York (2003)
7. Galhardas, H., Florescu, D., Shasha, D., Simon, E., Saita, C.: Declarative Data Cleaning: Language, Model, and Algorithms. In: Very Large Data Bases, pp. 371–380. Morgan Kaufmann Publishers, Rome (2001)
8. Etzioni, O., Banko, M., Soderland, S., Weld, D.S.: Open information extraction from the Web. Commun. ACM 51(12), 68–74 (2008)
9. Löser, A., Lutter, S., Düssel, P., Markl, V.: Ad-hoc Queries over Web page Collections – a Case Study. In: BIRTE Workshop at VLDB. Lyon (2009)
10. YahooBoss service, `http://developer.yahoo.com/search/boss/fees.html` (Last visited 01/06/10)
11. OpenCalais, `http://www.opencalais.com/comfaq` (Last visited 01/06/10)
12. Liu, J., Dong, X., Halevy, A.Y.: Answering Structured Queries on Unstructured Data. In: WebDB 2006 (2006)
13. HSQLDB, `http://hsqldb.org/` (Last visited 01/06/10)
14. Fung, G., Yu, J., Lu, H.: Discriminative Category Matching: Efficient Text Classification for Huge Document Collections. In: ICDM 2002, pp. 187–194 (2002)
15. Feldman, R., Regev, Y., Gorodetsky, M.: A modular information extraction system. Intell. Data Anal. 12(1), 51–71 (2008)

16. Fortune 500,
`http://money.cnn.com/magazines/fortune/fortune500/2008/full_list/` (Last visited 01/06/10)
17. Croft, W.B., Metzler, D., Strohman, T.: Search Engines, Information Retrieval in Practice, pp. 313–315. Addison Wesley, Reading (2010)
18. Dong, X., Halevy, A.Y., Madhavan, J.: Reference Reconciliation in Complex Information Spaces. In: SIGMOD Conference, pp. 85–96 (2005)
19. Löser, A., Hüske, F., Markl, V.: Situational Business Intelligence. In: BIRTE Workshop at VLDB (2008)
20. Battré, D., Ewen, S., Hueske, F., Kao, O., Markl, V., Warneke, D.: Nephele/PACTs: a programming model and execution framework for web-scale analytical processing. In: SoCC 2010, pp. 119–130 (2010)
21. Löser, A.: Beyond Search: Web-Scale Business Analytics. In: Vossen, G., Long, D.D.E., Yu, J.X. (eds.) WISE 2009. LNCS, vol. 5802, p. 5. Springer, Heidelberg (2009)

Handling of Uncertainty and Temporal Indeterminacy for What-if Analysis

Katrin Eisenreich[1], Gregor Hackenbroich[1], Volker Markl[2], Philipp Rösch[1], and Robert Schulze[1]

[1] SAP Research Center Dresden, Germany
firstname.lastname@sap.com
[2] TU Berlin, Germany
volker-markl@tu-berlin.de

Abstract. Enabling experts to not only analyze current and historic data but also to evaluate the impact of decisions on the future state of the business greatly increased the value of decision support. However, the highly relevant aspect of representing and processing uncertain and temporally indeterminate data is often ignored in this context. Although the management of uncertainty has been researched intensely in the last decade, its role in decision support has not attracted much attention. We hold that not considering such information restricts the analyses users can run and the insights they can get into their data. In this paper, we complement large-scale data analyses with support for what-if analyses over uncertain and temporally indeterminate data. We use a histogram-based model to represent arbitrary uncertainty and temporal indeterminacy and allow its processing in a flexible manner using operators for analyzing, deriving, and modifying uncertainty in decision support tasks. We describe a prototypical implementation and approaches for parallelization on a commercial column store and present an initial evaluation of our solution.

Keywords: Uncertainty, what-if analysis.

1 Introduction

In today's decision making processes, the analysis of large amounts of data is a central task. Users pose queries against historic data to derive insights into the past development of relevant figures and do forecasting to prospect *probable* future states of the business. Going beyond those approaches, the derivation of alternative scenarios for the evaluation of different *possible* future states is an important means to address evolving risks and chances. Scenarios answer the question what happens if an assumption about potential developments (internal or external to the business) or about effects of managerial decisions comes true. Their derivation involves a high degree of uncertainty both with respect to the planned figures and the temporal development of the plan. Although management of uncertainty has been researched intensely during the last decade, its role in decision support has not attracted much attention.

M. Castellanos, U. Dayal, and V. Markl (Eds.): BIRTE 2010, LNBIP 84, pp. 100–115, 2011.

In this paper, we address this application field and argue for the need to manage two kinds of uncertainty: (i) uncertainty of measure values and (ii) temporal indeterminacy of the occurrence and duration of events, that is, uncertain allocation of facts in the temporal dimension. We use a histogram-based approach to flexibly represent *arbitrary* distributions and describe operators for derivation and management of uncertainty. To enable analyses over temporally indeterminate events we introduce a special aggregation operator, extending previous research on temporal aggregation and temporal indeterminacy (e.g., [1,2,3]). Its application allows us to investigate scenarios where the allocation of events in time is not precisely known but has an impact on some target figure.

Although our approach is independent of a specific implementation we also consider performance as an important aspect for decision support. In this work, we use a column store for reasons of efficiency and flexibility; their performance benefits have made column stores the preferred choice for analysis-intensive applications. Also, support for planning and forecasting on column stores and the development of hybrid row-column systems for integration of OLAP and OLTP [4,5] have lately gained attention. We further investigate different schemes for parallelization of operators and evaluate their potential for a selected operator for histogram derivation.

Throughout this paper, we use running example tasks to illustrate the introduced concepts and their application. Section 2 introduces those tasks followed by a discussion of important features of uncertainty in decision support. Section 3 describes the logical data model and introduces a set of operators for analyzing, deriving, and modifying uncertainty. In Section 4, we describe the physical model and a prototypical implementation of our solution on a commercial column store. We exemplify parallelization approaches and discuss initial evaluation results in Section 5. Section 6 relates our work with previous research. Finally, we conclude the paper and provide an outlook on future work in Section 7.

2 Scenario and Features for Decision Support

In our scenario, we consider a user who wants to analyze and plan the processing (shipment, delivery, and deployment) of orders for a variety of products, as modeled by the TPC-H[1] benchmark. For illustration, we use the following two tasks:

- **T1: Delivery time forecasting** What will be the maximum number of days from receiving an order to delivery (see the task considered previously in [6])? After which time will 95% of all orders received today have been delivered?
- **T2: Uncertain resource demand analysis** Assume each delivered order induces a demand for deployment at the customer. What are the overall resources required for deployments during the following days?

In the following, we describe important features of uncertainty and indeterminacy; we relate them to the described tasks where appropriate.

[1] `http://tpc.org`

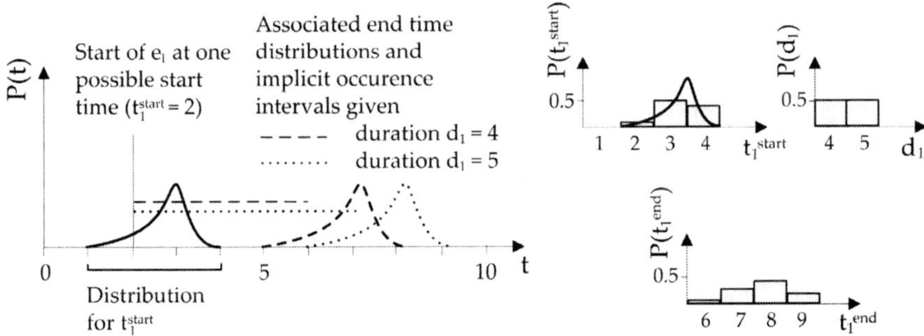

(a) Event e_1 with uncertain start time and associated uncertain end time distributions

(b) Start time, deployment duration and end time for event e_1

Fig. 1. Illustration of indeterminate temporal allocation

Uncertain Data and Temporal Indeterminacy. To appropriately handle uncertainty for decision support, we must consider the different characteristics of uncertain and indeterminate data involved in this context. Firstly, we require the representation of uncertainty on the level of attribute values defined either over a discrete or continuous domain. For example, predictions are often described as continuous distributions for a series of time steps, e.g., as a Gaussian distribution describing the prediction error for each time step. In other cases, users might want to model only a number of discrete cases with respective probabilities of occurrence to simulate alternative future scenarios. Another highly important aspect of real-world data is that they often are subject to correlation. Most existing approaches such as [7,8] assume independence in input data and do not allow the introduction of correlation information, thereby restricting the kind of analyses we can conduct. The interesting aspect of representing and processing arbitrary correlation structures complements this work and is described in [9].

Secondly, we address both the aspect of *(a) uncertainty of measure values* over arbitrary domains and the specific aspect of *(b) temporal indeterminacy*, that is, uncertainty in the temporal dimension of a fact. Case (a) occurs whenever we deal with planned or forecast values for some measure, such as next year's prospective sales numbers. Case (b) is especially relevant in processes of planning and forecasting as they involve events that can occur and extend over time indeterminately. An example is the occurrence of some deployment request we must fulfill after an uncertain delivery date (see T2). In this context, we define *events* as facts (represented by tuples from an *Event* relation) associated with some temporal extension.[2] Thus, an event e has a start time, a duration, and an implicit end time, all of which can be indeterminate, as depicted in Figure 1. Further, an event can have additional attributes describing its dimensions or measures X to be analyzed. As an example, consider a deployment in task T2 as an event e_1 involving some resource costs x_1 (certain or uncertain). Neither

[2] Note that we apply interval-based semantics as opposed to the time-point semantics mostly associated with the term "event" in the literature.

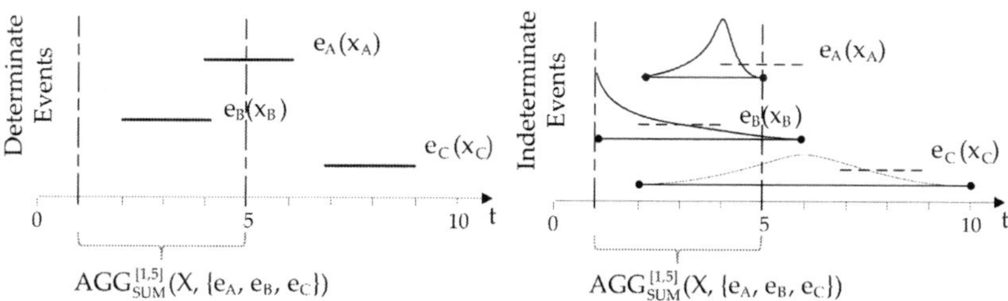

(a) Events with determinate temporal occurrence

(b) Events with indeterminate temporal occurrence

Fig. 2. Temporal aggregation over temporally determinate and indeterminate events

the start nor the duration of such an event are known exactly. In Figures 1(a) and 1(b) we indicate the start time t_1^{start} of e_1 by means of a skewed Gaussian distribution and an according histogram which approximates the distribution. Similarly, the histogram associated with d_1 in Figure 1(b) indicates two equally probable durations of 4 or 5 days for e_1 with a probability of 0.5 each.

For sound analyses over such data, we must consider the described facets of uncertainty. One key analysis functionality is the aggregation of some measure within a time interval of interest. In Figure 2, we illustrate the difference of aggregation over temporally determinate and indeterminate event data. As Figure 2(a) shows, events e_A, e_B, and e_C occur during some time interval and are associated with possibly uncertain measure values x_A, x_B, and x_C. We now want to compute a sum over values associated with those events occurring (partially) within a time interval $\underline{T}$, e.g., $\underline{T} = [1, 5]$. In the example, both e_A (partially, with one half of its duration) and e_B (fully) contribute to our result. To compute the aggregate we can apply a temporal aggregation approach such as reported in [2]. Analyses over temporally indeterminate events are more complicated. The reason is that we do not know whether an event actually lies within the interval or which fraction of its duration lies in the interval. Note that this situation occurs for T2, where we want to compute the demand for deployment resources within a time interval. This aspect is illustrated in Figure 2(b) where e_A, e_B, and e_C are associated with an indeterminate starting time, as indicated by the respective interval and distribution function. The dashed lines indicate one *possible* location of those facts in time (e.g., e_A might start at $t = 4$ as indicated). In the figure, we assume a duration of two time units for each event and do not show the indeterminacy of durations for reasons of simplicity. For the illustrated case, the complete occurrence of e_B and a fraction of e_A lies in $\underline{T}$, but there are many more possible instantiations contributing to the resulting aggregate.

We come back to this aspect in the next section, where we describe an aggregation operator that considers events associated with indeterminate temporal allocation. Before, we introduce the representation of uncertain and indeterminate data in our data model.

3 Uncertainty Modeling and Processing

This section introduces our data model and a set of operations over this data model, illustrating their application in the context of the example scenario.

3.1 Data Model

Histogram-Based Representation of Arbitrary Distributions. We address the representation of arbitrary distributions in a generic manner using histograms as a discrete approximation, similar to [10]. Consider an uncertain attribute value x of attribute X within a support interval $I = [l_X, h_X]$ according to some distribution P. The interval I restricts the set of distinct values that x may take. A distribution P can be provided either by a continuous function or by a set of discrete values from I, e.g., taken from historic data. A histogram $\overline{P}^{\beta}$ over x is an approximative representation of P, built by partitioning P into β mutually disjoint bins $B = \{b_1, ..., b_\beta\}$. Each b_i represents a sub-interval $I^{\beta_i} = [l_i, h_i]$ of I and is associated with the relative frequency (mass) of values falling into that particular bin. This mass is computed by either aggregating the count of values in I^{β_i} or integration over I^{β_i} for discrete or continuous distributions, respectively.

Histograms are a versatile choice for modeling uncertainty as they can be used to represent arbitrary distributions flexibly, applying different partitioning schemes (see, e.g., the classification in [11]) depending on the distribution to be modeled, a user's needs, and given resource constraints.

Indeterminate Instants and Durations. We represent indeterminacy in time by means of indeterminate *instants* t and *durations* d, similar to [1]. Both are defined over the domain of time; the smallest time unit representable is called a *chronon*. The representation of indeterminacy of a temporal instant t or duration d is similar to that of uncertain values over arbitrary domains. We specify the support interval I_t of possible chronon values for an instant and a corresponding distribution over those chronons P_t. Accordingly, I_d and P_d represent the support and distribution of durations. For example, Figure 1(b) depicts histograms for an uncertain start time (date) t_1^{start}, duration d_1, and the respective end time t_1^{end} of an event e_1. Each possible allocation of an event e_i to a specific start $t_{ip} = v_p, v_p \in I_t$ and duration $d_{iq} = v_q, v_q \in I_d$ yields a possible occurrence interval $I_{pq} = [v_p, v_p + v_q]$. Since we assume t_i and d_i independent, the probability of e_i occurring exactly during the interval I_{pq} computes as $p(t_{ip}, d_{iq}) = p(t_{ip}) \cdot p(d_{iq})$. The complete distribution of t_1^{end} then results as the convolution of t_1^{start} and d_1.

As stated before, we consider indeterminacy in time with the aim to enable analyses of facts associated with indeterminate start times and durations. The next section will introduce—amongst other functionality—an operator that provides basic functionality for such analyses.

3.2 Operators

We now introduce operators for derivation, analysis, and modification of uncertain values. The choice of operators is based on a breakdown of real-world tasks in decision support as well as an investigation of common libraries for statistic computation.

Representation of Uncertainty. We provide operators to derive and convert uncertain values as well as functions to access their basic statistical properties.

Statistical properties: We can access function values of the density ($pdf(x)$), distribution ($cdf(x)$), and inverse distribution ($invcdf(p)$) functions and the moments of distributions. Those functions are similar to the approach of *kernel functions* in [7] and are applied in the operators described below.

Derivation and conversion of uncertain values: $DRV(\{v_1, ..., v_n\}, tgt) = P_i$ computes an approximate distribution from input values $\{v_1, ..., v_n\}$ for an attribute depending on the target distribution specification tgt. An operator $CNV(P_1, tgt) = P_2$ serves us to convert distribution P_1 to P_2. We further provide an operator $TST(P_1, P_2)$ to compute the fit of a distribution P_2 to a (hypothesis) distribution P_1 based on the χ^2 test.

Analysis and Computation of Uncertain Values. We support standard analysis operators similar to those provided by relational algebra for selection and aggregation over uncertain values. Additionally, we address the aggregation of values associated with facts with an indeterminate temporal allocation.

Value selection and aggregation: To enable the selection of uncertain values that fit some condition, $FIL(X, cond, prob) = \{x_i | p(cond(x_i)) > prob\}$ applies predicate $cond = (op \in \{<, =, >\}, const)$ over values x_i of attribute X, complemented with a threshold value $prob$ indicating the smallest required probability P of $cond$ holding.

The generic aggregation operator $AGG(\{x_1, ..., x_n\}) = x_{Agg}$ computes aggregates over uncertain data values, such as their sum (AGG_{SUM}) or maximum (minimum) (AGG_{MAX}, AGG_{MIN}). Summation is performed by convolution over the associated distribution histograms $\overline{P}_i^{\beta}$. Alternative semantics and various algorithms for aggregation of probabilistic attribute values have been investigated, e.g., in [12] and will not be elaborated further here.

Example 1. In T1, to compute the total delivery durations d^{total} we sum up the uncertain durations of shipment d^{ship} and delivery d^{del}. Similarly, we can compute uncertain delivery dates t^{del} as sum of the (certain) order date t^{order} and d^{total}. Then, assuming $t^{start} = t^{del}$ as start of the deployment, we compute the uncertain deployment end times as $t^{end} = t^{start} + d^{depl}$. The resulting end time distribution for our exemplary event e_1 is shown in Figure 1(b).

Interval-based aggregation: $AGG^{\underline{T}}(X, E, \underline{T})$ enables aggregation of values $X = \{x_0, \ldots, x_n\}$ associated with temporally indeterminate events $E = \{e_1, \ldots, e_n\}$ within a time interval $\underline{T} = [l, h]$. As stated before, this operator is a central contribution to facilitate the consideration of temporal indeterminacy in the analysis process. The indeterminacy is reflected by an uncertain start time t_i and duration d_i associated with an event e_i.
In the following, we focus on $AGG^{\underline{T}}_{SUM}$. The fraction to which a value x_i of e_i contributes to the summation result depends both on t_i and d_i. To compute the relevant fraction ϕ_i of each x_i we must therefore compute and aggregate the *overlap* and the *occurrence probability* for all possible combinations of values $v_{ip} \in I_{t_i}$ and $v_{iq} \in I_{d_i}$, i.e., for all possible intervals $I_{ipq} = \left[t^s_{ip} = v_{ip}, t^e_{ipq} = v_{ip} + v_{iq}\right]$ in which e_i can occur. Since we consider t_i and d_i independent, the occurrence probability $P(t_i = v_p, d_i = v_q)$ is given by the product $P(t_i = v_p) \cdot P(d_i = v_q)$. The overlap means exactly that part of I_{ipq} that lies within $\underline{T}$ and therefore contributes to the aggregate result for $\underline{T}$. It is computed as

$$overlap_{ipq} = \begin{cases} (h-l)/d_{iq} & \text{if } t^s_{ip} \le l \wedge t^e_{ipq} \ge h \\ (t^e_{ipq} - l)/d_{iq} & \text{if } t^s_{ip} \le l \wedge t^e_{ipq} > l \\ 1 & \text{if } t^s_{ip} > l \wedge t^e_{ipq} < h \\ (h - t^s_{ip})/d_{iq} & \text{if } t^s_{ip} < h \wedge t^e_{ipq} > h \\ 0 & \text{else} \end{cases}$$

We then compute contributions ϕ_i of e_i with

$$\phi_i = \sum_{p,q} overlap_{ipq} \cdot P(t_i = v_p, d_i = v_q)$$

and compute the final result as $AGG^{\underline{T}}_{SUM}(X, E, \underline{T}) = \sum_i x_i \cdot \phi_i$.
For computing AGG_{MAX} and AGG_{MIN}, the set of contributing events $E^{incl} \in E$ are those events that have *any* I_{ipq} that overlaps $\underline{T}$. The resulting aggregate can then be computed similar to the "standard" minimum or maximum computation over the associated x_i.

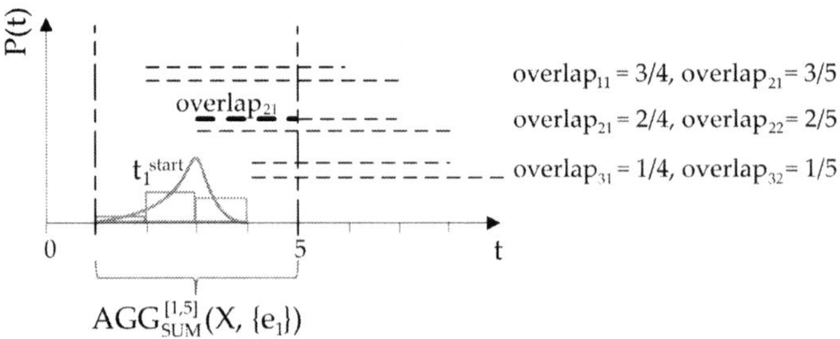

Fig. 3. Aggregation over indeterminate events illustrated over the single event e_1

Example 2. In T2, a user wants to compute the aggregated costs X for deployments within the next days, corresponding to $\underline{T} = [1, 5]$. We consider deployment events with indeterminate start times t_i^{start} and deployment durations d_i. The start times t_i^{start} correspond to the uncertain delivery dates derived from the results of Example 1 since a deployment starts after delivery. Figure 1(b) depicts exemplary distributions for t_1^{start} and d_1 of deployment event e_1. Figure 3 exemplifies $AGG_{SUM}^{[1,5]}(X, E)$ for the single event $e_1 \in E$. The occurrence probabilities p_{pq} are computed by multiplying the individual probabilities of start instants and durations, e.g., $p_{21} = P(t_1^{start} = 3) \cdot P(d_1 = 4) = 1/2 \cdot 1/2 = 1/4$. Similarly, the associated overlaps are computed as described above, e.g., $overlap_{21} = (h - t_{12})/d_{11} = (5 - 3)/4 = 2/4$. The aggregate is then built as the sum of all products $p_{pq} \cdot overlap_{pq}$ multiplied with the cost x_1 associated with e_1.

Modification of Uncertain Values. Since we consider the incorporation of assumptions as a central task in the decision support process, we also provide functionality for modification of values to create scenarios.

Modify: $MOD(P_{old}, P_{new}) = P_{\Delta}$ allows modification of an uncertain value represented by P_{old} to a value P_{new}. Note that we do not perform in-place updates but store updates together with a reference to the updated value. The distribution P_{Δ} is computed as a delta (histogram) of P_{new} to P_{old}.

Example 3. Assume the aggregated deployment demand computed in T2 (see Example 2) exceeds available resources. The user wants to evaluate the option of express delivery, resulting in lower (express) delivery durations d^{exp}, for a group of orders. Therefore, he modifies deployment start times to $t^{startexp} = t^{order} + d^{exp}$ for those orders. The resulting (probable) influence of using express delivery on the overall deployment demand in $T = [1, 5]$ can then be evaluated by computing $AGG_{SUM}^{[1,5]}(deploycost, E)$ anew.

4 Prototypical Implementation

We implemented an initial prototype to evaluate the described functionality on the SAP column store database TREX. As stated before, we use a column-based system due to its benefits with respect to data storage and processing in OLAP scenarios and apply parallelization in order to improve runtimes of expensive operators.

4.1 Physical Representation and Processing

Column-Based Access. Column-based systems outperform row-oriented databases when it comes to large-scale analysis tasks. This is due to both the column-oriented focus of analysis queries and the high compression rates achievable for columnar data, which allow to keep data in-memory and further speed up processing over the data (see, e.g., [5]).

The superior analytical performance suits decision support processes as they involve a large fraction of analyses and aggregations as basis for further steps. Similar to the analysis of data, the derivation and processing of uncertain values is also conducted accessing the values of individual columns rather than accessing data by rows (tuples). For example, the DRV operator essentially corresponds to a custom function over the relevant column containing the values whose distribution we want to derive.

Parallelization. Similar to tables in row-based systems, we can partition columns such as to enable parallel access and execution. This brings benefits particularly in contexts where a high percentage of overall query costs is determined by operations over individual columns which can be parallelized (i.e., executed independently) and return relatively small results which are merged in a final step. This applies to distributive aggregation functions (SUM, MIN, MAX, $COUNT$) but also to algebraic measures such as the average or variance of a measure, as well as to operators whose computation relies on such functions (e.g., the DRV operator).

4.2 Operator Implementation and Composition

We extended the TREX engine for the computation of complex analytical queries over so-called Calculation Views (CV). Those views enable OLAP analysis functionality as well as application of custom operations provided as Python or C++ implementations. Each CV can be queried like a base table or serve as input to further CVs. The topmost CV along with its ancestors forms a directed acyclic graph and is stored as a Calculation Scenario. We implemented our operators by creating and stacking several views as described above. Similarly, sequential or parallel operator applications for deriving a specific scenario are created by stacking the views that result from individual operator applications. We use custom operators implemented in C++ where native functionality (e.g., aggregation, filtering, application of formulas) does not suffice. Since the use of custom operators largely prevents automatic optimization, we apply different schemes for parallelizing their execution "manually" to speed up processing. While intra-view parallelization is implemented by threaded execution of custom operators within a single view, inter-view parallelization relies on several views being computed in parallel over partitions of the data. Initial results of those approaches are described in Section 5.1.

Figure 4 illustrates the application of our operators to implement T1. The operators are composed in a graph and consume and produce data as indicated in the figure. The shown example calculates the maximum number of days until all parts ordered today are delivered. As an alternative, users might wish to compute the days in which, e.g., 95 % of all orders will be delivered. To do so, we can preceed the MAX operator with a MOD operator to modify the values of d^{total} such as to eliminate (possibly irrelevant) tails of the distributions at $d = invcdf(0.95)$.

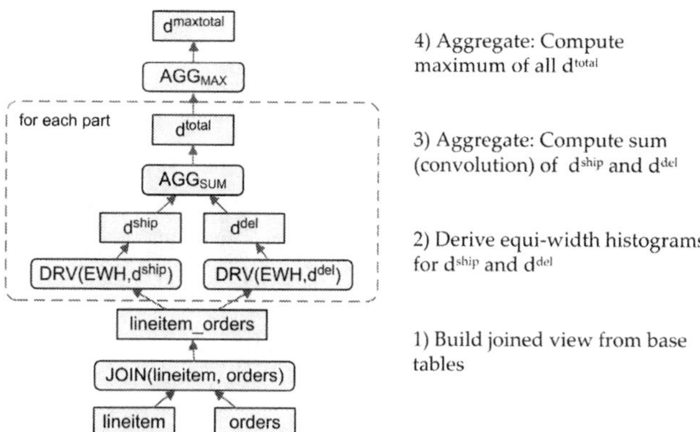

Fig. 4. Graph of applied operators and resulting (intermediate) views depicting the implementation of T1

5 Evaluation

We ran the following evaluations on a server with 2 AMD Opteron Dual Core processors with 2,6 GHz, 32 GB main memory, running SUSE Linux EE 64bit. The goal was to investigate required runtimes for selected operators and for executing the implementation of T1 as shown above. The underlying TPC-H data was generated with different scaling factors depending on the evaluation. We investigated processing times for the following cases:

T1 query performance: We evaluated the implementation of T1, applying a sequence of operators as depicted in Figure 4. We measured execution times for different sizes of the underlying data set.

T2 query performance: We evaluated one possible case of T2, using artificially generated start times and durations for deployments. We show analysis results for two basic scenarios and provide exemplary run times.

Individual operator performance: We evaluated the performance for derivation (*DRV*) of histograms from underlying data using different parallel execution schemes, as well as the modification (*MOD*) of histograms resulting from T1.

5.1 Histogram Construction

We evaluated the runtime performance of the *DRV* operator, deriving a 10-bin histogram per part from the `discount` attribute of the `lineitem` table. We applied different parallelization schemes to *DRV* in order to investigate how we can leverage available hardware resources. For those tests, we fixed the scaling factor to 20, resulting in a total of 120 million rows for the `lineitem` table. The results for *intra-view* and *inter-view parallelism* are displayed in Figures 5(a) and 5(b), respectively. Considering the thread-based intra-view parallelization

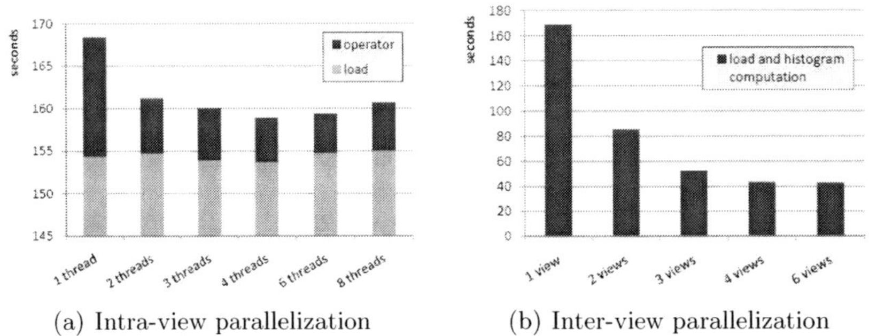

(a) Intra-view parallelization

(b) Inter-view parallelization

Fig. 5. Varying degree of parallelism for execution of *DRV* over 120 million rows

we see how the histogram computation times decrease (though not linearly) until reaching the minimum at 6 threads. With decreasing computation times the time required for loading the `discount` column becomes the dominating factor. Using parallel views circumvents this pitfall as it enables parallel loading of data from split partitions. Figure 5(b) shows how the computation times decrease almost linearly up to 4 parallel views (using more than 4 views does not improve results since we use 4 cores). Although we have only tested scaling out to multiple cores, we assume that the system can be extended to multiple nodes with similar results. We further applied the best setting from above (i.e., computation on 4 parallel views) to evaluate how the performance scales for different sizes of datasets. Table 1 shows a close to linear increase of processing times for scaling factors 0.1, 1, 10, and 20. For the small datasets, the relative performance is slightly worse, which most probably is due to the relatively higher costs of setting up parallel views and merging their results.

5.2 T1: Delivery Time Forecasting

The runtime results for T1, with different scaling factors (resulting in a total of 0.1, 1, 10, and 20 GB of data) for the underlying TPC-H dataset, are also shown in Table 1. The scaling factor $s = 20$ is included for a rough comparison with the results reported for the equivalent query Q2 in [13]—although we are aware of the great difference of our approach to the pure sampling approach. The resulting data set contains a total of 120 million and 30 million rows for the `lineitem` and `orders` tables, respectively. Running the query with intra-view parallelization with 4 threads yields total execution times of $1.1s$, $9.9s$, and $92.4s$ for $s = 0.1$, 1, and 10, respectively. We observe execution times of 190 seconds (or about 3 minutes) for the largest dataset ($s = 20$) compared to the 36 minutes reported for a variable number of Monte Carlo iterations in [13]. While a runtime of three minutes is certainly not acceptable for an interactive scenario, it is often not necessary to perform computations over the complete fact data every time anew. Rather, we can store and reuse computed results, updating them once a

Table 1. Runtimes for *DRV*

Scale	*DRV* (4 views)	T1 (4 threads)
0.1	$0.27s$	$1.1s$
1	$1.85s$	$9.9s$
10	$19.7s$	$92.4s$
20	$43.3s$	$192.1s$

Table 2. Run times for *MOD*

Scale	Modification fraction			
	0.1	0.3	0.5	1
0.1	$0.40s$	$0.54s$	$0.58s$	$1.02s$
1	$4.33s$	$6.69s$	$8.29s$	$15.03s$

certain amount of fresh data has been recorded and needs to be incorporated to the "old" state of our data. Naturally, the applicability of this approach depends on whether the applied query allows for such a composition.

5.3 Histogram Modification

Since we stated the modification of uncertainty as an important aspect to enable scenario creation, we evaluated the corresponding operator MOD for different fractions of modification to the original histogram. We applied the operator to the histograms resulting from the histogram derivation described in Section 5.1, computed from datasets with $s = 0.1$ and 1. Consequently, the operator modifies 20,000 and 200,000 histograms (one for each part in the `parts` table) with 10 bins each, respectively. We vary the fraction of modified data between 10% and 100%, depending on some criteria such as their frequency falling below a threshold. Applying a fraction of 100% means that all the histograms are modified, i.e., 2 million bin values are modified in the "worst case" (for $s = 1$). The results for the application of MOD for different combinations of scaling factors and modification fractions are shown in Table 2. As stated before, we store the result of MOD as the delta of the new to the old values rather than storing the complete histogram. Therefore, we observe a clear decrease of runtimes as the fraction of modification becomes smaller, since we must write delta values only for a smaller part of the histograms. This is beneficial, for example, when we only want to "eliminate" the probability of values at the tails of represented distributions. However, the numbers also indicate high initial time requirements for loading the data. Those dominate the runtimes recorded for small modification fractions, thus preventing a linear decrease.

5.4 T2: Uncertain Resource Demand Analysis

To evaluate T2, we consider a basic example with three deployments e_A, e_B, e_C, each inducing a cost of 100. Their start times are distributed as illustrated in Figure 6(a), with relatively similar t_A^{start} and t_B^{start} and a high t_C^{start} (e.g., due to some customization prior to shipping). For simplicity, assume that durations d_A, d_B, and d_C are uniformly distributed in $[0, 5]$, resulting in end times t_A^{end}, t_B^{end}, and t_C^{end}. Considering those temporal assumptions as basis for a first scenario, an aggregation of costs within the intervals $[0, 5]$, $[5, 10]$, and $[10, 15]$ results in low costs of 90 during $\underline{T}_1 = [0, 5]$ and high costs of 190 during $\underline{T}_2 = [5, 10]$, as indicated in Figure 6(b). Since this violates some constraint, the user evaluates

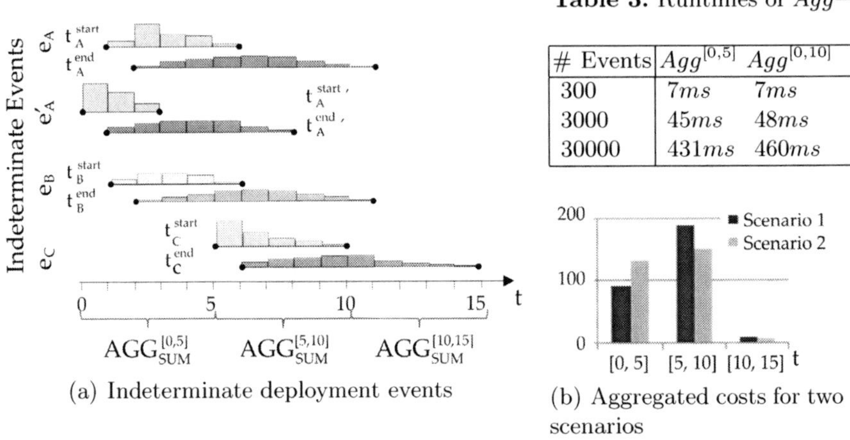

Table 3. Runtimes of $Agg^{\underline{T}}$

# Events	$Agg^{[0,5]}$	$Agg^{[0,10]}$
300	$7ms$	$7ms$
3000	$45ms$	$48ms$
30000	$431ms$	$460ms$

(a) Indeterminate deployment events

(b) Aggregated costs for two scenarios

Fig. 6. Aggregation of deployment costs over indeterminate deployments

a second scenario, assuming express delivery for all orders associated with deployment e_A. This results in earlier start and end times $t_A^{start\prime}$ and $t_A^{end\prime}$ and a more balanced cost distribution over $[0, 5]$ and $[5, 10]$. Table 3 shows exemplary runtimes for aggregating over 300, 3000, and 30000 generated instances of e_A, e_B, and e_C in an interval of 5 or 10 chronons, respectively. We see that the runtimes increase linearly with the number of aggregated events, whereas, in the evaluated case, the influence of the aggregation interval length is negligible.

6 Related Work

Uncertainty management has been an important field of database research during the last decade. Most approaches, such as the prominent TRIO [14] and MayBMS [8] systems, address the modeling and querying of discrete uncertainties relying on model-extension approaches—tuple and attribute alternatives are associated with a probability of occurrence in a possible world. In recent developments one can observe growing support for continuous distributions, e.g., in Orion 2.0 [10] and in proposals described in [7]. We take a similar approach to [10], modeling continuous uncertainty in a generic way using histograms as an approximation. An alternative approach to model extension is the sample-first approach employed, most prominently, by MCDB [13]. This approach is very flexible, allowing the computation of complex stochastical models using pseudo-random variable generation (VG) functions. However, opposed to the histogram-based approach applied in this paper, the VG functions completely encapsulate the models and intermediate (uncertain) results can not be retained for later use. The authors of [13] investigate approaches to deal with the high CPU-costs implied by the sample-first approach by means of parallel processing. Similarly, we address the optimization of expensive operators via parallelization.

Representing and querying indeterminate temporal data and analysis over interval-based data have been addressed comprehensively, e.g., in [2,1]. The work reported in [15] describes a generic approach to represent and query probabilistic fact characterizations with special focus on spatial data, but does not consider events associated with uncertain temporal extent (duration). Handling indeterminacy of both the start and duration of events and the application of operators allowing insight into changing assumptions about such events have not been focused so far. Our definition of the interval-based aggregation operator and its application in combination with modifications to indeterminate event data constitute an interesting contribution to both fields.

The introduction and modification to uncertainty for what-if scenario creation have not received attention in most previous research. The MayBMS [8] system includes a "repair-key" operator to provide for introduction of uncertainty to initially certain data, but considers only discrete probabilities on tuple level while we allow modifications over (histogram-based representations of) continuous distributions. The approach presented in [6] is situated in the decision support context and investigates some interesting tasks including forecasting and what-if analysis. As stated above, the proposed approach arguably offers the greatest flexibility for uncertainty modeling. A drawback is that any assumptions are introduced through encapsulated variable generation functions and the whole model must be recomputed if a new assumption is to be considered.

Lineage for tracking and managing different versions of data is stated as a highly relevant factor in the context of scientific data management in [16]. Many existing approaches such as [7,10] capture lineage information for tracing data derivation through query processing and late computation of result probabilities. We currently use a basic form of lineage information, capturing operator applications and storing modified values with a reference to their original value, which we can use to track and compare related scenarios.

Column-oriented database systems have gained major attention during the last decade due to their superiority for analyses over huge data volumes (see, e.g., [17]). Recently, the extension of column stores to the field of planning and forecasting and the development of hybrid row-column stores for integration of OLAP and OLTP have received attention [4,5]. Representing, querying, and modifying probabilistic data on column stores has not been addressed in previous research.

7 Summary

In this paper, we addressed the handling of different aspects of uncertainty for decision support. Concretely, we considered *uncertainty of measure values* as well as *temporal indeterminacy*. To efficiently represent uncertainty we proposed a histogram-based data model for representation of *arbitrary* distributions. Based on that data model, we presented a set of operators for handling uncertainty; most importantly, we proposed operators for deriving and modifying uncertainty as well as for the interval-based aggregation over indeterminate data.

To demonstrate the feasibility of our approach we presented a prototypical implementation. For an efficient execution, this prototype is based on a column store database. We considered further speedup by using inter- and intra-view parallelization. The evaluation of runtimes for histogram construction, forecasting and uncertainty modification are promising and demonstrate that our approach is not only flexible but also efficient. So far, we have not comprehensively evaluated the performance of the $AGG^{\overline{T}}$ operator. Initial applications yielded largely varying run times depending on both the aggregation interval and the nature of the start times and durations associated with the aggregated events. We aim at a comprehensive evaluation considering a range of variations of those aspects to get full insight into the operator performance.

Future work includes further optimization of the described implementation both with respect to runtimes and the flexibility of scenario composition. As stated in the beginning, decision support processes evolve iteratively. Therefore, an implementation must enable a truly iterative and interactive composition of operators for ad-hoc creation of scenarios. We currently also address an extension of our approach to enable flexible handling of correlation in data. Previous research does neither consider the *introduction* of correlation amongst marginal distributions, nor the modeling of different dependency structures over continuously distributed values on the database level. Investigating those aspects and integrating an appropriate approach with our existing solution are promising topics for our future research.

Acknowledgments. We would like to thank Wolfgang Lehner for his academic supervision of a thesis in the context of this work. We also thank Bernhard Jäcksch and the TREX team for their continuous support.

References

1. Dyreson, C.E., Snodgrass, R.T.: Supporting Valid-Time Indeterminacy. ACM Trans. Database Syst. 23(1), 1–57 (1998)
2. Böhlen, M.H., Gamper, J., Jensen, C.S.: Multi-dimensional aggregation for temporal data. In: Ioannidis, Y., Scholl, M.H., Schmidt, J.W., Matthes, F., Hatzopoulos, M., Böhm, K., Kemper, A., Grust, T., Böhm, C. (eds.) EDBT 2006. LNCS, vol. 3896, pp. 257–275. Springer, Heidelberg (2006)
3. Timko, I., Dyreson, C.E., Pedersen, T.B.: Pre-Aggregation with Probability Distributions. In: DOLAP 2006: Proceedings of the 9th ACM International Workshop on Data Warehousing and OLAP, pp. 35–42. ACM, New York (2006)
4. Jaecksch, B., Lehner, W., Faerber, F.: A Plan for OLAP. In: EDBT, pp. 681–686 (2010)
5. Plattner, H.: A Common Database Approach for OLTP and OLAP Using an in-memory Column Database. In: Proceedings of the 35th SIGMOD International Conference on Management of Data, pp. 1–2. ACM, New York (2009)
6. Jampani, R., Xu, F., Wu, M., Perez, L.L., Jermaine, C., Haas, P.J.: MCDB: A Monte Carlo Approach to Managing Uncertain Data. In: SIGMOD 2008: Proceedings of the 2008 ACM SIGMOD International Conference on Management of Data, pp. 687–700. ACM, New York (2008)

7. Agrawal, P., Widom, J.: Continuous Uncertainty in Trio. In: MUD, Stanford InfoLab (2009)
8. Huang, J., Antova, L., Koch, C., Olteanu, D.: MayBMS: A Probabilistic Database Management System. In: Proceedings of the 35th SIGMOD International Conference on Management of Data, pp. 1071–1074. ACM, New York (2009)
9. Eisenreich, K., Rösch, P.: Handling Uncertainty and Correlation in Decision Support. In: Proceedings of 4th Workshop on Management of Uncertain Data at VLDB 2010 (September 2010)
10. Singh, S., Mayfield, C., Mittal, S., Prabhakar, S., Hambrusch, S., Shah, R.: Orion 2.0: Native Support for Uncertain Data. In: SIGMOD 2008: Proceedings of the 2008 ACM SIGMOD, pp. 1239–1242. ACM, New York (2008)
11. Poosala, V., Haas, P.J., Ioannidis, Y.E., Shekita, E.J.: Improved Histograms for Selectivity Estimation of Range Predicates. SIGMOD Rec. 25(2), 294–305 (1996)
12. Ross, R., Subrahmanian, V.S., Grant, J.: Aggregate Operators in Probabilistic Databases. J. ACM 52(1), 54–101 (2005)
13. Xu, F., Beyer, K., Ercegovac, V., Haas, P.J., Shekita, E.J.: E = MC3: Managing Uncertain Enterprise Data in a Cluster-Computing Environment. In: SIGMOD 2009: Proceedings of the 35th SIGMOD International Conference on Management of Data, pp. 441–454. ACM, New York (2009)
14. Agrawal, P., Benjelloun, O., Sarma, A.D., Hayworth, C., Nabar, S., Sugihara, T., Widom, J.: Trio: A System for Data, Uncertainty, and Lineage. In: VLDB 2006: Proceedings of the 32nd International Conference on Very Large Data Bases, VLDB Endowment, pp. 1151–1154 (2006)
15. Timko, I., Dyreson, C.E., Pedersen, T.B.: Probabilistic Data Modeling and Querying for Location-based Data Warehouses. In: SSDBM 2005: Proceedings of the 17th International Conference on Scientific and Statistical Database Management, pp. 273–282. Lawrence Berkeley Laboratory, Berkeley (2005)
16. Stonebraker, M., Becla, J., DeWitt, D.J., Lim, K.T., Maier, D., Ratzesberger, O., Zdonik, S.B.: Requirements for Science Data Bases and SciDB. In: CIDR 2009 (2009), www.crdrdb.org
17. Boncz, P.A., Manegold, S., Kersten, M.L.: Database Architecture Evolution: Mammals Flourished Long Before Dinosaurs Became Extinct. PVLDB 2(2), 1648–1653 (2009)

NEEL: The Nested Complex Event Language for Real-Time Event Analytics

Mo Liu[1], Elke A. Rundensteiner,[1] Dan Dougherty[1], Chetan Gupta[2], Song Wang[2], Ismail Ari[3], and Abhay Mehta[2]

[1] Worcester Polytechnic Institute, USA
{liumo,rundenst,dd}@wpi.edu
[2] HP Labs, USA
{chetan.gupta,songw,abhay.mehta}@hp.com
[3] Ozyegin University, Turkey
Ismail.Ari@ozyegin.edu.tr

Abstract. Complex event processing (CEP) over event streams has become increasingly important for real-time applications ranging from health care, supply chain management to business intelligence. These monitoring applications submit complex event queries to track sequences of events that match a given pattern. As these systems mature the need for increasingly complex nested sequence query support arises, while the state-of-art CEP systems mostly support the execution of only flat sequence queries. In this paper, we introduce our nested CEP query language *NEEL* for expressing nested queries composed of sequence, negation, AND and OR operators. Thereafter, we also define its formal semantics. Subtle issues with negation and predicates within the nested sequence context are discussed. An E-Analytics system for processing nested CEP queries expressed in the *NEEL* language has been developed. Lastly, we demonstrate the utility of this technology by describing a case study of applying this technology to a real-world application in health care.

Keywords: Nested Query, CEP, Syntax, Semantics.

1 Introduction

Complex event processing (CEP) has become increasingly important in modern applications, ranging from online financial feeds, supply chain management for RFID tracking to real-time business intelligence [1,2]. There is a strong demand for CEP technology that can be applied to process enormous volumes of sequential data streams for online operational decision making as demonstrated by several sample application scenarios below. CEP must be able to support sophisticated pattern matching on real time event streams including the arbitrary nesting of sequence operators and the flexible use of negation in such nested sequences. The need for such sophisticated CEP technology is motivated via several example applications next.

M. Castellanos, U. Dayal, and V. Markl (Eds.): BIRTE 2010, LNBIP 84, pp. 116–132, 2011.

Motivating Example 1. In the web business application context, the query Q_1 = *SEQ(Create-profile c, Update-profile u, NOT (Answer-Email ae OR Answer-Phone ap, ae.uid = c.uid = u.uid, ap.uid = c.uid = u.uid))* detects customers not answering an email or a phone call after creating and then updating online profiles within a specified time. This query could be used for checking customer inactivity with the goal to understand customer behavior, to subsequently delete unused customer profiles as well as to adopt marketing strategies to retain customer interest. Efficient execution of such complex nested CEP queries is critical for assuring real-time responsiveness and for staying competitive in an increasingly fast paced business world.

Motivating Example 2. Another example of applications in need of complex nested event queries are organizations that need to track the status of their inventory. Consider tracking inventory within a hospital setting. For instance, reporting contaminated medical equipments within the daily workflow [3,4,5]. Let us assume that the tools for medical operations are RFID-tagged. The system monitors the histories of the equipment (such as, records of surgical usage, of washing, sharpening and disinfection). When a healthcare worker puts a box of surgical tools into a surgical table equipped with RFID readers, the computer would display approximate warnings such as "This tool must be disposed". A query Q_2 = *SEQ (Recycle r, Washing w, NOT SEQ(Sharpening s, Disinfection d, Checking c, s.id = d.id = c.id), Operating o, r.id = w.id = o.id, o.ins-type = "surgery")* expresses this critical condition that after being recycled and washed, a surgery tool is being put back into use without first being sharpened, disinfected and then checked for quality assurance. Such complex sequence queries contain complex negation specifying the non-occurrence of composite event instances, such as negating the composite event of sharpened, disinfected and checked subsequences.

Motivating Example 3. In a supply chain management scenario, suppliers may need to monitor the transport of RFID tagged medical goods. It is important to neither break the cold chain of pharmaceuticals nor to overrun the expiration of any of these goods. During transportation and temporary storage, pharmaceuticals can be exposed to environmental conditions that may damage the goods. The temperature in the cooling trucks of the carrier may exceed the allowable limits, leading to spoilage. It is thus critical to monitor all ongoing transports in real time for tracking patterns of "safe" and "unsafe" transport. The pattern query Q_3 = *SEQ(Distribution-Center dc, OR(Hospital h, NursingHome n, h.id = d.id, n.id = d.id), DrugStore d, dc.id = d.id, d.temperature* $<$ *5° Celsius)* is submitted together with the required conditions to track the paths of each truck to its destination. Such pattern query is executed continually during daily operations to reliably identify possible violators or locations of violation. With suitable technology, decision makers reduce the risk of loss of products, danger to health of our communities, and even potential lawsuits. In this scenario, CEP technology is poised to help cut production costs and to increase the quality of goods for human consumption and health.

Beyond these three motivating examples, numerous other real-time monitoring scenarios are emerging for supply chain management (SCM), financial systems, sensor networks, and e-commerce. What is common across these scenarios is a need to query large volumes of sequence data in real-time. However, each scenario has its own characteristic in terms of streaming data volumes, query latency goals and event query complexities. We believe enabling complex nested CEP queries would allow us to efficiently correlate trends and detect anomalies on sequence data for real-time business intelligence.

While nested queries are commonly supplied by SQL engines over static databases, the state-of-art CEP literature [1,2,6] does not support such nested queries. While the Cayuga system [2] mentions composable queries, they assume the negation filter is only applied to a single primitive event type within the SEQ pattern. Our objective instead is to allow the specification of negation within any level of the nested query as demonstrated in the scenarios above. While CEDR [6] allows the application of negation over composite event types, authors didn't provide formal semantics for the specification of such nested pattern queries. In addition, existing CEP systems [1,2] don't provide query semantics concerning the handling of predicates in nested CEP queries. Design of a clean syntax and semantics for nested CEP queries is a delicate task. In this work, we address this gap by carefully designing the syntax, semantics and algebraic plan for complex nested sequence queries. Preliminary experiments with processing nested query plans expressed in the *NEEL* language are reported in [16]. Last but not least, we describe a case study of applying this technology to health care applications.

Organization of Paper: The rest of the paper is organized as follows: Section 2 introduces the event model. Section 3 presents our proposal of a nested query language *NEEL*. Sections 4 defines the nested query semantics of *NEEL*. Section 5 discusses our E-Analytics system. Sections 6 describes the case study. Section 7 discusses related work, while Section 8 concludes the paper.

2 The NEEL Event Model

An event instance is an occurrence of interest in a system which can be either primitive or composite as further introduced below. *A primitive event instance* denoted by a lower-case letter (e.g.,'*e*') is the smallest, atomic occurrence of interest in a system. e_i.ts and e_i.te denote the start and the end timestamp of an event instance e, respectively, with $e_i.\text{ts} \leq e_i.\text{te}$. For a primitive event instance e_i, $e_i.\text{ts} = e_i.\text{te}$. For simplicity, we use the subscript i attached to a primitive instance e to denote the timestamp i. *A composite event instance* is composed of constituent primitive event instances $e = < e_1, e_2, ..., e_n >$. A composite event instance e occurs over an interval. The start and end timestamps of e are equal to $\text{e.ts} = \min\{e_i.\text{ts} \mid \forall\ e_i \in \text{e}\ \}$ and $\text{e.te} = \max\{e_i.\text{te} \mid \forall\ e_i \in \text{e}\ \}$, respectively.

An *event type* is denoted by a capital letter, say E_i. An event type E_i describes a set of attributes that the event instances of this type share. An event type can be either a primitive or a composite event type [7]. *Primitive event types* are

Table 1. NEEL Query Language

<table>
<tr><td><<b>Query</b>>::= PATTERN <event-expression>
WITHIN <window>
[RETURN <set of primitive events>]</td></tr>
<tr><td>E_v = <event-expression> <var>
<event-expression> ::=
SEQ((E_v | ! (E_v, [<q>]))*, E_v, (E_v | ! (E_v, [<q>]))*, [<q>])
| AND((E_v, (E_v | ! (E_v, [<q>]))*, [<q>])
| OR((E_v)+, [<q>])
| (<primitive-event>, [<q>])</td></tr>
<tr><td><primitive-event> ::= E_1 | E_2 | ...
<var> ::= event variable e_i
<q>::= (<elemqual>)*
<elemqual> ::= <var>.attr <op> <var>.attr |
<var>.attr <op> constant
<op> ::= $<$ | $>$ | $\leq$ | $\geq$ | = | ! =
<window>::= time duration w</td></tr>
</table>

pre-defined in the application domain of interest. *Composite event types* are aggregated event types created by combining other primitive and/or composite event types to form an application specific type. $e_i \in E_j$ denotes that e_i is an instance of the event type E_j. We use e_i.type to denote the type E_j of e_i. Suppose one of the attributes of E_j is attrj and $e_i \in E_j$, we use e_i.attrj to denote e_i's value for that attribute attrj.

Event History H is an ordered set of primitive event instances. Details of event history can be found in Section 4. *Cross product* ($\times$) *of event histories* for A[H] = $\{a_1, a_2, ..., a_n\}$ and B[H] = $\{b_1, b_2, ..., b_m\}$ is A[H] $\times$ B[H] = $\{ \sum_{1\leq i \leq n; 1 \leq j \leq m}$ $\{a_i, b_j\}$ with $a_i \in$ A[H] and $b_j \in$ B[H]$\}$.

3 NEEL: The Nested Complex Event Query Language

We now introduce the *NEEL*[1]. query language for specifying complex event pattern queries. *NEEL* supports the nesting of AND, OR, Negation and SEQ operators at any level of nesting.

The Backus Normal Form (BNF) syntax for *NEEL* is shown in Table 1. In *NEEL*, the PATTERN clause retrieves event instances specified in the event expression from the input stream. The qualification in the PATTERN clause further filters event instances by evaluating predicates applied to event attributes. The WITHIN clause specifies a time period within which all the events of interest must occur in order to be considered a match. In our language, the time period is expressed as a sliding window, though other window types could be easily plugged in. A set of histories is returned with each history equal to one

[1] NEEL stands for **Ne**sted Complex **E**vent Query **L**anguage

query match, i.e., the set of event instances that together form a valid match of the query specification. Clearly, additional transformation of each match could be plugged in to the RETURN clause.

Operators in the PATTERN clause. SEQ in the PATTERN clause specifies a sequence indicating the particular order in which the event instances of interest should occur. The components of the sequence are the occurrences and non-occurrences of events [1]. Any component of SEQ including at the start or the end of the pattern can be negated using "!". **AND** also specifies events occurrences and non-occurrences but their order does not matter. **OR** operator specifies disjunction of events.

We now explain step by step the proposed *NEEL* language using the earlier RFID-based hospital tool management scenario. Again, RFID tags are assumed to be either embedded in or attached to surgical knives, clamps, scissors, etc. Sensors transmit the events performed on the equipment in an input event stream of event types washing, sharpening, disinfection, etc. For example, the query Q_4 below detects activity related to surgical knife management. The PATTERN clause contains a SEQ construct that specifies a sequence consisting of a Recycling, a Washing instance followed by the occurrence of an Operating event instance.

```
Q4 = PATTERN SEQ(Recycle r, Washing w, Operating o)
```

Nested expressions and variable scope. If E_1, E_2 ,..., E_n are event expressions, an application of SEQ, AND and OR over these event expressions is again an event expression [7]. In other words, nesting of AND, OR and SEQ operators is supported. An event expression exp_i can be used as an **inner** component to construct an **outer** expression exp_j. The operator construct optionally also includes an event variable (<var>). The benefits of using such an event variable are that it is (1) more concise to refer to an event expression in a predicate, (2) easier for the user to interpret predicates, (3) and avoids ambiguity if the same expression occurs twice, e.g., $Washing\ w_1$, $Washing\ w_2$. The event variable in an outer expression exp_j is visible within the outer expression exp_j as well as within the scope of any of its own nested inner expressions exp_i. For example, the PATTERN clause of the query Q_5 extends the query Q_4 by nesting the occurrence of a sub-sequence consisting of a Sharpening, a Disinfection and a Checking instance within the outer sequence of a Recycling, a Washing and an Operating event instance. Event instances "r", "w" and "o" declared in the outer SEQ expression are visible both in the outer and inner SEQ operators. Event instances "s", "d", "c" declared in the inner SEQ expression are visible only within this inner SEQ operator.

```
Q5 = PATTERN SEQ(Recycle r, Washing w,
             SEQ(Sharpening s, Disinfection d, Checking c),
             Operating o)
     WITHIN 2 hours
```

Window Constraints. We currently work with simple sliding windows, though other window models could be adopted in the future. The window constraint in the WITHIN clause imposes a time duration constraint on all instances involved in a match of the query. For a nested event expression, the same window clause w is applied to all nested subexpressions as a constraint. However, this window constraint w will be further restricted implicitly in each nested subexpression based on its context within its outer expression. For example, the window for the query Q_5 is 2 hours. The window for the subexpression SEQ(Sharpening s, Disinfection d, Checking c) is bounded by the timestamps of events w and o, namely by the interval [w.te, o.ts]. Explicit time windows for the inner SEQ can also be supported in the future as longas they do not violate the window constraints of the outer nested sequences.

Predicate specification. The optional qualification in the PATTERN clause, denoted by *qual*, contains one or more predicates. Predicates only referring to events in the local expression exp_i (**simple predicates**) are specified directly inside exp_i. Predicates referring to event instances both from an outer and an inner expression are **correlated predicates**. They must be placed with the innermost expression where a variable used in the expression is declared. For example, in Q_6 the correlated predicate "s.id=d.id=c.id=o.id" referring to both inner ("s", "d" and "c") and outer ("o") events must be placed within the inner SEQ operator where any of the variables are defined. The simple predicate "o.ins-type = surgery" is placed with the outer SEQ operator where the variable "op" is declared. Predicates across the OR arguments are not allowed as only one of the OR arguments will match at a time. Correlated predicates involving two sibling expressions are not allowed since the event instances in one expression are not visible within the scope of the other expression.

```
Q6 = PATTERN SEQ(Recycle r, Washing w,
             SEQ(Sharpening s, Disinfection d, Checking c,
                 s.id=d.id=c.id=o.id),
             Operating o, o.ins-type="surgery")
```

Q_7 below is not a valid query as the subexpression SEQ(Washing d, Sharpening s) contains a correlated predicate (w.id = c.id) referring to the Checking event c which is not within the scope of this predicate because it is declared in a sibling SEQ operator. Similarly, the event w is not within its proper scope, yet is referred to, in the subexpression SEQ(Disinfection d, Checking c).

```
Q7 = PATTERN SEQ(Recycle r,
             SEQ(Washing w, Sharpening s, w.id = c.id),
             SEQ(Disinfection d, Checking c, d.id = w.id))
```

Negation. The symbol "!" before an event expression E_i expresses the non-occurrence of E_i and indicates that E_i is not allowed to appear in the specified position. If there is a ! (Negation) symbol before an event expression, we now say that the event expression marked by ! is a **negative event expression**, otherwise, it is a **positive event expression**. At least one positive event expression must exist in SEQ and AND operators. Event instances that satisfy the positive event expressions of a query with no events existing in the input stream satisfying the negative event expressions in the specified positions are said to be a **valid match**. For example, the query Q_8 specifies the non-occurrence of Washing events anywhere between Recycle and Operating events.

```
Q8 = PATTERN SEQ(Recycle r, ! Washing w, Operating o)
```

If several adjacent event types are marked by ! in a SEQ operator such as in Q_9 below, the query requires the non-existence of **any** *Washing* and *Sharpening* events between our matched pair of *Recycle* and *Operating* event instances. In other words, SEQ(*Recycle* r, ! *Washing* w, ! *Sharpening* s, *Operating* o) is equivalent to SEQ(*Recycle* r, ! *Sharpening* s, ! *Washing* w, *Operating* o) as no ordering constraint holds between *Washing* and *Sharpening* events. Events of either types can't exist in the location between our *Recycle* and *Operating* matches.

```
Q9 = PATTERN SEQ(Recycle r, ! Washing w, ! Sharpening s, Operating o)
```

Scoping of Negation. Pattern matching involving negation is different from matching on positive event types. Let us consider query Q_4 with only positive event types. It looks for the existence of Recycle, Washing and Operating events in the proper order. But Q_8 is different. We do not look for three instances, the first matching Recycle, the second matching ! Washing, and the third matching Operating. If we were to follow this interpretation, for event history H = $\{r_1, w_2, s_3, o_4\}$, we would return $\{r_1,\ o_4\}$, since s_3 would match "! Washing". However, $\{r_1,\ o_4\}$ should not be returned in this case because $w_2 \in$ Washing exists between r_1 and o_4. Clearly, the role of the "!" Washing in this context is different from the role of positive event types in the same position. Mainly, the "!" in a SEQ operator has a "for all" semantics and not an "exists" semantics. Put differently, in Q_8, "! Washing" doesn't mean matching one particular ! Washing instance between Recycle and Operating events. Rather, the query requires the non-existence of Washing events anywhere in the input stream between the matched Recycle and Operating events.

Nested Negation. A negative event expression exp_i can be used as an inner expression to filter out the construction of other outer event expression exp_j. For example, in Q_{10} the negative event type "Disinfection" is a sub-component of the negative event expression SEQ(*Sharpening* s, ! *Disinfection* d, *Checking* c). The later in turn is a sub-component of the outermost SEQ expression of Q_{10}. Q_{10} states that $< r, w, o >$ is a valid match if either no *Sharpening* and *Checking* event pairs exist in the input stream between our *Washing* w and *Operating* o events in the outer match $< r, w, o >$, or otherwise if they do exist, then disinfection events must also exist between all *Sharpening* and *Checking* event pairs.

```
Q10 = PATTERN SEQ(Recycle r, Washing w,
                  ! SEQ(Sharpening s, ! Disinfection d, Checking c),
                  Operating o)
```

Predicates with Negation. Consider the query Q_{11} below.

```
Q11 = PATTERN SEQ(Recycle r, ! Washing w, Operating o,
            r.attr1 + w.attr1 = o.attr1)
```

Assume the history H = { r_1, o_5} and r_1.attr1 = 1 and o_5.attr1 = 1. Here we assume that no negative *Washing* events exist in this history. Should query Q_{11} return {r_1, o_5}? The question is how do we decide whether the condition is true or false since there is no value for a Washing event to participate in the predicate?

One answer might be that the predicate (r.attr1 + w.attr1 = o.attr1) will be treated as true whenever it refers to attributes of negative events (like w.attr1 above). This would lead to awkward semantics because the logic of the predicate will be unexpected. For example, if P is any formula and w is the "excluded" event, then (P ∨ (w.attr1 !=w.attr1)) will evaluate to true. This logic would clearly not be sensible. Or, we could have the above predicate evaluate to false. {r_1, o_5} would not be returned in this case as a result. It is also unexpected as no Washing events exist so no sequence results of the outer positive event expression should be filtered. Instead, we adopt a third strategy of interpreting nesting similar in spirit to that of our interpretation described above for the ! symbol in the primitive case.

```
Q12 = PATTERN SEQ(Recycle r, Washing w,
          ! SEQ(Sharpening s, Disinfection d, Checking c),
            Operating o)
      WITHIN  1 hours
```

```
Q13 = PATTERN SEQ(Recycle r, Washing w,
          ! SEQ(Sharpening s, Disinfection d, Checking c,
                s.id=d.id=c.id=o.id),
            Operating o, r.id=w.id=o.id)
      WITHIN  1 hours
```

For this, we now propose that the way we write predicates influences its meaning and thus its results. Simple predicates involving negative event types are placed with negative event types. We require that all predicates referring to only positive events are stated separately, as they refer to instances that must exist. And we require all predicates involving negative event types are stated separately with the negative event types. During pattern matching, we first match events of the positive event expression and predicates only involving thse positive events. If and only if we find a match, then we check events for the non-existence of instances to match the negative event expression and thus we then check their associated predicates. Assume the history H = $\{r_1, w_2, s_3, d_4, c_5, o_6\}$ and r_1.id = w_2.id = o_6.id = 1, s_3.id = 2, d_4.id = 3 and c_5.id = 4. Assume one user requires all event instances in Q_{12} have the same id. If the user put the condition "r.id = w.id= o.id = s.id = d.id = c.id" in the end of the outer SEQ in Q_{12}, this is an invalid query by earlier definition. However, now assume that the user represents the predicate as "r.id=w.id=o.id" associated with the outer SEQ expression, and "s.id=d.id=c.id=o.id" associated with the inner SEQ expression as shown in

Q_{13}. Then during Q_{13} pattern evaluation, we first construct the outer sequence $< r_1, w_2, o_6 >$ with r_1.id $= w_2$.id $= o_6$.id. Then we check between w_2 and o_6 if one or more matches for the inner expression a SEQ(Sharpening s, Disinfection d, Checking c) sequence exist with "s.id=d.id=c.id=o_6.id". $< r_1, w_2, o_6 >$ is a match for Q_{13} as no such inner sequence is found.

```
Q14 = PATTERN SEQ(Recycle r, Washing w,
                  ! SEQ(Sharpening s, Disinfection d,
                       ! (Checking c, c.id = d.id),
                       s.id=d.id=o.id),
                  Operating o, r.id=w.id=o.id)
      WITHIN  1 hours
```

When a negative event type is nested in another negative component such as the *Checking* event in Q_{14}, the user is required to put predicate requirements for the *Checking* event directly with the *Checking* event type. Predicates referring to *Sharpening* and *Disinfection* events but not involving the *Checking* event are specified in the end of the inner SEQ operator as shown in Q_{14}. During Q_{14} pattern evaluation, we first construct outer <r, w, o> sequences with r.id=w.id=o.id. Then we check between w and o pairs if one or more matches for the inner expression a SEQ(Sharpening s, Disinfection d, ! Checking c) sequence exist with "s.id=d.id=o.id". If not, <r, w, o> sequences are matches for Q_{14}. If yes, we then check if one or more Checking event exist with "c.id = d.id". If such c event exists, <r, w, o> sequences are matches for Q_{14}. If not, the query filters this intermediate match.

4 Formal Semantics of NEEL

We now define the operator semantics using the notion of event histories. Below, we define the set of operators that *NEEL* supports in the PATTERN clause of a query and the semantics of the expressions that they form. Below E_i represents an event expression of either a primitive or composite event type.

For closure, the input and output data types are the same. The cross product of event histories A[H] and B[H] is a power set over H denoted by A[H] × B[H]. This in turn could be the input of another operator which then would generate a power set over H again by working on one event history at a time (pow(H) → pow(H)).

Definition 1. *Assume the window size for a nested event expression is w. For sliding window semantics, at any time t, we apply a query to the window constrained event history H_w = H[ts, te] with te := t and ts := t-w such that:*

$$H_w = \{e | e \in H \wedge (ts \leq e.ts \leq e.te \leq te)\}. \tag{1}$$

Definition 2. *$E_i[H_w]$ selects events of event type E_i from H_w.*

$$E_i[H_w] \;=\; \{\{e\} | e \in H_w \wedge e.type = E_i\}. \tag{2}$$

Definition 3. *Union of event histories.* $H_1 \cup H_2 = \{ e_i \mid e_i \in H_1 \vee e_i \in H_2 \}$. *Duplicates of* e_i *that appear in both histories* H_1 *and* H_2 *are removed from the result set.*

The notation $\overrightarrow{e_{1,n}}$ denotes an ordered sequence of event instances $e_1, e_2, \ldots, e_n$ such that for all pairs (e_i, e_j) with i < j in the sequence, e_i.ts $\leq e_i$.te $< e_j$.ts $\leq e_j$.te holds. The notation $\widehat{e_{1,n}}$ denotes a set of event instances $\{e_1, e_2, ..., e_i, ..., e_n\}$ without any ordering constraints. The notation $\uplus E_{1,n}$ denotes the cross product (defined in Section 2) of event histories. Namely, $\uplus E_{1,n}[H_w] = E_1[H_w] \times E_2[H_w] \times \ldots E_i[H_w] \times \ldots \times E_n[H_w]$. We use the notation $\mathcal{P}_{1,j}(\widehat{e_{1,n}})$ to refer to predicates $P_1, ..., P_j$ on events $\{e_1, \ldots, e_n\}$. Namely, $\mathcal{P}_{1\ldots j}(\widehat{e_{1,n}}) = P_1(\widehat{e_{1,n}}), ..., P_j(\widehat{e_{1,n}})$.

Definition 4. *SEQ specifies a particular order in which the event instances of interest* $e_1, e_2, ..., e_n = \overrightarrow{e_{1,n}}$ *should occur.*

$$\begin{aligned} &SEQ(E_1\, e_1, E_2\, e_2, ..., E_i\, e_i, \ldots, E_n\, e_n, \mathcal{P}_{1\ldots m}(\widehat{e_{1,n}}))[H_w] \\ &\quad = \{\widehat{e_{1,n}} | (\overrightarrow{e_{1,n}} \in \uplus E_{1,n}[H_w]) \wedge \mathcal{P}_{1\ldots m}(\widehat{e_{1,n}})\}. \end{aligned} \tag{3}$$

Example 1. *Given SEQ(Recycle r, Washing w) and* $H = \{r_1, w_2, w_3\}$, *SEQ(Recycle r, Washing w)[H] generates 2 histories:* $\{r_1, w_2\}$ *and* $\{r_1, w_3\}$.

Definition 5. *Equation 4 defines the SEQ operator with negation.*

$$\begin{aligned} &SEQ(E_1\, e_1, ..., E_i\, e_i, !(E_{i+1}\, e_{i+1}, P_{i+1}(\widehat{e_{1,n}})), E_{i+2}\, e_{i+2}, ..., E_n\, e_n, \mathcal{P}_{1\ldots i}(\widehat{e_{1,n}}), \\ &\quad \mathcal{P}_{i+2\ldots m}(\widehat{e_{1,n}}))[H_w] \\ &\quad = \{\{e_1, ..., e_i, e_{i+2}, ..., e_n\} | (\{e_1, ..., e_i, e_{i+2}, ..., e_n\} \in (\uplus E_{1,i}[H_w] \times \uplus E_{i+2,n}[H_w])) \wedge \\ &\quad (\overrightarrow{e_{1,i}} \wedge \overrightarrow{e_{i+2,n}} \wedge e_i.te < e_{i+2}.ts) \wedge \mathcal{P}_{1\ldots i}(\widehat{e_{1,n}}) \wedge \mathcal{P}_{i+2\ldots m}(\widehat{e_{1,n}}) \wedge (\neg \exists e_{i+1} \in E_{i+1}[H_w] \\ &\quad \textit{where } (e_i.te < e_{i+1}.ts < e_{i+1}.te < e_{i+2}.ts) \wedge \mathcal{P}_{i+1}(\widehat{e_{1,n}}))\}. \end{aligned} \tag{4}$$

Equation 4 defines the SEQ operator with negation in the middle of a list of event types. P_{i+1} involves predicates referring at least once to an instance of type E_{i+1}. In Equation 4, events $\{e_1, ..., e_i, e_{i+2}, ..., e_n\}$ of the positive event expression satisfying the associated predicates are first constructed. We then check the non-existence of E_{i+1} instances satisfying the predicate P_{i+1} with timestamps between e_i and e_{i+2} events. Once constructed, the sequence results involving negation in NEEL will not be changed during evaluation. Namely, our semantics are iterative such that for nested negation the order of resolution is to establish patterns within patterns. Thus unlike in the well-known problem of stratified negation for handling logical recursion with negation [22], an event instance extracted by a NEEL expression that is deemed positive (or negative) cannot switch its status in evaluation.

Negation could equally exist at the start or the end of the SEQ operator. If negation exists at the start, the non-existence left time bound should be $e_n.te - w$. Similarly, if negation exists at the end, the non-existence right time bound should be $e_1.ts + w$. If negations are specified at both the start and the end of the SEQ operator, we need to bound them conservatively into both directions simultaneously from the leftmost and the rightmost positive components. Multiple negations could exist in the SEQ operator. For example, SEQ(E_1 e_1 ,..., E_i e_i, ! (E_{i+1} e_{i+1}, $P_{i+1}(\widehat{e_{1,n}})$), ! ($E_{i+2}$ e_{i+2}, $P_{i+2}(\widehat{e_{1,n}})$), ..., ! ($E_{i+j}$ e_{i+j}, $P_{i+j}(\widehat{e_{1,n}})$), E_{i+j+1} e_{i+j+1} ,..., E_n e_n, $\mathcal{P}_{1...m}(\widehat{e_{1,n}})$. It requires the non-existence of E_{i+1}, E_{i+2}, ... and E_{i+j} event instances between e_i and e_{i+j+1} with those qualifications.

Definition 6. *AND operator computes the cross product of the input events.*

$$\begin{aligned} &AND(E_1\, e_1, E_2\, e_2, ...E_n\, e_n, \mathcal{P}_{1...m}(\widehat{e_{1,n}}))[H_w] \\ &= \{\widehat{e_{1,n}} | (\widehat{e_{1,n}} \in \uplus E_{1,n}[H_w]) \wedge \mathcal{P}_{1...m}(\widehat{e_{1,n}})\}. \end{aligned} \tag{5}$$

Definition 7. *Equation 6 defines the AND operator with negation.*

$$\begin{aligned} &AND(E_1\, e_1, ..., E_i\, e_i, !(E_{i+1}\, e_{i+1}, P_{i+1}(\widehat{e_{1,n}})), E_{i+2}\, e_{i+2}, ..., E_n\, e_n, \mathcal{P}_{1...i}(\widehat{e_{1,n}}), \\ &\mathcal{P}_{i+2...m}(\widehat{e_{1,n}}))[H_w] \\ &= \{\{e_1, ..., e_i, e_{i+2}, ..., e_n\} | (\{e_1, ..., e_i, e_{i+2}, ..., e_n\} \in (\uplus E_{1,i}[H_w] \times \uplus E_{i+2,n}[H_w])) \wedge \\ &\mathcal{P}_{1...i}(\widehat{e_{1,n}}) \wedge \mathcal{P}_{i+2...m}(\widehat{e_{1,n}}) \wedge \neg\exists e_{i+1} where\ (e_{i+1} \in E_{i+1}[H_w] \wedge P_{i+1}(\widehat{e_{1,n}}))\}. \end{aligned} \tag{6}$$

Again, negative event expressions just like positive ones could be composed of SEQ, AND and OR operators.

Definition 8. *Formally, the set-operator OR is defined as follows. Predicates across the OR arguments are not allowed as arguments are independent, i.e., only one of the instances will constitute the result history for each match.*

$$OR(E_1\, e_1\, , ..., E_n\, e_n, \mathcal{P}_{1...m}(\widehat{e_{1,n}})[H_w] = (E_1[H_w], P_1(e_1)) \cup ... \cup \quad (E_n[H_w], P_n(e_n)). \tag{7}$$

Example 2. Assume the query Q_{15} = OR(*Checking*, *Sharpening*, *Checking*.id > 10, *Sharpening*.id > 15)[H] and the event history $H_w = \{c_1, c_2, c_6, s_8\}$ where c_1.id = 5, c_2.id = 20, c_6.id = 2 and s_8.id = 25. Then Q_{16} = (*Checking*[H_w], *Checking*.id > 10) ∪ (*Sharpening*[H_w], *Sharpening*.id > 15) = {{c_2}, {s_8}} as c_2.id > 10 and s_8.id > 15.

5 E-Analytics System

E-Analytic Architecture. Figure 1 shows the overall architecture of our E-Analytics system. Our E-Analytics framework is implemented inside a Java-based complex event processing prototype called ECube [23]. Input adaptors read event streams from different devices and of different formats. Queries are first compiled into query plans, then optimized and lastly submitted to the query executor for processing. The execution engine will instantiate the query plan by

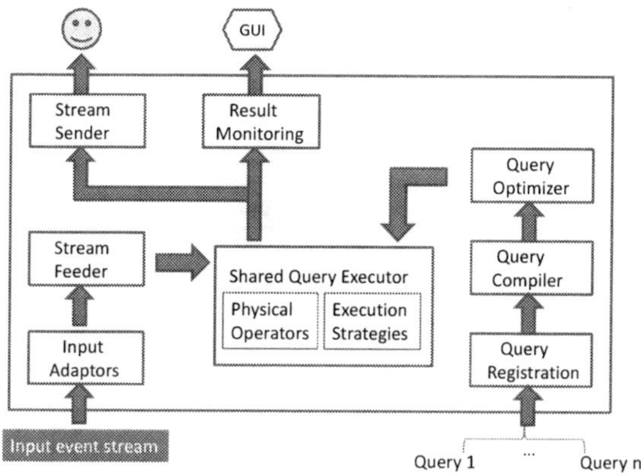

Fig. 1. E-Analytic Processing System

instantiating the corresponding physical operators in the query plan. Thereafter, execution of the query is activated which then will continuously consume the input event stream and produce complex events that match the query pattern. The resulting streams will then be fed continuously to the monitoring business applications. These applications can either have a Graphical User Interface (GUI) for visual analytics or can be console-based. The system will help track the critical conditions for scenarios described in Section 1. A more detailed case study of this technology can also be seen in Section 6.

Query Compiler. A query expressed by *NEEL* is translated into a default nested algebraic query plan composed of the following algebraic operators: Window Sequence (*WinSeq*), Window Or (*WinOr*) and Window And (*WinAnd*). The same window w is applied to all operator nodes. During query transformation, each expression in the event pattern is mapped to one operator node in the query plan. *WinSeq* first extracts all matches to the positive components specified in the query, and then filters out events based on negative components as specified in the query. *WinOr* returns an event e if e matches one of the event expressions specified in the *WinOr* operator. *WinAnd* computes the cross product of events of its component event expressions. The operator node for an outer expression is placed on top of the operator nodes of its inner expressions. For queries expressed by *NEEL*, predicates are placed in their proper position in nested event expressions as discussed in Section 3. A leaf node, labeled by a primitive event type E, selects instances of the primitive event type E from the input event stream S and passes them to its parent nodes.

Example 3. Figure 2 shows the basic query plan for the sample query SEQ(*Recycle* r, *Washing* w, ! SEQ(*Sharpening* s, *Disinfection* d, *Checking* c, s.id = d.id = c.id = o.id), *Operating* o, r.id = w.id = o.id, o.ins-type = "surgery"). The two SEQ operators are transformed into two WinSeq operator

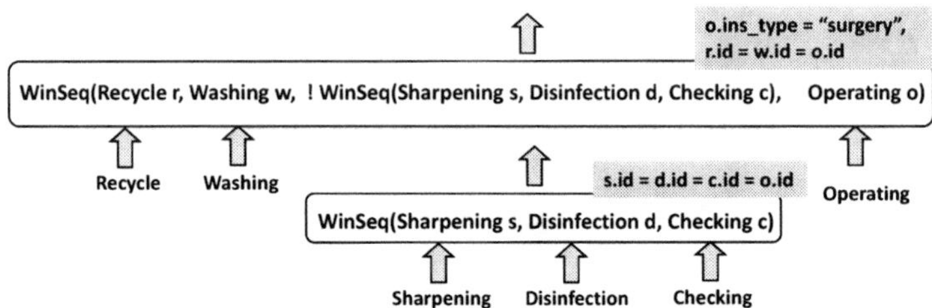

Fig. 2. Basic Query Plan

nodes in the query plan. The simple predicate o.ins-type = "surgery" is attached to the topmost WinSeq operator node containing the Operating event type. The correlated predicate is attached to the inner WinSeq operator node.

Query Executor. Following the principle of nested iteration for SQL queries [12,13], we apply the iterative execution strategy to queries expressed by *NEEL*. The outer query is evaluated first followed by its inner sub-queries. The results of the positive inner queries are passed up and joined with the results of the outer query. For every outer partial query result, a constrained window is passed down for processing each of its children sub-queries. These sub-queries compute results involving events within the constraint window. Qualified result sequences of the inner operators are passed up to the parent operator. The outer operator then joins its own local results with those from its positive sub-queries. The outer sequence result is filtered if the result set of any of its negative sub-queries is not empty. We apply iterative execution until a final result sequence is produced by the root operator. Finally, the process repeats when the outer query consumes the next instance e. A more detailed description with preliminary experimental evaluation of the nested execution strategy can be found in [16].

Query Optimization. With precise semantics in place, we now have laid a solid foundation for developing optimization strategies for E-Analytics. For instance, in [16], selective caching of intermediate results is introduced as technique for optimizing iterative execution. In addition, interval-driven cache expansion and interval-driven cache reduction are proposed in [16]. Clearly, other optimization opportunities could be identified. However, it is beyond the scope of this paper.

6 Case Study with Real-Time Health Care Monitoring Application

We are collaborating with medical staff in the University of Massachusetts Memorial Medical Center in the context of a project entitled "Development and Testing of an Electronic Infection Control Reminder System for Healthcare Workers" [17]. We aim to tackle one of the major concerns in healthcare today of the spread of human infectious diseases in hospital settings. It has been established by the medical community that one of the simplest yet most effective methods for prevention of hospital-acquired infections is to have healthcare workers cleanse their hands and follow other precautions (such as wearing masks for H1N1, gowns, etc) before and after they see patients. Unfortunately, compliance for hand hygiene even in the best practicing hospitals in the country is below acceptable levels (75% to 80% in the best case) and methods of enforcement are minimal to non-existent.

Thus, our objective is to overcome this problem by building a Hospital Infection Control System (HICS) that continuously tracks healthcare workers throughout their workday for hygiene compliance and for paths of exposure to different diseases and unhygienic conditions. Our system would alert healthcare workers at the appropriate moments, for instance, if they are about to enter an operation room without first performing the required disinfection procedure. Such events are detected in real time by our system using queries such as Q_{17}.

```
Q17 = PATTERN SEQ(!(Sanitize-Area s, s.wID = o.wID),
                   Enter-Operating-Room o)
             WITHIN 1 minutes)
```

Similarly, in intensive care units we need the capability to conduct path analysis determining who went into an operating room, left for a break or to visit a different patient, and returned without washing and drying hands. Such logic could be expressed in *NEEL* by query Q_{18}. On finding matches, officials may then need to find out which operating rooms and/or patients are potentially at risk to undertake the needed actions to remind the healthcare workers.

```
Q18 = PATTERN
      SEQ(Operating Room o1,
          OR(Break Room br, Patient Room pr,
             br.wID = o2.wID, pr.wID = o2.wID),
          ! SEQ(Washing w, Drying d, w.wID = d.wID = o2.wID),
          Operating Room o2, o1.wID = o2.wID)
      WITHIN 1 minutes
```

If a significant number of violations occur at a certain room, the supervising staff may want to review all violation patterns related to this room to deduce potential causes of this phenomenon. Or, the supervising staff may want to identify the violator causing such an abnormal violation pattern who possibly may be a young physician or intern not well versed in required safety regulations or simply a worker neglecting usual precautions distracted by an overly busy schedule. Clearly, real-time analysis to not only track sequences of events in real time, but also to analyze their frequency relative to prior behavior of the same health care work, prior patterns by the overall staff within this intense CPU unit also across the overall care facility may be time critical, potentially, mitigating risks before they spread.

As an example of the type of services our *HyReminder* system provides, consider our real-time monitoring console in Figure 3 that displays the current hygiene compliance state of every HCW for the head nurse to supervise. The map-based monitoring window displays each worker as a moving object in the

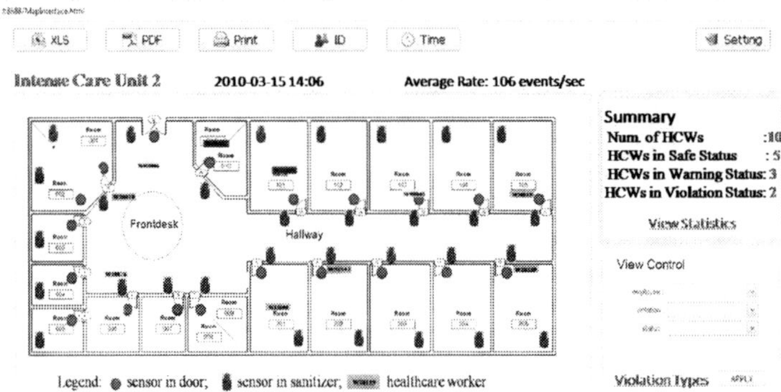

Fig. 3. Real-time Hand Hygiene Monitoring

intense care unit map. Real-time statistics about the hand hygiene violations can be accessed and filtered by specifying conditions in the "view control" panel. A more detailed description of the *HyReminder* system can be found in [24].

7 Related Work

Most event processing systems, such as SNOOP [20], do not support scope. The Cayuga [2] query language is a simple mapping of the algebra operators into a SQL like syntax, similar in spirit to the complex event language in SASE [1]. In Cayuga [2] and SASE [1], scope is expressed respectively by a duration predicate and a window clause. *NEEL* adopts basic query constructs similar to the ones in SASE [1] for expressing a flat query. Negation is not treated as an operator in *NEEL*. Instead, negation is scoped within the context of other algebra operations to act as filter of positive matches, namely, within SEQ and AND operators. As compared to previous event languages such as *ODE* [19], SASE provides a compact CEP query language which is easy to read. For instance, "*relative(deposit, ! before interest) and withdraw*" is used to express the pattern "deposit followed eventually by withdraw with no intervening interest" in *ODE* [19]. Using *SASE*, the pattern can be simply expressed as PATTERN SEQ(deposit, ! interest, withdraw). However, *SASE* [1] has several limitations. It only supports SEQ and $SEQ_{WITHOUT}$ operators which allow you to express flat sequence queries. In addition, it only allows queries to transform events from primitive types to complex types, but has not looked at transforming from complex types to (even more) complex types. Even though *SASE+* [21] claims to support query composition, *SASE+* doesn't support the nesting of complex operators. This is our key focus.

While CEDR [6] allows the application of negation over composite event types, they didn't provide a clear syntax for the specification of such nested pattern queries. The *SEL* language [18], while supporting nesting of operators, focuses in particular on temporal relationship specification. Semantics of nested negation appear ambiguous as negation itself is an operator and thus a match (or, negation match) presumably would need to be returned from the negation operator if nested. Subtle issues with predicates in the presence of negation operators are not explored in [18], but can be found in our work (see Section 3).

8 Conclusions

In this paper, our proposed nested CEP query language *NEEL* succinctly expresses nested queries composed of sequence, negation, AND and OR operators. *NEEL* allows users to specify fairly complex queries in a compact manner with predicates and negation over query nestings both well-supported. We also introduce the formal query semantics for *NEEL*. An algebraic query plan for the execution of nested CEP queries is designed. The proposal presented here permits a simple and direct implementation of nested CEP queries following the principle of iterative nested query execution for SQL queries. Our case study in health care confirms the utility of applying nested complex event processing support for enabling real-time event analytics.

Acknowledgements. This work is supported by HP Labs Innovation Research Program and National Science Foundation under grants NSF 1018443 and NSF IIS 0917017, Turkish National Science Foundation TUBITAK under career award 109E194. We thank Di Wang, Han Wang and Richard T. Ellison III for the case study. We thank Database System Research Group members at WPI for many valuable comments.

References

1. Wu, E., Diao, Y., Rizvi, S.: High-performance complex event processing over streams. In: SIGMOD Conference, pp. 407–418 (2006)
2. Demers, A.J., Gehrke, J., Panda, B., Riedewald, M., Sharma, V., White, W.M.: Cayuga: A general purpose event monitoring system. In: CIDR, pp. 412–422 (2007)
3. Boyce, J.M., Pittet, D.: Guideline for hand hygiene in healthcare settings. MMWR Recomm Rep. 51, 1–45 (2002)
4. Shnayder, V., Chen, B., Lorincz, K., Fulford-Jones, T.R.F., Welsch, M.: Sensor Networks for Medical Care. In Harvard University Technical Report TR-08-05 (2005)
5. Stankovic, J.A., Cao, Q., et al.: Wireless sensor networks for in-home healthcare: Potential and challenges. In: Proceedings of HCMDSS Workshop (2005)
6. Barga, R.S., Goldstein, J., Ali, M., Hong, M.: Consistent streaming through time: A vision for event stream processing. In: CIDR, pp. 363–374 (2007)
7. Chakravarthy, S., Krishnaprasad, V., Anwar, E., Kim, S.K.: Composite events for active databases: Semantics, contexts and detection. In: VLDB, pp. 606–617 (1994)
8. Gupta, C., Wang, S., Ari, I., Hao, M., Dayal, U., Mehta, A., Marwah, M., Sharma, R.: Chaos: A data stream analysis architecture for enterprise applications. In: CEC 2009, pp. 33–40 (2009)
9. Inetats, I.: Stock trade traces, `http://www.inetats.com/`
10. Seshadri, P., Pirahesh, H., Leung, T.Y.C.: Complex query decorrelation. In: ICDE, pp. 450–458 (1996)

11. Beeri, C., Ramakrishnan, R.: On the Power of Magic. J. Log. Program. 10, 255–299 (1991)
12. Wong, E., Youssefi, K.: Decomposition - a strategy for query processing. ACM Trans. Database Syst. 1(3), 223–241 (1976)
13. Smith, J.M., Chang, P.Y.-T.: Optimizing the performance of a relational algebra database interface. Commun. ACM 18(10), 568–579 (1975)
14. Guravannavar, R., Ramanujam, H.S., Sudarshan, S.: Optimizing nested queries with parameter sort orders. In: VLDB, pp. 481–492 (2005)
15. Seshadri, P., Pirahesh, H., Leung, T.Y.C.: Complex query decorrelation. In: ICDE, pp. 450–458. IEEE Computer Society, Los Alamitos (1996)
16. Liu, M., Ray, M., Rundensteiner, E., Dougherty, D., et al.: Processing strategies for nested complex sequence pattern queries over event streams. In: 7th International Workshop on Data Management for Sensor Networks (DMSN 2010), pp. 14–19 (2010)
17. Wang, D., Rundensteiner, E., Ellison III, R.: Active complex event processing: applications in realtime health care. In: VLDB (2010) (demonstration paper)
18. Zhu, D., Sethi, A.S.: SEL - A new event pattern specification language for event correlation. In: Proc. ICCCN 2001, Tenth International Conference on Computer Communications and Networks, pp. 586–589 (2001)
19. Gehani, N.H., Jagadish, H.V., Shmueli, O.: Composite event specification in active databases: model & implementation. In: VLDB 1992, pp. 327–338 (1992)
20. Chakravarthy, S., Krishnaprasad, V., et al.: Composite events for active databases: semantics, contexts and detection. In: VLDB 1994, pp. 606–617 (1994)
21. Diao, Y., Immerman, N., Gyllstrom, D.: SASE+: An Agile Language for Kleene Closure over Event Streams, UMass Technical Report 07-03
22. Greco, S., Sacca, D., Zaniolo, C.: Datalog queries with stratified negation and choice. In: Vardi, M.Y., Gottlob, G. (eds.) ICDT 1995. LNCS, vol. 893, pp. 82–96. Springer, Heidelberg (1995)
23. Liu, M., Rundensteiner, E.A., Greenfield, K., Gupta, C., Wang, S., Ari, I., Mehta, A.: E-Cube: Multi-dimensional event sequence processing using concept and pattern hierarchies. In: ICDE 2010, pp. 1097–1100 (2010)
24. Wang, D., Rundensteiner, E.A., Ellison, R., Wang, H.: Active Complex Event Processing: Applications in Real-Time Health Care. In: PVLDB, pp. 1545–1548 (2010)

Author Index